AT THE MERCY OF EXTERNALS

✦

Righting Wrongs and Protecting Kids

✦

2ND EDITION

David L. Roberts, BA, MS, MS, Ph.D.

iUniverse, Inc.
Bloomington

At the Mercy of Externals

iUniverse books may be ordered through booksellers or by contacting:

iUniverse
1663 Liberty Drive
Bloomington, IN 47403
www.iuniverse.com
1-800-Authors (1-800-288-4677)

ISBN: 978-1-4759-1637-9 (sc)
ISBN: 978-1-4759-1638-6 (hc)
ISBN: 978-1-4759-1639-3 (e)

Library of Congress Control Number: 2012907262

Printed in the United States of America

iUniverse rev. date: 4/19/2012

Dedication

This book is dedicated to Granny, Melissa, Adan, Susan,
And to all of the kids I serve or have served,
Remembering especially those who have died.

Contents

Preface

The ideas contained within this book have been developing, at least experientially, since the day I was born. Now it is finally time to sit down and begin putting them on paper as a way of sharing with others what I have learned along the way. My original questions as to how to proceed with this project stemmed from both the dilemma of how to make the presentation, and from my concerns about being honest and open relative to my own personal life and history. Finally I recognized these as two separate yet connected perspectives. The sections dealing with my personal history are very different from the intended theme of this book and will be designated as "The Past that Lived in My Present", separating this information from information related specifically to the purpose of the material presented. I have decided to "listen to [and follow] the teachings my blood whispers to me" as indicated by Hermann Hesse in his prologue to <u>Demian</u>, a powerful book first introduced to me in college, at the age of 17. At that time I realized life is indeed a journey - or process as I now think of it. So, it is my desire to share with you, the reader, some of the insights I have gained along my own personal path. I believe this book will touch the lives of those who are intended to read it. Therefore, I am going to trust this process as well. As you will see, my book includes my 'author bio' embedded within the content primarily included in the first five or six chapters.

I am very proud to have reached a point where a work in progress has culminated in the writing of *At the Mercy of Externals: Righting Wrongs and Protecting Kids* – now a 2nd Edition. Most of the readers will be able to benefit from their own personal journey of assessment and discovery/recovery relative to histories of abuse and victimization. Each of you will then have an opportunity to pass this book and it concepts on to others as a way of sharing with them the benefits you have gained from the experience of reading and applying the concepts found herein to your own life and family.

For those readers who have an interest in teaching and are searching for materials to use for various self-help/therapy groups, the subject matter of this book offers countless opportunities to customize and present the concepts under several different headings. The beauty of my Roberts FLAGS Model and its related concepts is that it adapts well to any number of different group settings in need of educational materials. As you read the following pages you will be able to see how the entire process adapts very well to groups regardless of culture and ethnicity, educational level, or background. This is true because the very nature of the model allows individuals to apply the lists and diagrams to their own unique needs and circumstances, using the book itself as a textbook and training guide for each group member and leader.

For instance, if someone is leading a group for those dealing with chemical dependency issues, the title "A.D.U.L.T. Education: Acceptance, Determination, Understanding, Love, and Trust" serves as a very strong description of the focus of the group. A leader of such a group simply needs to apply the RFLAGS Model and related concepts to the goals of any program transforming it into a psychoeducational class that can be spread out over a four to six week period.

Another example would be that of using the RFLAGS Model to address specific issues and objectives within educational settings to address teacher and administrative effectiveness in the classroom and on the school campus. An appropriate program title would be "U.S.E.R. Friendly: Understanding Student Emotional Reactivity". The RFLAGS Model would be a great format to use in increasing awareness of why kids in school settings are not progressing and advancing in spite of maximum efforts by school personnel. A good example of this is related to the need for educators to understand that quite often the lack of success on the part of students goes beyond the context of school and is impacted by factors within other contexts especially within the home/family context described in this book. One of the most valuable aspects of *At the Mercy of Externals: Righting wrongs and Protecting Kids, 2*nd *Edition*, is that the model and related theories offer a clear explanation of the external factors often impeding a student's ability, and even their willingness and desire to learn. The chapters addressing other points of consideration within the scope of this text lend themselves well to open discussion and critical thinking in applying the concepts to any particular setting.

Other examples would include a group for parenting called "H.O.M.E. Improvements: Honoring, Opening, Mending, and Empowering". A class addressing domestic violence and victimization could use the title "B.E.A.T.E.N. Down: Battered, Emotionally Abused, Threatened,

Endangered, and Neglected". For at risk youth a great program name would be "K.I.D.S. With Hope: Kindness, Individuality, Determination, and Success". Finally a program title for those being trained to work with kids in such roles as volunteers, daycare workers, counselors or mentors would be "R.O.L.E. Models: Respect, Optimism, Love, and Encouragement". I am sure you will be able to come up with other program titles to meet the needs of any psychoeducational group, seminar, or workshop that you have the responsibility for and opportunity to lead.

When using this book and its content, encourage group members to participate fully in the discussions, and also in identifying and applying various topics as indicated relative to the goals of your group. As a group leader you can be creative in your presentation of the materials and can trust the process if you are well prepared and fully understand the concepts found within these pages. If you begin the process with your own efforts to conduct an open and honest evaluation of yourself and your history it will be easy to encourage others to do the same. Always keep in mind that nothing about the model and related materials creates any of the negative emotions associated with histories of abuse and victimization. These emotional scars are simply brought into conscious awareness where they can be faced and dealt with, sometimes through professional help and guidance if the realities seem to be too overwhelming and frightening. Remember that if we are not careful the past will live in our present as it did in mine (much less so now). It is only by addressing this reality and the realities creating the underlying negative emotions that we can move forward and right the wrongs and protect the kids in our care regardless of the role we play in their lives. After all, every adult is at least indirectly responsible for the world as it exists today relative to the kids who will be the adults of tomorrow. I truly hope *At the Mercy of Externals: Righting Wrongs and Protecting Kids, 2nd Edition,* will serve as a guide for adults and adolescents everywhere, and in all walks of life, to begin the process of both healing wounds and preventing all abuse and victimization of kids in the future. My greatest dream is that this book will serve as such a starting point.

CHAPTER I
Foundations of Beliefs

My desire to become a psychologist stemmed from my fascination with human nature and what makes people "tick" so to speak. Part of that desire included a need to understand myself, as well as the people who played significant roles in my life. Of particular interest were the members of my immediate family and my relationships with them. Because of my belief that the complicating factors from my childhood also complicated my adult years, I became determined to leave the past where it belonged and create more productive patterns of thinking and behaving to help me fulfill the roles I would assume as I matured. By using a metaphorical microscope to carefully examine my "self" and various factors from my past, I have discovered some amazing ways of understanding what makes people tick which have nothing to do with blaming or scapegoating. The alternative is to understand people for whom they are rather than for whom we might like them to be. This approach allows us to move forward without all of the hatred and resentment resulting from harmful experiences during childhood.

Another significant discovery was the understanding I gained of the importance of effectively fulfilling our adult roles and responsibilities as they pertain to children of all ages. My work as a psychologist has made me painfully aware of the damage done to kids when these roles are neglected and not taken seriously. In today's world of being so busy and self-absorbed it is easy to forget that the kids in our lives still deserve our complete

1

commitment to be the best we can be for them and for ourselves. One of the most rewarding outcomes from my interaction with kids is watching them learn and grow – even in my roles as father and grandfather. As you read this book you will learn how to facilitate the same process for kids more effectively and appropriately than ever before. In other words you will be able to optimize your effectiveness to match your intentions and hope of making a difference relative to the roles you choose. You will also have the opportunity in some cases to be that one adult who makes a positive difference in the lives of kids under your care. If you successfully apply these approaches to your role as a parent then you won't need to place so much hope on interventions from "outsiders". This level of effectiveness will occur only after each of us completes a thorough and honest process of self-assessment and evaluation, seeking professional guidance when the task appears to be too daunting and painful to complete alone.

I feel as though I have been given this process as an inspired task, one that I accept wholeheartedly, by sharing with the world the things I have learned over the last several years and especially intensifying about 1986. It was at that time I began to pursue what ultimately became my career as a licensed clinical psychologist. While this book is not *about* me, it comes from *within* me relative to almost unbelievable life-altering experiences I have had both on a personal and a professional level. Within the pages of this text I will share only a few very personal accounts associated with my journey through childhood and early adulthood as they relate to an understanding of how I know what I know. As I look back to 1986 and the years between then and now, I am amazed at how carefully and clearly my ideas have evolved. I firmly believe the process of writing this book originates from a Source much greater than myself alone, and actually is a gift from that Source through me to the world.

My younger brother recently asked me, as we discussed some sensitive historical family matters, why I get so emotional about such things. At that moment I didn't know how to respond and I simply indicated that my emotions are probably associated with my perception that I have been through a lot. In the months since that conversation I have come to realize how my training, education, and profession have made me intensely aware of and more sensitive to incredible hardship in the lives of people around the world. These experiences made it necessary early on that I participate earnestly in my own personal therapy as a continuation and amplification of an ongoing process of honest and open self-evaluation. I know this is one of the main reasons, as an important first step, for my successes and reputation as a licensed clinical psychologist. My decision to start my own therapy resulted directly from my desire to work continuously toward becoming the best person I can become;

always trying to be the best I can be at any given moment and yet still striving for more knowledge and wisdom as my process continues.

In spite of barriers often associated with race and culture, I have been able to go into geographical areas and interact with people of amazing diversity, and be accepted. For me this has been and is a very humbling experience making me extremely conscious of the never-outdated concept of "man's inhumanity to man". I see more and more how this lack of consideration and regard appears to be based in both arrogance and ignorance which often results in abuse/victimization of others within the contexts of home/family, school, community, society, politics, and religion.

While this book will focus primarily on the first three contexts of home/family, school, and community I will also attempt to address the last three more lofty and philosophical contexts of society, politics, and religion. The effort will be to propose ways my model, and its various components, are rather universally applicable. Within this text I hope to gain the attention of adults within all readily identifiable roles, as well as the attention of people in more global positions of power and influence over others. This list of adult groups will start with parents, relatives, and other individuals from the first three contexts who are directly responsible for children and for others who are in some ways vulnerable.

From there I will attempt to expand the list to include people and groups dominating the contexts of societal, political, and religious influences, and who are always at least ethically responsible for children and others who truly are at the mercy of numerous external factors. This second list will include: individuals, groups, and world leaders who set societal standards; politicians and political factions serving as policy and law makers; and religious leaders at all levels who in many cases unsuccessfully attempt to address spirituality and moral values. We will attempt to discover realities existing within the respective ideologies espoused by leading nations as they try to find a middle ground between the poles of extremism relative to an almost complete breakdown of antiquated traditional conservatism toward destructive and reckless forms of liberalism. This represents a shift from too much control and domination to a growing lack of regard and consideration for self and others. I will propose roles of leading nations to make efforts toward righting the wrongs in countries currently exhibiting overt examples of abuse and victimization resulting in horrific acts of terrorism. Frequently religion, gender-based violence, and race/ethnicity are the bases of both disagreement and justification in developing nations.

I do not intend to come across as someone who has all of the answers, or as one who whines about today's corruption and immorality, longing for a return to the "good ol' days". With my Roberts FLAGS Model I simply intend to propose ways of examining and understanding our current conditions to first recognize the urgent need for change and balancing. It is then possible to begin identifying, developing, and implementing opportunities somewhat systematically and formally, as a process of healing and repairing centuries of abuse and victimization present throughout history and currently within all contexts and around the world. This book, with the model and related materials, will give all adults, especially those serving in professional roles, a means to understand and teach the concepts offered within these pages.

Therefore, the purpose within these pages is to initiate the changing of this world toward the creation of a better world for us and for those generations to come. It is time to correct the errors in the ways adults and leaders view our responsibilities individually and collectively as compared to the relative context or contexts in which we act, or in some cases, act out our hopelessness and helplessness. This approach is better than blindly and foolishly denying the unfulfilled obligations we hold, especially to children. As we correct we also prepare a much more desirable existence for ourselves and for those yet to exist. We must identify both the abusers and those "underdogs" who are the victims, or who see themselves as the victims of abuse. This book is all about honest self-examination by adults and leaders who, by the very nature of these roles, are put in positions of power and influence whereby they either build up or break down.

It is time to teach to every man, woman, and adolescent the responsibility and obligation for ourselves, each other, and especially for the children who are constantly brought into our care, either directly or indirectly. This must be done regardless of whether we ignorantly and arrogantly deny, rather than acknowledge and accept, our unquestionable calling. Each generation prepares the way for the next. To stop the existing destructive cycles we must begin now to understand and correct ourselves on all levels and in all quadrants.

In both theory and reality the concepts of parents and leaders are the same and are, therefore, somewhat interchangeable. So true is this that the very leaders of nations and the world have a significant necessity to nurture all under their care, not to dominate, but to teach in the sense of guiding each "underdog" group to shake off its stigma of victimization and stand up to the abusers. I define "underdogs" as those who are vulnerable to people in any position of power and influence as determined by a number of both biological and environmental factors. Abusers are not leaders, nor effective parents. They are the destroyers of all that is good and pure within the innocence of those truly vulnerable enough to be abused.

This is the true representation of an "underdog" – the very real, rather than accepted and worn, vulnerability associated with Fear, Loneliness, Anger, Guilt, and Shame (FLAGS). An "underdog" is simply any child, adult, group, new idea, or new ideal which must be nurtured into reaching its full potential. Those who are truly vulnerable in life have few, if any choices and are indeed easy targets. Those who are not helpless, and yet claim to be victims, are merely buying into to the one-down position resulting from a history of victimization, and yet ironically coupled with a future of new opportunities. Traditional thoughts that bind and limit our motivation to learn and grow are no longer acceptable. Such traditions are often defended from a basis of Fear, Loneliness, Anger, Guilt, and Shame (FLAGS) based in unresolved issues rather than from actual ongoing abuse/victimization. This thinking insists that we keep acting out our emotion-based anxieties and frustrations, rather than deal with and correct a destructive past living within our present. To break such cycles requires nothing less than identifying, understanding, and facing the emotions fueling our frustrations and causing us to not care.

Most of my approaches to psychology, including the development of these concepts, are grounded in the Existential and Humanistic philosophies as applied to psychology from literature by the well known psychologists, Dr. Rollo May and Dr. Carl Rogers. These are the same philosophies beautifully implied within the pages of many of today's books dealing with spiritual approaches to viewing and reviewing life and existence. I was particularly inspired by the recent writings of James Redfield and the Celestine Prophecy collection; and by The Third Millennium, written by Ken Carey. My most recent inspirations come from Mick Quinn and The Uncommon Path; and Ken Wilber's 20+ works regarding Integral Spirituality and Psychology. These writers are true visionaries who, at the turn of the new millennium and beyond, both confirmed and expanded my own beliefs about the latent potential beginning to awaken within the universe and the souls of people.

In addition to a great deal of reading about philosophy, psychology, and spirituality, I have had many wonderful, and often times difficult experiences which have brought me to my present understanding of purpose in my own life. I feel I have an obligation, as we all do, to share with others those insights which have helped advance me through my process of living and growing. The title of this book, *At the Mercy of Externals*, is extracted from The Book of Runes, by Ralph Blum. It suggests that many of us spend our lives looking outside of ourselves for answers that can only be found within and in relation to ourselves and others. Furthermore, it indicates that those factors that are the most detrimental to our growth and development come from external sources and are often associated with abuse/victimization. Also taken from The Book of Runes is a powerful prayer, one which has advanced me rapidly forward in my process. When spoken with true commitment it opens one's life to all possibilities for learning and growth. The prayer is: "I will to will Thy will." At first read it may seem simple. However, I think it requires a great deal of exploration, and even translation into one's own words. For me the best translation is something to the effect that with all of my being, and from my heart, I desire to desire what You desire; or I want to want what You want, as the only spiritually based philosophy making any sense. True spiritual growth and maturity is indicated by the revision of the prayer to simply "I will Thy Will." "I want what You Want." "I desire what You Desire." If there truly is some overriding universal process, then why not tap into its Source and maximize its progression. I firmly believe that the Energy that is us is God or the Source within us.

The Past that Lived in My Present

Allow me to share with you a little of the educational and technical history of how some of my theories and continuing queries have evolved. None of my life had any sense of identifiable purpose until I began taking control of my life and destiny in my late 20's. My earlier experiences did not have any real conscious intention. I let go and began to follow my intuition, but my intention became directed only as I consciously and earnestly sought spiritual guidance from God as the Source (not the religious concepts of god) and stepped aside as much as I had learned to do. The point is that even though I was not consciously aware of how to proceed, I proceeded and trusted the urges coming from deep within my soul.

With an undergraduate degree in English Literature and a minor in music, and after many years of an unsatisfying career in the field of both retail and wholesale credit, I decided to return to school to work on a Master of Science degree in Administration at Georgia College. Close to the end of this endeavor, I realized I was only getting deeper into the credit field. After deciding I was too close to finishing this degree to quit, I completed the courses and graduated in June 1986.

Toward the end of this program, I decided to follow my heart and pursue a degree in Psychology as I had wanted to do for many years. So, in June 1986 I began taking two prerequisite courses which were required before I could qualify for the Master of Science degree in General Psychology, also at Georgia College. Needing a project for a research design class, I decided to study grief - not in the traditional sense of death and dying; but relative to unresolved losses and bereavement associated with and resulting from dysfunctional backgrounds of abuse and victimization. With this research project I began the development of the Roberts Grief and Loss Analysis Scale (RGLAS), an instrument designed to detect unresolved grief which impairs and complicates current adult functioning. I gained recognition for this initial effort at the University of Georgia PSI CHI Conference in April 1987, when I made my first research presentation. It was a graduate level competition, and I knew I would be disqualified because my initial research was conducted for an undergraduate class. However, I was told by the judges that I would have won "hands down" because my ideas were original and innovative, which are the bases of good research. This was the "go ahead" I needed.

From my initial efforts, I worked with the RGLAS questionnaire as the focus of my master's thesis, at which time I constructed and analyzed the current form of the RGLAS. I completed my MS in Psychology in June 1989, and then took a giant leap of faith. Using all the courage I could find at the age of 35 I quit my job, sold most of everything I owned, and left the southeast to attend the California School of Professional Psychology in Los Angeles (CSPP-LA), now associated with Alliant International University. I started this program in August 1989 only two months after completing my second master's degree. For the next four years I worked and sacrificed to earn my Ph.D. in Clinical Psychology, graduating from CSPP-LA in June 1993. CSPP accepted my master's thesis as Study I, and allowed me to continue my research with the RGLAS by conducting validity and reliability studies to further substantiate the RGLAS as a useful tool in the detection of unresolved grief resulting from dysfunctional family backgrounds. In other words, this research served to indicate whether or not the RGLAS works as a measurement of unresolved grief. Fortunately both my thesis and dissertation research yielded very successful results supporting the usefulness of the RGLAS.

My ideas for this particular research came from my own experience of growing up in a very conflicted, restrictive, and abusive family environment. Both of my parents were raised during the difficult time surrounding "The Great Depression", by very abusive fathers. Both were middle children in the sibling line up, my dad growing up in rural Mississippi, and my mother growing up in a city in Alabama. My parents were not bad people, and none of this is intended to serve some type of need to blame or find fault. I am simply talking about reality and the kinds of complicating factors which made their adult lives difficult both as a married couple and as parents. As we go through my model the terms reality, truth, and honesty will be major components in the self-examination required if this presentation is to be understood as applicable to people in general.

My beliefs are that adults have a responsibility to make sure we are stable emotionally, mentally, psychologically, and spiritually as the only hope for children to have a secure base from which to experience the world. Because my parents never resolved the losses and unresolved issues from their own abusive backgrounds, my younger siblings and I have had many problems trying to deal with life during childhood and adulthood. Each of us as siblings had a different experience with our parents because of the differences in our ages. I am the oldest, preceding my brother by four years and my sister by fourteen years. My memories of the problems and tragedies early in my parents' marriage are very different from the memories of my siblings, indicating that each respective experience in our family was different and very subjective. When thrown in with differences in personalities and factors of time and other life events, it is possible to see how each family member has a different perspective on what happened, and how the family dynamics changed and evolved over time.

The important factor to remember is that while some aspects of the environment changed, the basic personalities of our parents changed very little during the times in which we lived as children and adolescents under their roof. Through the end of my parents' lives there was a great deal of denial and an insistence there was "a lot of love in our home" during those years. The reality is that while our parents perhaps "meant well", and were truly using what they convinced themselves to be the right approaches, they were in actuality taking their anxiety out on us, rather than resolving it for and between each other. As you will see in the chapters to follow I have developed the Roberts FLAGS (RFLAGS) Model as a way to understand these patterns of dysfunction and how everyone tends to act out emotion-based anxiety. As we go through the model and the various components, you will see how this process evolves and continues, setting people up for a great deal of negative Karma, in the sense that whatever we set into motion is what comes back to us. Virtually every culture has some form of this concept as a part of its overall cultural philosophy. You will also be able to see how this negative and ineffective process can be broken and changed into something which works rather than something which destroys. The goal is to change negative patterns and perceptions into actions which will generate a positive future and heal relationships from within, between our "self" and our higher "Self", and between us and other people when and where there is an opportunity or a desire to do so.

Because of the experiences in my own life, along with my own set of complicating factors, I have spent most of my adult life trying to recover from my past. I can honestly say that while my recovery continues, I have made considerable progress and now I am ready to share my discoveries with you as I have with others during and after the years of my education and training in the field of psychology. My required formalized training has ended; however,

I see all of my future as an opportunity and obligation to myself to continue learning and growing. Even the revision and republishing of this book will certainly prove to be a valuable personal "training" experience now and into the future. I believe it will open many new doors as I continue seeking fulfillment of a process in life toward ultimately maximizing my spiritual growth, development, and maturity.

Of particular importance to the development of the RFLAGS Model and the writing of this book were the experiences I had while I was in my Ph.D. program and in the years since. Beginning in September 1990, my first two years of practicum and internship experience were within two different community-based, non-profit clinics. It was at this time I began to realize my future in psychology would be spent primarily in the provision of services to underserved populations. This approach made it difficult to pay back student loans, but for me it is the most satisfying and challenging.

For my third and final year of pre-doctoral training, I decided I wanted to work with "high risk youth", the only population with which I had not had any experience. I applied for and was accepted into an internship program with an emphasis in gang prevention. Services were provided to low income families through The Family Service Center within an elementary school located in East Los Angeles. Though quite nervous about what to expect and whether or not the community would accept me, I went in with an intense desire to learn, without an attitude of knowing it all or having all the answers. I had begun to study Spanish a few years earlier and found that the people in East LA, with whom I had the privilege of working, appreciated my efforts to learn and speak their language. My internship at this site continued for two years, at both the pre-doctoral and post-doctoral levels. As confirmation of my acceptance by the community I was even given the honor of speaking at the commencement exercises at the end of my second year of service. The invitation to speak was extended to me by the parents of the children at the school and was one of the greatest honors I could have ever received.

The staff and families associated with this school made me feel welcome. In an effort to address the needs of the children in East LA relative to the excessive violence they faced on a daily basis, I developed an anti-violence program, called "KIT Cadets: **K**ids **I**n **T**ouch Against Violence" (included in my third book *ProKids, Inc.: The Message and The Movement; A Guide for Parents and Professionals* – www.createspace.com/3526148). Each time a group of kids completed the six-week program we had a public assembly at school to award the certificates and invited the parents to the program. Because, at the time, this school was part of the Healthy Start Program within the state of California, the funding for the provision of services was made possible through a state grant.

During the first year of service at the site, I became fascinated with the gang culture given the fact I was working right in the middle of it on a daily basis. I began to understand the dynamics of gang involvement and decided I wanted to work specifically with this population as well. Six months prior to my assignment in East LA I had been jumped and robbed by three gang members close to where I was living. In spite of this I knew I wanted to understand how dysfunction and circumstance played a part in the lives of these kids, not only in their homes, but within the other contexts as well. Soon I was given another opportunity to obtain a part time job working under supervision and through a gang prevention grant at an additional school site just east of East Los Angeles. This school was an alternative community school established specifically for middle school kids with serious behavior problems, most of whom were gang kids. I had this job for almost three years, which gave me an incredible opportunity to work under supervision with gang kids and their families and the dysfunctional environments that provided the impetus for kids to act out by joining gangs.

One other factor relative to job opportunities came through employment at a private psychiatric hospital where I worked as a psychoeducational instructor with substance abusers diagnosed with other psychiatric conditions such as depression and anxiety. I was asked to co-facilitate groups with other therapists and was given the opportunity to develop my own group formats. The group topics included: abuse recovery, anger management, loss and grief, and family dysfunction. It was during this time I developed the earliest forms of my RFLAGS Model, as I tried to come up with a focus for each of these groups. The patients in the program were actually participants in my own initial program development.

One additional element that prepared me for the work I do currently was involvement for an extended period of time in my own therapy. I started therapy in my first year at CSPP-LA as a requirement for graduation, and as a way to help me deal with the stress of a Ph.D. program and the culture shock of moving from "the Deep South" to California. This, along with some other significant complicating factors in my personal life, kept me in therapy for several years. Therapy was the best investment I could have ever made in my "self" and my future. My therapist was an excellent guide, who helped me explore the answers I needed relative to my own history, and relative to my desire to be the best therapist I could possibly be. I firmly believe every therapist needs a solid background in having been "on the couch", so to speak, if they are to be effective. For it is in finding answers and insight into our own "dysfunction" that we are able to help others with the same process. How can we possibly help people solve their problems if we have not identified and resolved our own issues first?

Sometimes people with the best of intentions actually do the most harm simply because, quite often, people assume they need no personal assistance, or they have no personal issues or problems. In my opinion, virtually everyone can benefit from some degree of ongoing self-examination, simply because no one comes from the perfect family, a concept existing only as an ideal. Therapy is primarily an educational experience in which a *competent* licensed therapist shares with a client their wisdom gained through experience and education, representing my belief in each of us within the therapeutic context being both learner and teacher. Hopefully the therapist has more to offer than to gain from experiences and interactions with clients.

This last thought of the teacher continuing to learn is what kept me in therapy for so long. As I began to work with extremely dysfunctional families associated with gang kids and juvenile offenders, I found myself being faced with reflections of my own past relative to abuse/victimization and emotional neglect. I began to experience unresolved grief reactions as I listened to kids talk about the essential elements of childhood of which they were deprived for various reasons. Deprivation resulted not always because parents didn't care, but because the parents' unresolved issues interfered with their ability and responsibility to provide for the children in their care on every level. Parenting is a full time job and a lifelong commitment regardless of whether or not parents stay together in a successful relationship. It requires sacrifice as needed to provide effectively for children; not sacrifice of the self, but sacrifice in the sense that even after survival issues are satisfied, kids have to be the first priority until they reach the age when they can effectively care for themselves and live independently.

As I was confronted with these unresolved issues, I found my own anxiety level going up at times. I learned to use this as a gauge indicating a need to look at my own emotional state before I could help people find their respective answers. If parents do their job right, they successfully raise their children to leave them, and to become independent, responsible, and "functional" (as opposed to dysfunctional) members of society. Though my family provided me with the material factors such as food, clothing and shelter which I needed as a child, I never had the nurturing or guidance needed to teach me self-discipline, self-confidence, self-esteem, critical/creative thinking, or good problem-solving/decision-making skills. All of my decisions were made for me until I reached the age of 16 and to some extent until I got married at the age of 20 primarily as a means of escaping the very restrictive environment in which I was raised.

By continuing in therapy, I was able to take all of my concerns and questions back to my therapist who guided me through the often difficult and painful exploration of what I believe to have been the reality of my past.

As I found my own answers, I was able to take my insights into therapy with others and try them out in appropriate and professional ways on my clients. This served as a means of fine tuning them for me personally, and as a way of learning to generalize my experience and insight into situations which were at least similar to my own on an emotional level. I became, and still am, both teacher and learner. Once I resolved my issues I was able to terminate my personal therapy, but not my learning process.

The reality is there are some issues we cannot handle without professional guidance. It was as though my therapist gave me the parenting I needed, which went beyond basic physical necessities, to give me a solid basis from which to grow and learn on my own. At the same time, my therapist helped me find the ability to effectively work with one of the most difficult populations in psychology - "at risk or high risk youth". Other than a few very basic useful components, I have discarded most of the past that interfered with my ability to effectively deal with life as an adult. In other words I feel I have resolved much of the dysfunction I experienced as a child. Again, none of this is about blaming. It is only about reality, truth, and honesty, which are the same elements I introduce my clients to whether they are adults or kids. My model is rooted in these factors; with resolution of dysfunction being based in simple universally accepted and acknowledged spiritual concepts. Again, the object of my work is to help others heal one's relationship to "self" and then between self and others regardless of the context, or the nature of the relationship. This is why I consider my methods to fall under the heading of Spiritual Psychology.

In the chapters to follow I intend to share with you the RFLAGS Model which is the center of my understanding of how adults and kids tend to act out emotion-based anxiety, rather than face the negative emotions and their origins which create the anxiety. I will attempt to connect all concepts to this model; therefore it is important for each reader to have a clear understanding of how it works. Many of my insights come from the experiences I have had presenting my theories to others both as a psychologist and as a college instructor, and in addition to understanding my own personal experiences. Because the entire presentation has grown and continues to grow, I will also propose ideas for further consideration during this presentation. It is my hope that the RFLAGS Model will be expanded to fully achieve the status of being 'my gift from the Source to the world' through input and reciprocation from the readers.

Because the RFLAGS Model actually comes toward the end of the conceptual sequence, after the presentation of the model in the next chapter,

I will back up to the beginning so we can explore the actual adult roles and responsibilities we are suppose to adopt. We will look at how some key words have different meanings to different people, especially looking at labels and often times unconscious prejudices/biases adults possess and convey to kids. In the process I will refer directly to the model as a means of tying everything together at all levels of the presentation.

Conceptually the sequence flows from Adult Roles and Responsibilities; Abuse/Victimization; Contexts of Abuse/Victimization; Complicating Factors; Losses and Grief; Personality Traits; the RFLAGS Model; to Breaking the Cycle. Within these pages we will: start with what we hopefully are doing right and the good things we have experienced; move into what we actually may be doing or have experienced; and look at the environments in which victimization occurs. From there we will identify adult patterns of dysfunction; see how all of these components create the need to act out emotion-based anxiety; and finally move into changing perspectives and resolving the negative influences from the past. The final chapters will be more along the lines of a where-do-we-go-from-here approach, in which I will suggest some possible expansions of the presentation to more universal perspectives and applications. Within the first half of this book you will be directed to a number of appendices. These lists are in some cases too long to be embedded within each chapter. So, please bear with me relative to the importance of these lists and take the time to study them as suggested and at the time suggested relative to each respective appendix.

As I guide you through this process of self-examination, problem identification, and ultimate resolution, I hope you will find the faith and courage to be both open-minded and honest. I also hope you will continue to see in my writings the courage I have discovered and used to get beyond fear, even as I present several different personal aspects of my history and process. As I said earlier, this book is not *about* me. It is from *within* me relative to insights I have gained to date in my own life process. I believe my ideas are valid and have been successfully developed and shared since 1986 within various settings and with extremely diverse audiences from many walks of life. Based of my successes as a psychologist I know these methods and theories have been tried and proven many times over. Countless numbers of kids and families have benefited from my outreach to those who appear to be hopeless and helpless relative to their life perspective and circumstances.

Now, with courage as our banner, LET'S GO!

CHAPTER II
Roberts FLAGS Model

Different theorists have many different ways of attempting to explain how human behavior develops. By now people in general readily accept the influences of both genetics and the environment upon the ultimate result of who we become as adults. No one denies the significant interactions between the personality traits and other genetic factors we are born with, and the factors outside of ourselves which help determine how these traits ultimately manifest themselves behaviorally as we grow up and mature. I personally believe the interaction between us and the external environmental factors continues until the day we die. However, I also believe the most critical interactions relative to shaping personality characteristics occur when we are children, especially during the early years. While I believe it is possible to overcome and compensate for deficiencies during those significant early years, I believe even more strongly in giving kids what they need so ideally there is nothing, or at least very little, to mend.

The main developmental theorist I want to focus on relative to understanding my model and the development of maladaptive behavior is Erik Erikson. He was one of the first psychologists to view personality development as a process occurring across the entire lifespan. His first five stages, which cover infancy through adolescence, are the most relevant to this text. Without successful mastery and completion of these early stages, the adult stages of development will likely be quite complicated, with very few productive accomplishments possible throughout the remaining lifespan.

Erikson's "eight stages of man" are:

> Trust vs. Mistrust (infancy);
> Autonomy vs. Shame and Doubt (ages 1-3);
> Initiative vs. Guilt (ages 3-5 or 6);
> Industry vs. Inferiority (ages 5 or 6-12);
> Identity vs. Role Confusion (ages 12-18);
> Intimacy vs. Isolation (ages 18-35);
> Generativity vs. Stagnation (ages 35-60);
> Integrity vs. Despair (age 60-death).

As you look over the above list, think about a couple of factors. First of all, each of us is born with the unspoken assumption the world will be a safe and friendly place. Secondly, we innately assume we will be loved and nurtured, with all of our needs hopefully being met as they were prior to birth. Finally, we assume our parents will be the ones who make all of this happen. Unfortunately, depending on many different possibilities, *none* of the above may turn out to be reality. As children we cannot control either our environment or the people in it, much less the conditions of the environment into which we are introduced.

Take a little time to think about the quality of the people and the environment as they existed at the time you were born. Really spend some time looking honestly at what was happening, and at the personalities of those within your birth reality. Hopefully, for many of you this awareness is a positive one, as it was for me initially. On the other hand, there are likely a number of readers for whom this reality is rather disappointing and even shocking and traumatic. For others like me, the first few years may have been relatively safe and stable. However, this environment may have taken on a rather tragic twist as life began to throw some very difficult realities into the mix which then changed everything in the future. Even if we are not abused by people we can feel abused by life's events.

The Past that Lived in My Present

By all accounts my birth reality on Friday, May 7, 1954, at 2:12 P.M. must have been quite stable and hopeful, with the exception of having been born breech. Rather than being delivered normally, I was reportedly pulled into the world with a pair of forceps. Perhaps my reluctance to be born was prophetic, possibly even setting me up for some of the distance between my mother and myself which lasted throughout her life. Maybe she never forgave me for the 36 hours of painful and difficult labor she reportedly endured.

When I was born my parents had been married for nearly two years, with both of them working and enjoying the post World War II boom. At the time of my birth we were living in a small apartment close to the downtown area. After about two years my parents built a small house north of the city of Mobile, Alabama and in a newly incorporated area called Chickasaw advertising itself as "The All White City", as printed on the welcome signs until the Civil Rights Movement in the 1960's. My dad was apparently proud to have a son for his first child. Even though he worked as a mortician at the time of my birth, he took a job two years later in December 1956 at a newly opened textile mill, where he worked until he retired. This kind of stability is an important factor relative to his philosophies of security and his priorities which resulted for many people who were products of "The Great Depression".

My dad's jobs as a mortician, and later as a worker at the factory, required him to work rotating shifts. Because both of my parents worked, most of my time was spent with my maternal grandmother; with my dad on his days off; and later with Bell, our housekeeper my parents hired after they moved from the main city and into the suburban community. I have only a few memories of my mother prior to the time when my brother was born in June 1958. Unfortunately, they are not pleasant ones. I can only wonder if mom was ever happy. However, all of my memories prior to June 1958 of my maternal grandparents, my dad, and Bell are very positive. I believe they gave me a reasonably stable basis upon which to begin my life. According to Erikson's stages of development, I gained trust, autonomy and initiative given their love and support.

All of this changed drastically, beginning with the birth of my brother on June 3, 1958. My mother quit her job just prior to his birth, apparently with some resentment and probably at the insistence of my dad who reportedly wanted her home "to raise his children". Shortly after these events, my parents sold their first house and started construction on another one in the same area. Because the first house sold so quickly, we moved into a government housing project to wait for the new house to be completed. Very soon after this move, I have the first really vivid memory of hearing my mother scream upon receiving the news by phone that her father, brother and brother-in-law had all drowned while fishing at a reservoir in or near Paducha, Kentucky. All of the families were visiting my mother's brother who lived there with his wife and two children. Suddenly our family was faced with an unpredictable tragedy that left three women widows and four children fatherless. My dad would likely have died as well if not for the fact he was unable to get the time off for vacation.

This tragedy was especially difficult for my mother to face because of her own unresolved issues from the past relative to her father, issues that I would not understand until a few years after her death (that is another book!). While I never knew him as such, my grandfather reportedly had been a very abusive, violent alcoholic who would disappear for extended periods of time, leaving my grandmother to provide for her three children as best she could during and after the Great Depression and through World War II. My grandmother remarked once with tears in her eyes, "there are some things far worse than divorce", indicating the zeitgeist of the times when women were oftentimes powerless over such abuse and victimization.

As you can imagine, with all of these family tragedies my life also took a traumatic turn for the worse. In June 1958 I found myself with a mother I hardly knew. I could no longer spend the same amount of time with my dad, maternal grandparents, or Bell because of the changes initiated by my brother's birth, which included the fact I was no longer an only child. We then moved from the only home I had known for two years, and my grandfather and two uncles tragically died.

All I remember from the years during childhood after that horrible summer are the constant fights between my parents, and my attempts to take care of and console this unpredictably vicious, depressed, anxious, angry woman I called "Mama". My dad, whom I had loved and trusted, suddenly became this angry, sadistically cruel, frightening man who started abusing me both physically and emotionally because of the tension between him and my mom. All of my time was spent trying to please them in an effort to protect myself from their attacks which were impossible for me to understand as a child. My love for my dad turned to hatred and what he called respect became nothing more than fear, resentment, and compliance. My dad was, and continued to be a control freak throughout virtually all of his life. His love turned to total emotional neglect as my world, as I had known it, fell apart. My mother continued to be vicious, angry, unpredictable, and manipulative throughout her life until just before she died in April 2000. The two of them managed to keep the family divided to meet their own needs for control and revenge. As for many people, my anger toward them lies in the fact they got away with this, with many outsiders thinking we had the perfect family. How can I forgive my parents for things they wouldn't even acknowledge much less apologize for doing?

The only good thing for me that came out of the tragedy is that my maternal grandmother moved into a basement apartment my parents offered to her in the new house. This meant my grandmother moved into my environment and lived there all of my years while growing up from 1958 forward. My initial separation from her lasted only about six months. She was clearly the saving grace that kept me from becoming a total emotional wreck. Even at the age of 100, my grandmother's love for me never changed, except to grow stronger. Interestingly enough, in many settings I have found the love of a maternal grandmother to have been a stabilizing factor in the lives of others who have also endured very dysfunctional backgrounds. During all of the years following the tragic deaths, Granny continued to give me the love and support I needed. She sensed my vulnerability from all of the conflict and abuse that I endured in the house just above her basement apartment.

The important point here is that even a relatively solid basis was subject to being torn apart at a crucial point in my emotional development. This resulted in part from a series of unavoidable and unpredictable events, and also by the unresolved issues from childhood present in the lives of both of my parents; events brought to the surface by the tragedy. Also illustrated is the fact that early on the emotional void with my mom was filled by two "mother" figures in my life – my grandmother and Bell, whom I loved as much as I loved my grandmother. Without these first few good years I cannot begin to imagine how many more emotional scars I would have had to deal with as an adult. So many people lack even the relatively solid basis I had at the beginning of my life. I don't know how I would have survived without this factor.

Following the deaths my trust turned to mistrust as I tried to carry on in the ways I had known previously as my reality. At age four it was hard to comprehend how any environment can change so quickly, and so permanently. The very people I had trusted were not available to me because of their own processes of bereavement and adjustment. The woman I should have been able to trust as my mother turned out to be emotionally unstable and unpredictable during all of my remaining years at home. My dad became unavailable emotionally, with the only remaining experiences with him being very negative and extremely unpleasant. As my home/family environment or context fell apart, the stage was set for me to develop many maladaptive ways of dealing with emotions and life. Into this already negative mix, abuse was introduced in the forms of extreme conflict between my parents, exposure to very fundamentalist and extreme religious views, and actual physical and emotional abuse from both of my parents. My dad even took on the same apparent characteristics of both of my grandfathers who were often gone, certainly unavailable emotionally, and very abusive when in the home. Without intentionally doing so, my parents recreated much the same kind of environment each of them endured as children, though possibly not quite as extreme in the present as in their respective pasts. My dad's father was apparently very similar to my mother's father, especially relative to the physical and emotional abuse and neglect.

Referring back to Erikson's model, take note as well of how these events also turned my trust into mistrust, my sense of confidence and autonomy into shame and doubt; and turned my sense of initiative into guilt. Along with all of this came a real sense of being totally confused about every facet of life. At this time religion became the only model presented to me as a way of making sense out of chaos. However, the Baptist religion into which I was introduced taught me I was a worthless sinner whom God would punish harshly for wrongdoing. Even "God" was abusive and I thought all of this was my fault. After all, the adults in my environment told me they were the ultimate authorities next to God. Questioning of their authority resulted in seriously abusive consequences. Fear and intimidation told me they were "right" on all counts and that to doubt them or God would result in more bad things happening. You can only imagine how all of these factors set me up to fail miserably at the next stage of development – industry vs. inferiority. What a way to start out in my experiences with school and the world outside of the home/family context!

Hopefully, I have successfully set the stage for you to understand the concept of emotion-based anxiety, and then to begin seeing how we tend to act this out behaviorally, rather than deal with it, explore it, and learn from it. It is important to explain that the details I have presented about my past are a presentation of my own reality. While I am sure most of it is true, I am not actually sure of the accuracy of some of the details or the perspective of some of what I consider to be facts. Remember, these are the memories of a young child recalled with no ability to discuss them for clarification with any of the characters involved. I am absolutely sure, however, of the emotional scars resulting from the behaviors I clearly remember from my parents. The only things I may have some confusion about are details, not the overall experiences.

However, this doesn't matter because, regardless of the facts, this was and <u>is</u> my reality. Of utmost importance is the awareness that my emotions connected to this reality are factual and are the result of the past as I recall having experienced it, even though I may be a little confused about details of some of the circumstances. In other words no one can dispute how I feel in the present about and because of the past. Furthermore, any distortion of the past I may have is not my fault. As children we will fill in the blanks on anything which does not make sense, certainly when there is no opportunity for questioning and correction. The unfortunate reality is that a child tends to internalize these past emotions, even to the point of denial and unawareness, coupled with the tendency to blame themselves for all of the negative experiences.

As in many families, no one in my family is willing to talk about any of this at a level where we could understand each perspective and correct any misperceptions. These subjects are taboo in the sense they are the past and the past is better left alone – "let sleeping dogs lie". The other factor is that the realties of everyone involved are subjective, and after so many years who can say with any certainty what is factual any more for anyone, other than a few "newspaper-like" details. Reality is subjective and each of us has to deal with our own subjective reality as best we can. Keep in mind, too, that everyone involved in these dramas now have their own likely subjective distortions of what actually happened and why. I have also found many times the perpetrators of abuse tend to suppress the memories of what they did to others who were the unfortunate targets of their victimization.

"The past" is a scary subject for a significant number of people. Even many of my clients and friends say they see no point in living in, or re-living the past. I actually agree with the notion of not living in the past. However, because the past often lives in our present on an unconscious level, I believe it is necessary to at least review the past as honestly and openly as we can in an effort to understand our historic reality and deal with the effects which often complicate our current lives. This needs to be done both by adults and adolescents, and usually with professional guidance. An unhealthy past results in later years being filled with doubt, insecurity, deprivation, and unpredictability, all generating a complicated emotional repertoire which we then act out behaviorally and emotionally. The "scary past" is the very one which seriously needs to be exposed, not necessarily in great detail, but in whatever detail is necessary to define it. Also, whenever and if ever possible, the details of the past should be checked out and either verified or corrected. However, this is possible only if those involved are open to communicating about the past. Certainly this is not a requirement, but can be beneficial if the option is available and desirable.

As we go through the RFLAGS Model and the other concepts associated with it, please understand that none of the process I present is about blaming, judging, or scapegoating. Rather than being seen as accusatory, I hope you will see the process simply as the expression of reality-based awarenesses and observations; in other words, an expression of our own subjective "Truth", and in many instances when sharing with you my past, *my* own subjective "Truth".

Over the years I have come to understand the difference between judging another person or situation, as opposed to simply stating a reality-based perception or observation. Sometimes people really are superficial and abusive, and to say so is simply to state a non-judgmental observation. To go any further and put a value of good or bad, right or wrong on it then makes it judgmental. The observed characteristic just is, and is part of the other person's subjective process, and is open to change and reevaluation on the part of the observer if improvements are made by the one being observed. The trick is to learn the difference between the two ideas and to also check our motivation for the expression of such awarenesses. Sometimes these kinds of observations should be kept to ourselves and filed away for our own information and at times for our own protection, being careful not to turn these observations into judgmental ways of dealing with or categorizing someone. In spite of the awareness, I believe we need to look behind and beyond what we see in an effort to see the person we are actually observing, thereby learning to *separate what people do from who they actually are.* This, however, is much easier to do with kids than with adults, because behaviors become more permanent parts of who we are if they are not checked and corrected at least during late adolescence. People can change, but the more permanent a behavior becomes, in the sense of being automatic and unconscious, the less likely people are to make those changes.

The RFLAGS Model serves as a visual and intellectual way to understand the development of maladaptive behavior. It is a means of helping us to understand that behavior is not necessarily representative of who we are as a person. It certainly is not representative of who we could be with the opportunity and willingness to resolve the emotions fueling the anxiety and the need to act out rather than feel bad or deal with the emotional basis. *Separating who we are from what we do is a key part of this concept!*

I do not believe in or support the use of labels, especially for children, because we tend to treat people according to the label(s) we impose upon them. For instance, I believe there are no such categories as "bad kids", "incorrigibles", or "a problem child". There are simply kids who do bad things or make bad choices, and kids who have problems. Though fairly subtle, this rather minor change in wording greatly affects the implications and perceptions. It amazes me how children are often referred to as bad kids, incorrigibles, and problem children even in professional circles and research literature. Check out research presented in the various psychological and psychiatric journals dealing with the subject of "The Problem Child" and other such stigmatizing terminology. To me this is extremely offensive and serves as a means of perpetuating the focus on behavior as being a true representation or manifestation of the actual character of the person behind the acts. Much of this goes back to the psychoanalytic notion of "characterological disorders" and is clearly associated with outdated religious philosophies focusing on sinners and condemnation.

Even though Sigmund Freud, often referred to as "the father of modern Psychology", set the stage for the investigation into human nature, many of its originators and subsequent followers have done a great deal of damage. They did so by labeling people as the problems or symptoms they exhibit, even labeling some lifestyles and personal identities as problematic when indeed they are not. We have come to accept as fact that if we make mistakes we are flawed in some way, especially if we tend to repeat the same mistakes, or appear to continuously make new mistakes. This thinking allows us to trap ourselves into believing "this is just the way I am. What I do wrong is an innate part of who I am and it cannot be changed." As we start with the RFLAGS Model and move into the other topics, hopefully each of you - who can see the need to do so - will be able to find the courage and the willingness to change your perspective relative to yourself and others. Clearly this is where the concept and implementation of honest self-assessment/evaluation/ examination comes into the process.

Visually the Roberts FLAGS (RFLAGS) Model contains four segments: Negative Emotions, Anxiety/Depression, Hopelessness/Helplessness (giving up), and Acting-Out Behaviors (see diagram below and Appendix A). This serves as a very useful graphic of the process evolving from negative emotions into the maladaptive acting-out behaviors which generally result from the unresolved issues and emotions.

Roberts FLAGS Model

Negative Emotions	**Anxiety/ Depression**	**Hopelessness/ Helplessness**	**Acting Out Behaviors**
Fear			
Loneliness			
Anger			
Guilt			
Shame			

Between Anxiety and Acting Out is the element of hopelessness/helplessness derived from the perception and choice of giving up or not caring, and/or feeling like no one else cares either. Conceptually the RFLAGS Model works in a cyclical fashion, always moving in a clockwise direction. The process is to identify each individual's respective terminology, patterns and elements under each of the segments of Anxiety/Depression, Helplessness/Hopelessness, and Acting-Out Behaviors to bring these into conscious awareness, and ultimately into conscious control. The goal then becomes that of understanding the emotion-based state of anxiety which is generally acted out rather than dealt with and resolved.

Starting with the emotions, note that the "F" is "Fear"; the "L" is "Loneliness"; the "A" is "Anger"; the "G" is "Guilt"; and the "S" is "Shame" - FLAGS. These are all negative emotions and certainly are not the only emotions which can be experienced. They are, however, the emotions which I believe, from both personal and professional experience, to be the most problematic, especially when they occur simultaneously and were created within and from a history of abuse and victimization. The result is a state of anxiety and possibly depression, which can be overwhelming and debilitating. Depression alone tends to be experienced in a passive manner, while depression associated with emotion-based anxiety tends to be acted out behaviorally, and often to extremes with extreme consequences resulting either immediately or ultimately.

The idea with the model is that the "FLAGS" are *waving* as an indication something is happening and going wrong. You can think of someone's life as being "stormy". However, the problem is most people are cut off from awareness of their emotions and, therefore, never identify them or deal with them. The focus tends to be on the resulting emotional state of anxiety/depression which is undesirable and something to be eliminated or avoided by whatever means available - often times in a maladaptive manner which only complicates and intensifies the emotional basis existing beyond conscious awareness. Elimination and avoidance of the unpleasant emotional state becomes the focus and eventually becomes second nature and unconscious as well in the sense of becoming an automatic reactive choice. The resulting problematic behaviors have the potential to become so completely habitual as to become permanent maladaptive coping styles.

I also believe depression generally accompanies anxiety, possibly even at times resulting from it as people realize their lives (rather than acknowledging their emotions) are out of control. On the other hand, I do not believe anxiety always accompanies depression, which when experienced as the only emotional state tends to be very passive and non-motivational. However, as I indicated above, a state of anxiety and/or anxious depression tends to be acted out rather than resolved. All of this is by degree in the sense that the stronger the negative emotional basis is, the more intense the resulting negative emotional state will be.

The acting-out behaviors then become an external means of trying to soothe, control, and/or eliminate the unpleasant internal negative emotional state. Even though the behaviors may originate from an internal impetus, they manifest themselves as something which can be seen as an external factor. Therefore, rather than looking inside for the source of control, we look outside of ourselves for tangible and/or conceptually solid means of feeling better and trying to cope. This then leaves us *"at the mercy of externals"* as the book title indicates. Rather than serving as solutions, these external elements also become part of the problem and a further source of fuel for the negative emotions already creating the emotional state we seek to escape or eliminate. Having been at the mercy of environmental factors as children, it is easy to accept also being at the mercy of all external factors as we grow older.

Let's examine each of the emotions. Fear is an emotion experienced by everyone at various times and in various contexts. Unfortunately it is difficult for people to admit fear, feeling that doing so indicates they are in some ways cowardly and vulnerable. Sometimes there is even a sense of shame associated with fear, especially for men who are taught culturally that any degree of fear is a shameful sign of weakness often associated with women. I see this quite often in the gang kids and juvenile offenders I work with as clients. People don't always see fear as being subject to degree, ranging from simple nervousness to sheer panic; nor do they see fear as normal and necessary to survival. Sometimes fear can be experienced without the other emotions being present. But think about how complicated fear becomes when it is accompanied by a feeling of loneliness and the "fear" this loneliness will continue. Fear can even be seen as a basis for the other emotions in this model. Perhaps these first two emotions are accompanied by anger related to the feelings of being lonely and afraid. Couple these three negative, unpleasant emotions with the feeling of guilt that I should be able to be strong or brave, and the shame of feeling flawed, weak, and out of control.

Clearly this combination of FLAGS has the potential to lead to an emotional state which will possibly include both anxiety and depression. Now assume the individual with this emotional combination is cut off from and unaware of the emotions fueling the resulting physical/behavioral manifestation of the emotion-based condition. Both anxiety and depression are experienced as physical conditions, as well as emotional states. Anxiety seems to reside in the chest or in "the pit of the stomach". This person has only the awareness of feeling bad, often accompanied with the intense desire to eliminate and/or escape this reality. Rather than use the emotional state as an indication of the need to examine and deal with the emotions causing this state, let's assume the individual becomes so overwhelmed they give up out of a sense of helplessness/hopelessness. This individual will then move into some means of acting out and reacting to the emotional state in a maladaptive, problematic manner.

The entire process of acting out emotion-based anxiety originates in the general condition of being cut off from emotions, which I believe is learned in childhood from adults who, in one extreme, stifle the honest, appropriate expression of emotions. In the opposite extreme another possibility is that children learn inappropriate expression of emotions, believing it is okay to act out rather than face emotions because emotional needs are neglected or appropriate behaviors are not modeled and encouraged. Either way children often become adults with no idea of how to deal with frustration, loss, anger, and/or disappointment; and with little or no ability to cope or to soothe themselves appropriately. Beginning in childhood and continuing into adulthood, these children seek outside sources of relief to guard against simply feeling bad, making them even more vulnerable to external factors. This results in a population of adults and kids who take their frustrations out on themselves individually, and on others by targeting people either in isolation or within groups or contexts. This process has led to what I call "moral bankruptcy", present within people of all ages in our societies and cultures globally.

It is important to also see that the emotions do not necessarily occur together. Sometimes we are just afraid, lonely or angry. Even when emotions occur in isolation, we still need to be in control of them to avoid acting out toward ourselves and/or others. I tell my kids and adult clients all the time: "Just because you can, doesn't mean you should". Many times people will use an emotion as an excuse to act out in some manner. For instance some people will say "I hit the wall because I have a bad temper." My response is that it is necessary to control the temper rather than use it as a reason to proceed with the maladaptive behavior. By blaming the "temper" as the culprit, thereby using this as an excuse, we never have to take responsibility for our actions and willingness to follow through.

Think about guilt and shame for a moment. Infants are not born with a sense of either guilt or shame. Of the three FLAGS, these are the only ones which I believe are exclusively learned emotions, often being taught to us at early ages by adults. However, fear, loneliness and anger can easily be identified in infants as survival skills which get them the attention they need for their care and inclusion. My favorite example is the parent(s) at the mall with a small child. The child begins to act out the fact they are tired, bored, frustrated, etc. I am not talking about the child who throws a temper tantrum because they can't have the toy they want, but the screaming child who really is tired. The parent usually starts telling the child to "stop that! Everyone is looking at you". What is the truth in this situation? Who is everyone actually looking at?

The answer is everyone is looking at the parent and thinking: "why can't you see your child is tired and either needs a nap or at least an opportunity to have some fun?" The parent, on the other hand, is telling the child how ashamed he or she should feel for what is a natural reaction for any kid under those kinds of circumstances. This inaccurately teaches them the whole world is looking at *you* and misjudging what *you* are doing as being a bad child who embarrasses mommy or daddy, and who has no consideration for the feelings of others. Oh the guilt of feeling responsible at the age of four for having screwed up your parent's day simply by being tired and bored, and having the nerve to express these feelings in a manner which causes your parents to come under scrutiny. How dare you bring attention to the inappropriateness of your parents' lack of consideration for your feelings and needs?

With time (and therapy) it is possible to get rid of most of the guilt and shame instilled in us as children. Some of it seems to last forever, especially if the people who instilled these emotions continue to make the same attempts in our adult lives. Always remember that if you are doing nothing wrong to yourself or to others, there is no need to feel either guilt or shame. Remember, people in the world who are supposedly watching us spend too much time worrying about what everyone else is thinking about them to ever spend much time thinking about the rest of us.

People have no right to impose their beliefs upon others. There are things about my own life and nature that many people might disagree with and object to. However, I don't care what they think as long as I know my heart is pure and my intentions are good. I have learned that most people will not express their opinion to your face unless they are given the opportunity to do so. I simply never ask what people think unless I truly want to know. Certainly there are times when the impression we make upon others is important, but those times are generally by our own choice such as job interviews and following rules at work to get a good performance appraisal or a promotion. These situations are different from the unnecessary negativity imposed on us by others.

As we talk about abuse and victimization later you will see how people often feel entitled to pass judgment, quite often based on some closed-minded set of religious, political, and/or social beliefs. The very act of passing judgment is often an act of victimization and therefore a way of acting out an individual's own anxiety present in their life and history. If we have something in our life which brings feelings of guilt and shame upon ourselves from within rather than simply from standards placed upon us from others, then these behaviors need to be looked at and dealt with. Otherwise throw away all unnecessary feelings of guilt and shame, and learn to protect yourself from them. After all, why not get rid of as much unhealthy emotional baggage as possible?

Let's examine a little more closely the segment in the RFLAGS Model entitled "Anxiety", and look at other words people use to describe the emotional state of anxiety, and how it manifests itself physically. As I indicated earlier anxiety is experienced on a physical level as well. Anxiety is even hard to distinguish from its opposite physical state of excitement. Both are accompanied by muscle tension, increased heart rate, fatigue, headaches, agitation, faster breathing rate, sleep disturbance, changes in eating habits, and changes in other bodily functions. I know when I am excited about something, and if the excitement is intense and continues for a long period of time, I experience these physical changes. I am not talking about sexual excitement (even though I guess an extended state of sexual excitement could also qualify). I am talking about a state of anticipation based in positive emotions such as joy, confidence, love, pleasure, etc., rather than anticipation based in the negative FLAGS. The difference between anxiety and excitement lies in the emotions creating the state.

Even without guilt and shame, the other three, fear, loneliness and anger are quite enough to still create anxiety. Moving from only one emotion to acting out is not the same as acting out anxiety. Emotion-based anxiety is created by a combination of emotions which may grow from just one to others. The very act of acting out an emotion can create the conditions to bring on the other FLAGS as well. As we act out we tend to complicate our lives and the emotions associated with our condition, rather than find solutions to the problems that created the emotions in the first place.

To further understand the state of anxiety or anxious depression, consider some terms and phrases we tend to use to describe this state. Study the list in Appendix B to see how we identify and experience anxiety. This list is the first of several throughout the book, all of which are extremely important in the understanding of and application of the model. It is, therefore, critical that you take the time as each list is mentioned to study it and understand how it applies to the concept being illustrated. This current list is by no means complete, so feel free to add your own descriptive terms to it. It comes from my own perspective and from the classes I teach when I present the RFLAGS Model to various groups.

From the list in Appendix B you can see how some of the terms used may seem redundant. However, keep in mind that sometimes when people say "I'm angry", or "I'm anxious", they are expressing a more complicated condition than they realize by virtue of the fact they may be cut off from the awareness of a combination of emotions which actually might be involved. Many times kids are taught they are to be seen and not heard. They are also taught their feelings either don't matter or are unimportant and irrelevant. It's no wonder people don't know how to identify emotions when many of us were taught at an early age to suppress them, or were taught in some way not to trust our perceptions of emotions. Children learn this from phrases such as: "You can't possibly feel that way;" or "How dare you feel that way;" or "If you do that or express that again, I'll…." There is also the assumption children don't really have feelings or the ability to understand life events prior to the onset of puberty. Any emotions prior to then which don't correspond to adult perceptions of what is appropriate are frequently squelched. Oh the confusion from being treated as something less than human when we were children.

Finally, let's look at the last phase of the cycle, the Acting-Out phase. For a reactive choice to be identified as acting-out behavior it must be preceded with a degree of hopelessness/helplessness, giving up, and/or not caring. This is usually expressed in some form of thought or statement like: "Screw it! No one else cares, so why should I?" At this point the individual will likely give up on the hope of feeling better and will then make a maladaptive choice in an effort to eliminate, avoid, or escape the emotion-based state of anxiety. This state of anxiety is also similar to anxiety associated with physical feelings of withdrawal and detox from any maladaptive behaviors such as drinking, using drugs, or smoking. Remember, the person is about to act out emotion-based anxiety rather than use the physical feeling of anxiety as a gauge to identify the emotions needed to be faced and dealt with appropriately. In order to avoid relapse relative to substance abuse a person needs to also remind herself or himself the anxiety associated with physical withdrawal is temporary and will pass. However, the state of anxiety remaining once the feeling of actual physical withdrawal subsides will be based in the emotions originally fueling the need to escape the emotion-based anxiety in the first place.

Take a few minutes and look carefully at the next list (Appendix C) of possible acting-out behaviors and impulsive reactions from which people can choose. While this list is rather long, it is not necessarily all-inclusive. Chances are many of you will be able to identify with some of the possibilities. Some of you may even come up with a few more of your own which I have not thought about yet. As you look over the list, remember this model is usually presented to an audience of people seated in front of me. The presentation is very interactive, with participants providing their own list of items at any given part of the seminar. If you find others that I missed I would like to hear from you so I can add your items to my list – www.DavidLRobertsPhD.org.

As you reviewed the list you may have even been a little shocked at how many of the items pertain to your own coping style. Please do not be overly alarmed by this, as this is not uncommon. Remember that many of the items are problematic only when they are out of balance or out of control. For instance, we all have needs for eating, sleeping and sex. Exercising, reading, watching TV, and withdrawing all can be positive things to do unless they are excessive. The key factor for some of the possible choices is control and balance. As you can clearly see, however, some of the remaining possible choices should never be made, or should be eliminated if they are already part of your coping patterns and personality. Any extreme distress you may experience now or in the future relative to any of the lists and issues included in this book will hopefully signal your need to explore these issues with a mental health professional who can guide you through them safely and successfully.

One other list (Appendix D) I want to include in this chapter is a list of the problems/issues we seek to escape from by acting out our emotion-based anxiety. As with the previous list, this list is not necessarily all inclusive, so feel free to come up with some other items and pass them along to me so I can update my records. Generally the problems and issues underlying our negative emotions of Fear, Loneliness, Anger, Guilt, and Shame (FLAGS) are numerous and depend upon the degree of dysfunction we experienced in childhood. So, do not be alarmed or surprised if you find quite a few in the list that again pertain to your own life and history. Remember, too, none of this is intended to make anyone feel they have a lot wrong with them. There is nothing *wrong* with any of us who have been abused or victimized in the sense of being inherently and permanently flawed relative to personality characteristics. The purpose is to help people recognize the dysfunction in the present, which is based in the past, and which will impede progress in the future. View these lists with both hope and courage, and then find the determination and commitment to make changes which will uncomplicate your existence from this point forward.

Much of the elimination of this maladaptive process lies in the need and ability to face unpleasant feelings rather than seek to avoid them. Instead of moving forward into the acting-out phase, one should back up and sit with the emotional state until something can be learned from it. The only exception would be with any psychological state which is out of control and/ or debilitating (as with major depression, bipolar disorders, or more serious mental disorders which are primarily chemically/physiologically based), or is potentially life threatening. It is important to recognize one's limits relative to dealing with emotions which may in reality be overwhelming, and which may require professional guidance and assistance.

If an individual lacks the ability to deal with the emotional state of anxiety and the feeling of physical discomfort, they will then make one or more reactive choices. These choices will represent either an act of victimization of self, victimization of other, or some combination of both. Any choice made at this point has the potential to become reinforced as a way to feel better by escaping or avoiding, without the realization that the behavior chosen is only an escape or avoidance and not a solution. The probability of the behavior becoming part of the complicating factors creating the emotional basis of the anxiety increases substantially as the psychological connection between the behavior and false feeling of relief becomes stronger. The maladaptive behavior then further complicates the person's life by increasing the negative emotions already present. This is a process whereby an individual learns to unconsciously abuse self and/or others as a way of perpetuating the history of victimization. Certainly if these types of coping choices start early enough in life, they will likely become part of someone's adult personality, thereby creating and recreating the same kind of chaos the individual experienced in childhood and adolescence.

Clearly there is a connection to this process and any process of addiction. However, while I believe in a possible genetic predisposition for addiction to alcohol and other substances, I believe addiction comes in many forms. Furthermore, I believe every maladaptive behavior is based in, and/or perpetuated by anxiety and the need to act out anxiety rather than learn to face it. After all, the existence of a genetic predisposition alone does not account for the initial choice to drink or use. For example, my parents did not drink; but, they acted out in some very maladaptive, habitual ways which only served to complicate their own lives and the lives of those around them.

I am not saying everyone who feels anxiety will act out in a maladaptive way. Much of the choice to act out depends on history; the degree of emotion-based anxiety; and on an individual's ability to cope effectively and soothe herself or himself appropriately. Perhaps the genetic predisposition is not to addictive tendencies, but rather to an inability to effectively deal with anxiety. The more likely someone is to be wired for extreme anxiety relative to genetic and environmental factors, possibly the more likely it is they will choose to act out rather than learn to face negative emotions and cope with them. Even though addiction becomes physical relative to substance use, I believe the strongest form of addiction is the psychological addiction to a euphoric escape experience derived from external acting-out factors, rather than generated internally through appropriate coping skills consciously, willfully developed and applied from within.

For instance, I suspect there is likely a genetic predisposition toward anxiety on my mother's side of the family. The other possible explanation could be that a complicated environment could somehow wire the brain to always be on the alert for incoming negativity and other unpredictable factors. Either way I can see a pattern of anxious personality styles with my mother's maternal aunt, my mother, myself and my sister, and my daughter. All of us would be described by my dad as being "high strung and overly sensitive, and nervous". This seems to come back to the basic assumption of an interaction between environment and genetically based personality factors.

The only way for me to achieve zero anxiety is through meditation and self-hypnosis. Otherwise, I seem to experience some degree of "feeling" anxious much of the time. My therapist helped me to identify this factor in my personality. Once it was brought into my conscious awareness I vowed to work on it and change it. To accomplish this I am learning more and more to use any state of anxiety as a gauge and as a motivator for change; and I am learning to reduce the degree of anxiety I feel by identifying and understanding the emotions underlying and fueling it. I do this during meditation by telling myself I am actually "rewiring" my brain to function from a level of calm rather than from a level of anxiety. This is an especially useful tool for visualization during both meditation and self-hypnosis. The effort is a very conscious one, and one which takes a great deal of practice. But with time I find this process of working to calm myself down is becoming more second nature, like the anxiety has been in the past.

I am also learning to allow myself time to process feelings and review negative experiences from the past as a way of understanding them and learning from them. In other words I allow myself to stress out a little at a time without stressing out about the fact I am stressing out. This comes after the awareness that my state of anxiety is telling me there is more to learn. I no longer see anxious depression as something to be acted out. I see it as an opportunity to find increased understanding for the purpose of re-parenting myself and simplifying my emotional nature. It is nothing more than a process of undoing the damage which was done to me unintentionally by my parents and undoing damage which also resulted from the events in my life which I could not control or avoid.

This chapter is one of the most important in the book simply because the RFLAGS Model is the core to understanding all of the material. You will likely want to refer back to this chapter from time to time for further clarification as we move through the other parts of the overall concept. We will now move backwards to see how the negative emotions develop and where they come from. So, hold onto your hats. For some of us this will be a bumpy, yet exciting and enlightening ride!

Chapter III
Adult Roles and Responsibilities

Now that we have looked at and understood the RFLAGS Model it is time to back up and see how the negative emotions (FLAGS) develop. In this chapter we will explore what we as adults should be doing compared to the reality of what we actually are doing in many cases. All of us should take our role as adults in the lives of children very seriously. This is true regardless of whether the role is that of a parent, grandparent, aunt, uncle, teacher, administrator, law enforcement official, counselor, therapist, social worker, lawyer, judge, clergy, volunteer/mentor, or any other type of authority figure or role model. Children will model what they see as their only way of acquiring new behaviors and coping styles. As adults it is important to remember we are modeling something at all times. My hope is we will all work to make sure we are modeling positive characteristics rather than negative ones.

During my years of training and work experience in the field of psychology I have had many occasions to study and learn about human behavior. As I mentioned earlier everyone is a product of both their genetic predisposition's and of the environmental factors present in our lives. With regard to environmental factors, I think everyone agrees the years since World War II have been filled with many rapidly changing aspects. Of particular importance are the emphases on human rights in all regards, and the advances in technology. In my lifetime I have seen societal values swing from the extreme right to the extreme left and back to the right, with both extremes being dangerous and destructive relative to emotional/psychological well being. I believe we are currently witnessing and participating in a balancing act whereby we are seeking a somewhat middle ground which can facilitate the most beneficial stance for healthy growth and development for people of all ages.

The changes I am most concerned with are those changes that have affected, and continue to affect "the family", even as the traditional definition of "family" continues to evolve and change. Over the last few decades we have watched as families changed from working father and mom at home, to both parents having to work for families to survive economically. From there we went to an unprecedented decline in family stability as evidenced by rapidly rising rates of separation and divorce. The statistics we see today relative to such factors as violence, youth "at risk", and teen pregnancy all result from the world which we as adults have created for "our" children. I use the word "our" to emphasize the global responsibility each of us has to create a safe and hopeful environment in which "our" children can live and grow. As adults we have not done a very good job in recent years of creating such a world.

On the other hand I do not believe our adult predecessors did such a good job either. If you were born and raised prior to the 1970's there were few laws to protect children or women from abuse. People turned their heads away from all forms of domestic victimization believing these issues to be a "private family matter". This was a time in the United States of America when white men ruled supreme and control over kids was intended to break wills and bring them into submission and into compliance with the rules. Religion even found ways to justify abuse and victimization toward women, children, and people of "color". This was a time of boom rather than bust for some, and a time of increasing educational opportunities for young people, opening their eyes to many of the world's injustices.

During this time and since, attempts have been and are being made to redefine respect, fairness and acceptance as significant, but almost unconscious issues. We talk about these issues as they pertain to conscious human and civil rights outside of the home. However, I believe there was, and is, a struggle for equality going on inside the home as well. This is especially true with children who have gained enough sophistication in recent years to understand that respect toward anyone, even toward adults, must be won rather than demanded or expected as some kind of entitlement which somehow comes with adult status. Kids are way ahead of adults in this regard. This is evident as adults struggle within all contexts to retain positions and powers of unquestionable authority and control. For instance, I was taught to respect all adults without questioning their respectability. Failure to do so resulted in rather severe consequences within any setting or context. These kinds of one-up approaches toward kids no longer work. This fact needs to be accepted and dealt with as an obvious factor within today's reality.

During the decades since the 1960's adults in many roles taught us by example to be materialistic, hedonistic, self-absorbed, selfish, and uninvolved/underinvolved relative to our responsibilities to one another. People wanted to give children everything they never had, and in so doing took away some of the very principles needed to survive and grow. Such principles include: a work ethic, delayed gratification, regard for human life, and common sense fear which in the past kept many of us from experimenting with risky choices that could have proven to be self-destructive. Sure we can place responsibility for much of this on the media, movies, music, toy manufacturers, and technology, but who are the profit seeking beings behind these institutions? Adults!

It is my goal in this book to get each of us to examine where we are relative to our roles and responsibilities to and for children. I want each of us to realize that the very problems existing for and with children were created and facilitated by proceeding generations. It is time to stop blaming children for their problems and begin to see our parts in creating those behaviors. It is time to stop expanding juvenile justice lock-down programs and start working as adults to discover the very elements which are missing for ourselves so we can then help teach these values to the children we have neglected and continue to neglect.

The only way to teach such values is to connect children of all ages with positive role models inside and outside the home. Too many of us are detached from our own very real responsibility for the chaos and violence we see in the lives of children today. This is something I see very clearly being modeled and reflected in the lives of children who take no responsibility for their actions either. Rather than seek to "fix" ourselves as adults, we seek opportunities to "fix" the children in ways where we as adults do not have to be involved, generally because we are too busy and too detached to see the truth. There is also the factor in many instances where adults are uninvolved simply because they are so self absorbed and choose to listen to the messages of punish, conquer, and control; rather than assist, guide, respect, and redirect.

As indicated previously, I believe many adults seem to have a feeling of arrogance and entitlement relative to respect from kids. The old "just because I said so" attitude doesn't work anymore. Kids are too sophisticated for that. Even kids know they have the right to be treated with respect. After all, they are simply adults in the making. The old ways of beating, yelling, threatening, and intimidating required very little time. With the right combination of these destructive approaches any child could be brought under "control", or, rather, into compliance and submission. With the exception of my maternal grandmother, my parents and other adults involved in my childhood were unbelievably adept in convincing themselves that their negative approaches to child rearing were right. They were also adept in their denial that children have emotional needs which must be recognized and attended to with care. Failure to fulfill our roles and responsibilities results in permanent scarring which will impact a child negatively on into adulthood, thereby creating the FLAGS.

I believe many adults use kids as a punching bag, both literally and figuratively, upon which to act out their own emotion-based anxiety resulting from various unresolved issues. Rather than take the time to learn new approaches to interaction and communication between kids and adults, many adults still resort to the outmoded standards that didn't really work in the past. After all, 'who are children anyway, that I should take time out of my materialistic pursuits of pleasure and satisfaction to fulfill my unspoken obligation to be an effective role model?' I see this quite often in schools where some teachers seem to be more interested in control than they are in teaching. For some educators, as with others in positions of authority over children, respect is demanded and expected, rather than earned. Think about the arrogance of many law enforcement officials as well who feel because they enforce the law they are entitled to also be above the law within their codes of silence and "good ol' boy/girl" networks. I see this quite often within juvenile justice systems as I follow the progression of kids from arrest to juvenile hall, through the court process, and on to sentencing. Control by adults within these settings needs to be monitored carefully and regularly. Those in any position of power and authority/control which can be used abusively should be reprimanded and removed when necessary if they are unwilling to comply with reasonable, ethical principles and standards. Overloaded systems are no justification for preying upon the vulnerability of minors, regardless of their patterns of acting out emotion-based anxiety, simply for the sake oftentimes of money, numbers, job security, and politics.

Respect is never a given in any situation. I cannot respect anyone whom I fear or hate for trying to bring me into submission before they are willing to interact with me in a positive and respectful manner. This seems to represent some kind of need to first establish a one-up position which is beyond challenge. No adult is ever better than any kid or other adult. It is only necessary to impose control onto a situation that is out of control. Once control is appropriately gained, the next step is to establish an atmosphere where an attempt at reasoning and understanding can be made as quickly as possible. This requires mutual consideration and respect which must be initiated and modeled by the adults involved, not demanded from kids first. To demand it from kids sets up the competition, leaving kids with no way to back down with dignity. As adults we often arrogantly demand things we could never expect or even hope to receive from other adults. Simply being an adult doesn't entitle *anyone* to respect!

Those who are jaded beyond any willingness to learn different approaches need to step aside. Educators are important, but only if they are effective in educating students on all levels. From my own experiences of working in the schools in different areas around Southern California and now in the deep south, I have seen many teachers who feel so victimized and unappreciated they hide behind union structures and contracts at the expense of educating children. They often do this rather than deal with the problems in an effective or considerate manner. They often focus so much on themselves as the victim that they fail to see how they in turn victimize the students through a blatant neglect of their responsibilities as teachers. Sometimes those who protest the most are the least effective in their roles as educators. Certainly no one should be victimized; but no one is any more special than any other person. The feeling of being important and essential has in many cases led to arrogance and a sense of entitlement. Many adults cannot stand the fact that respect is no longer a given because of their relative position of authority over kids, or because of their positions in life relative to other adults. Respect is necessary; but it must be earned not demanded. Above all else respect must be reciprocal under the new paradigm of human rights for all children and adults alike.

In my seminars and brochures I use the concept of: "in the competition between ADULTS vs. KIDS, no matter what the score, everyone looses." Really think about what this sentence is saying. In spite of this truth I see on an almost daily basis the struggle by adults to maintain control over kids just for the sake of control. In this kind of battle generally the adult will win, but what have they really gained by proving that in a position of authority I can control a kid? I understand in many settings some degree of control must be established and maintained. However, once that control is achieved the focus needs to then shift to that of modeling and teaching self control through some degree of positive interaction which, again, includes mutual respect and consideration. Systems need to allow for both the training and the time necessary for adults to learn and model such values if kids are to have the opportunity to change their behaviors and learn the values they are otherwise being forced without success to adopt. Being an effective role model is time consuming.

Again, as the title of my book indicates, control simply for the sake of control doesn't work except to gain some degree of compliance or submission which clearly represents the breaking of someone's will. Because the "one-up" position exists in many situations, in my work as a therapist with kids I teach them how to deal with this reality in a manner which will not further complicate their lives. Without the realization by a kid that self-control is a necessary and desirable characteristic in most situations, compliance is nothing more than a one-down position of being at the mercy of an external force which, without submission and obedience, can bring about some negative consequence or punishment. This kind of compliance feels to any individual like they are kissing someone's rear end. While I would never do this myself, in reality I do see the need on occasion to back down from the competition established by another person when it is in my best interest to do so until I can find another solution to the problem. This, however, is much easier for adults than it is for kids. I no longer fight defective systems directly. Instead, I do so through the communities affected and victimized. After all, most systems intruding upon the lives of kids are closed and protected by their own internal codes of silence, cover-up, corruption, and secrecy.

If nothing more is learned by the individual in compliance than external control imposed simply for the sake of control then, once the external force is removed, the source of control is also removed and the individual, whether child or adult, will resume some undesirable, possibly destructive, behavior. Look at how adults are often out of control in their unbridled pursuit of "happiness", consumerism, materialism, and success. For example, this is evident by the number of adults who recklessly and carelessly spend money and are overextended relative to indebtedness. I believe this lack of self control results from either the lack of internal control possibly taught to us when we were the kids, or from the imposition of excessive external control which when removed can lead to a destructive inability to establish appropriate self-control. On a more global scale this is also a risk when world powers intervene in abusive situations in other countries, with the only intent of bringing them into submission. Arrogant nations and world leaders, like individual adults, may be good at problem identification; but are themselves oftentimes still struggling with problem resolution within their own countries. This is as true in America as in any other country in the world.

Experience continues to teach me that any kind of acting out behavior results from the lack of intrinsic self-control which was not successfully taught to us by adults from previous generations. They tried to "scare" us into compliance with the rules through physical and emotional abuse, rather than helping us as young children learn to do things simply for our own best interest and the best interest of others. Or they neglected to teach any form of control at all. Many of the adults today try unsuccessfully to control adolescents for the sake of control. The mistake in this approach is in the lack of ability to enforce such approaches through fear and intimidation available to our predecessors. Thank God children can no longer be beaten, neglected, and ignored without consequences; and thank God people outside the home are no longer given permission to paddle or spank children in school and other settings, with the exception of some religious (faith-based) private schools in this country. These are commonly some of the groups seeking vouchers to support private education.

One additional mistake in this approach of control for the sake of control is the tendency for adults to wait until it is almost too late, during those adolescent years when the need for self-control is so critical. If a child has not learned self-control at an early age there is no point in establishing competition between adults and kids during adolescence in an effort to force control. The only way to deal with adolescents who are out of control is to help them see how being out of control is complicating *their* lives. It is necessary to give kids the opportunity to see how their actions are not getting them any of the considerations they are demanding. To accomplish this goal the adults must resolve their issues and be in control of their behaviors in order to model and explain appropriate means of gaining consideration and cooperation. Kids need to see that making demands doesn't work for them any more effectively than it does for adults. Please don't misunderstand me. Kids need rules and responsibilities with clear consequences for not following through on reasonable expectations. But, kids also need to have reasonable opportunities to gain rewards for positive behaviors.

Don't use guilt and shame by asking kids to feel sorry for adults in the sense of owing adults some consideration, especially when the child feels the consideration given to them previously in the form of unchecked, unsupervised freedom is being withdrawn. At this point parents and other adults must take the time to learn to communicate with and reason with any kid who is out of control, rather than panic and try to enforce control which never existed previously, or existed only on a limited basis. If given the opportunity to do so, many kids will eventually calm down and listen if they are approached from a position of respect relative to the fact kids are nothing less than future adults and human beings who deserve to be treated fairly. Realistically, kids need to see the advantages to *them* of behaving in an appropriate manner both in the present and into the future. Furthermore, kids and adults must learn to deal with boredom and frustration in an effective, rather than destructive manner, sometimes by simply learning to tolerate and learn from these aspects of life. Both can serve to motivate in positive ways if looked at in a different light.

My fear is that adults do not want to take the time out of their already busy schedules to learn new approaches to deal effectively with kids regardless of the role the adult plays in a kid's life. By writing this book I truly hope to give everyone an opportunity to understand that child-rearing principles are actually quite simple, though not necessarily easy. No one is exempt from responsibility for the well being of kids, even if only in some indirect manner, if there is such a thing. The complex task is that of unlearning negative patterns of interaction from the past and replacing those with the simple concepts found within these pages. The initial investment of time will be the most significant, because with time the ability to improve interactions between adults and kids will drastically reduce the wasted time and energy spent in conflict and open competition between adults and kids. Kids don't like chaos in their lives anymore than adults and will readily admit this when asked.

The most basic task is to make the new concepts as automatic and unconscious as the dysfunctional approaches already are; i.e. replace the old with the new on a conscious level until the new becomes second nature. My basic philosophy in working with adults and kids is: "if it hasn't worked so far, it probably will not work in the future. Therefore, rather than continue wasting energy by doing the same things, why not try something new?" I find most adults and kids to be very open to the possibility of making life simpler. This is what my work and writings are all about.

As we think about what adults should be doing as opposed to the reality of what we are actually doing in many cases, remember the use of labels we addressed in a previous chapter. I firmly believe the labels we use with kids and the categories into which we try to stick them reflects our general view of kids and our corresponding awareness of the kinds of responsibilities we believe we have toward them. If we think of kids only as "bad kids", "incorrigibles", or the "problem child", we will focus our attention and efforts only on the behaviors a kid exhibits. Our first goal should be that of looking beyond the negative behaviors to actually see the kid and the potential within every child for good.

In therapy with kids I always look to find at least a tiny piece of heart which I can then identify as the true, innate identity of who a child is meant to be or become with appropriate guidance. Also, I work very hard to be aware of the likelihood a child's behaviors may reflect or mask something or some set of factors which are not readily apparent. The phrase "for no apparent reason" doesn't imply there is no reason, only there is no reason that is easily identifiable. Bottom line is, I separate what a kid is doing from who they really are if the behaviors are negative. Every kid deserves that kind of respect and consideration. Kids know, at least on an unconscious level, what unfairness and disregard feels like. No kid will ever be able to interact with an adult in a positive manner if the odds are against the kid in the sense of the kid not having a chance to avoid being misjudged and misunderstood.

Adults in positions of authority generally talk about opposition and defiance from kids without seeing that sometimes this is simply active resistance to a no-win, unfair situation from which the kid cannot escape. So, as a kid why not fight the "opponent" rather than give in? Law enforcement officials frequently resort to this tactic as a means of getting kids to commit crimes so they can then be arrested, rather than helped, and removed from the streets and neighborhoods. Adults need to understand there really is no way to establish limits and boundaries with adolescents who are out of control unless the kids can see there is some benefit to their well-being to accept such restrictions. Any victories won during open competition and conflict between adults and kids are only temporary and are of no substance. However, if measures are taken during the earlier childhood years to instill intrinsic morals and values, then competition generally will remain at a lower level than if such groundwork is not laid, simply because one can appeal to the higher nature already established within the kid's psyche. On the other hand, if a positive foundation is not established early on, then adults must work very hard with kids to help them tear down the maladaptive bases and start over from the standpoint of what is in their best interest for now and into the future. The best interest of others will have to come later!

Our first responsibility as adults toward kids is that of questioning and understanding our commitment to kids and our motivation to work with them, regardless of our role(s) in their lives. No matter how indirect our role may be, we still impact the world in which kids are raised. I once heard a therapist refer to kids as "trolls". In another instance someone told me a teacher had referred to a student as an "undesirable element" in the classroom. There is no way anyone with these kinds of prejudices can go into any encounter with a kid and be successful. Labels always reflect prejudices and biases.

Child rearing, a responsibility shared by every individual involved in a child's life, requires an almost selfless approach to giving each child what they need individually in the effort to recognize and nurture both their uniqueness and potential. To do anything less is unjust and immoral. If we cannot be fully committed to giving children the very best care possible to insure healthy spiritual, emotional, intellectual, and psychological development, then we should limit our direct connections with kids. Individuals should not begin to take on the role of becoming parents until they have worked on their own issues and understand the commitment they are (or should be) making to the little ones they will create. This kind of thinking and commitment to individual well being should be taught even during the middle school and early high school years, given the fact that sexual activity often begins now in early adolescence.

Sadly, however, because of so many divisive groups within the political, social and religious contexts in this country, the real tragedy would be in the difficulty of developing a consensus of what the concept and definition of personal well being would actually be. The difficulty would exist within the many hidden and overt agendas which adults in differing factions espouse. This is especially true when considering extreme religious and political biases rather than focusing on common spiritual principles underlying all religions. These principles include: giving unconditional love and acceptance; being non-judgmental; practicing altruism; having an awareness of interconnectedness; and living the concept of Karma which is nothing more than the concepts of "The Golden Rule", or "what goes around comes around". As you can see in this example, the competition between groups exists within other settings and contexts, just as it exists between kids and adults. Part of my purpose in exploring these issues is to increase awareness about the victimization of many individuals and groups taking place within many different arenas. These concepts of victimization within contexts outside of the home will be explored further in a later chapter. Big powerful nations also can be viewed as "adults" with certain roles and responsibilities. Arrogance and ignorance have the same negative results on a much larger scale between countries/societies, and religious and political extremism.

Now that I have explored with you some of the negative factors relative to what adults are often times doing, let's take some time at this point to review the listing of actual Adult Roles and Responsibilities I have included as Appendix E. This list includes as many of the positive things adults should be doing as I have been able to identify to date. As with other lists please understand this list consists only of items identified by me and through the seminars I teach. The list can be amended to include other items that may be identified. Please review this list now.

After reading the first part of this chapter and then considering the list of things we should be doing, some of you may have been shocked at the contrast. In all references I make to the human condition, again please understand I am not judging or blaming. I am simply sharing my perceptions on what I have observed to be reality and truth relative to my own life and what I see exhibited in the lives of others through my personal and professional interactions. Rather than looking to find fault, I am seeking to do problem identification and then problem resolution. I am always open to amending and adapting my perspectives to new realities and truths. Furthermore, I am aware that my own truth is continuously evolving and growing. My goals within this writing are: to teach what I have learned to date; learn from the experience of writing down my own observations and thoughts; and provoke and encourage critical thinking in others. This process begins with individuals and moves out to groups and, in some cases, factions within the contexts identified previously that will be addressed in more detail as we go.

As you carefully look over the list, try to pick out any words or phrases which possibly could be interpreted in different ways by different people or groups. Such words and phrases would include discipline, control, punish, and limit. Each of these concepts has within it an opportunity for abuse/ victimization if defined in a negative and inappropriate manner.

Think about the concept of *discipline* and the different contexts and settings in which the word is used. When teaching this segment in my seminars, I always pull these words out and ask people to give me the first words they associate with each of them. Generally, the first word associated with discipline is some form of corporal punishment such as spanking. According to Webster's Dictionary the word "corporal" is defined as: "of, relating to, or affecting the body." Therefore, corporal punishment means bodily or physical punishment usually in some form of hitting, or at least in some form which could either hurt in the sense of abuse and victimization, or lead to death in the sense of corporal punishment as in a death sentence. Don't forget about military discipline that exists for the sole purpose of breaking wills and assuring compliance with orders from superiors during combat situations. This is necessary only in the military and not in other settings, especially involving kids.

Even today in some of the extreme conservative factions, people speak of the need to return to corporal punishment as a way of dealing with problematic behavior. Hopefully each of you will begin to see how this kind of approach or "remedy", if you will, simply involves only the time and effort necessary to hit, yell, and conquer. Nothing is gained and very little time is involved compared to the time it will take for each of us to unlearn inappropriate measures and learn new ones. With these old measures there is no investment of time into the well being of children, who are simply frightened, shamed, outraged, and broken down into compliance and submission. By these means adults can then remain in their positions of authority, arrogance and entitlement, keeping kids in their places of being seen and not heard. It is interesting to me how generally the older adults, people from within male dominated cultures and societies, and those within the contexts of abusive extremist religions who espouse the victimization of those who are different from themselves, are the only ones who adamantly support such notions. Reflected in this as well are varying degrees of education and cultural influences. Hopefully society will eventually progress beyond these puritanical efforts to control others so certain groups can simply maintain their positions of power. This concept can readily be applied on an international basis as well.

Think about figuratively how "corporal punishment" is dealt out within political, social, and religious contexts relative to issues such as race, ethnicity and other forms of diversity such as homosexuality. The goals in many settings of victimizing others is for groups in positions of perceived power to maintain their position by "bodily" or physically keeping others in their "places". Think about it! Was this country founded upon religious freedom as the impetus to leave Europe; or was it founded upon the religious victimization of others with white Anglo Saxon Protestants as religious extremists establishing themselves and their religious beliefs as the ideals? Look at how this kind of thinking continues to be carried out around the world today in the form of terrorism and terrorist acts.

As I near the end of this chapter about Adult Roles and Responsibilities, let me give you two more lists. In the first we can identify factors that constitute the "ideal family" (Appendix F), and in the second explore the mistakes adults are often times making (Appendix G) to varying degrees depending on each respective individual. As you review this second list remember that children have to live with the choices and mistakes made by adults. Children have little or no ability to shield themselves from any chaos created by adults. Therefore, one of the single most important characteristics to be modeled by adults is that of forethought, or the ability to consider the consequences to self and others of any decision to be made. Be sure to compare these lists to the list of things we should be modeling (Appendix E). The contrast is quite extreme between adult roles and responsibilities and the list of mistakes. However, the factors describing and defining the "ideal family" almost parallel the list of adult roles and responsibilities.

I believe these lists speak for themselves and tie very well into the next chapter where we will look at abuse and victimization. The mistakes made by adults generally set the stage for mistreatment, and for inappropriate and ineffective patterns of interactions with kids. Again, keep in mind we are exploring factors which create, establish and perpetuate the negative emotions (FLAGS) which lead to anxiety we then tend to act out in maladaptive and often self-destructive ways. Please see this as nothing more or less than an identification process of the negative factors impacting many of us everyday either as the target/victim, or as the "victimizer". As we learn to live out our appropriate roles and responsibilities we will begin to right the wrongs and move closer to the principles contained within any set of ideals

CHAPTER IV

Insult and Injury

After looking at the adult roles and responsibilities, what constitutes the "ideal family", and then at the mistakes often made by adults, we will now look more specifically at abuse and victimization. Remember we are moving from the ideal to the factors existing as reality in many cases. I will use the terms abuse and victimization somewhat interchangeably with more emphasis on the term victimization. I believe most people associate the word abuse with children more than they do with the victimization of adults. Generally the concept of abuse is associated more with child abuse and possibly with spousal abuse or elder abuse, but the term victimization applies to people on all levels, within all contexts and quadrants, and at all ages. Someone or some system victimizes most everyone at some time in their lives. Because I will try in later chapters to connect all of these concepts to larger contexts other than the context of home/family, it is important to use a term to which anyone can relate; and a term that is universally applicable regardless of culture. None of my ideas or theories is intended to be exclusively representative of North American culture as many of the wrongs I am addressing exist within numerous other countries and cultures around the world.

Hopefully, as you read the previous chapters you were able to find connections between the material presented and your own subjective past. Remember there is no such thing as "the perfect family", which exists only as an ideal. Therefore everyone comes from some degree of dysfunction in the sense there is always room for improvement. For some of you this experience may have been somewhat difficult. Again, if this is true I hope you will be aware of any limitations relative to your ability to deal with the intensity of your feelings on your own and that you will seek professional help if necessary. Some of you may already be recognizing the negative feelings of Fear, Loneliness, Anger, Guilt, and Shame (FLAGS). If this is true for you then I would ask you to be careful about how you proceed through this chapter.

Every reader is likely to discover some degree of abuse and victimization not only in her or his past, but possibly in the present as well. Some readers may also discover ways in which you are victimizing others, possibly even on an unconscious level. You may find this to be true within the context of current interactions and situations in the present with spouses, family members (extended or immediate), work associates, classmates, or various social, political, and religious contexts. As you come to not only understand abuse and victimization, but to see it in the things people say and do, you may become stressed beyond your ability to deal with these feelings on your own. If you experience such occurrences of intense anxiety and/or depression, please find a licensed mental health professional that can help you deal with whatever surfaces. Above all, find the courage to face whatever you discover rather than close this book and decide it is all too painful. Remember that courage does not mean facing a situation without fear. Courage means finding the ability to move forward and do what is best *in spite of* the fear which is there. If you are not afraid who needs courage?

Keep in mind that my book will not create any new feelings. My writings and public presentations regarding the RFLAGS Model will only bring into conscious awareness those emotions and memories which already exist. The process presented in the model cannot create histories of abuse/victimization and the resulting FLAGS; however, the recollection of them can be revived. Research to date with the Roberts Grief and Loss Analysis Scale indicates that in a situation where the RGLAS is given prior to and subsequent to the formal presentation of the entire RFLAGS Model, some scores may actually decline (worsen) at posttest. This possibly indicates that one's history of abuse and victimization may have been ignored as something either too painful or irrelevant, with the significance being realized by participation in the seminar. Don't be afraid to proceed; just be cautious. Be especially careful not to feel guilty or ashamed of feelings and thoughts that emerge. Remember we are only identifying your subjective experiences and emotions relative to the past. We are looking only to see if, how, and to what extent the past continues to live in our present often times without our conscious awareness of it. We are not looking for opportunities to blame or judge, only for opportunities to identify and understand.

Allow me to state again that many people, including adolescents, tell me they do not want to relive the past. As I stated earlier I agree with this sentiment. However, I believe it is critical to identify at least enough of the past to understand the dynamics and the sources of current distress. This is necessary even if that distress exists only on an unconscious basis fueling our current anxiety and motivating our acting out behaviors and feelings of hopelessness without our conscious control or understanding. This is the concept of being at the mercy of factors outside of ourselves (externals). The fear of looking at the past is what keeps many of us locked into current patterns of repeating the same mistakes over and over again. It also keeps us believing we are trapped and cannot make desired changes. This fear also keeps us from exploring, nurturing and reaching the full potential within ourselves and in the children for whom we bear the responsibility of being positive role models regardless of our connection.

Remember, too, that none of this is about bashing or hating. By identifying the reality of the past and possibly the present, you will likely learn about characteristics of significant people from the past that you may not like. As stated previously I believe it is always necessary to try and separate what people do from who they are. As you try to do this keep in mind you may find this to be much more difficult with adults because behaviors of adults tend to be more permanent, and tend to also more accurately represent the personalities of the individuals. The point I am trying to make is that the possibility exists of loving someone such as parents, siblings, spouses, and other significant individuals, but not being able to like who they are, what they do, or have done. Often times the rage associated with all of this results from the feeling these individuals got away with what they did or are still doing, with no accountability for their actions or the results of their victimization of others. Within this rage you can see the resentment toward the arrogance and feelings of entitlement with which adults do their misdeeds toward children, and misdeeds toward other adults whom they treat like children. This rage and resentment represents the abuse and victimization addressed within this chapter.

Allow me to address a little further the personalities of abusive individuals who feel the need to victimize and control others. Within the field of psychology, therapists currently use the Diagnostic and Statistical Manual, Fourth Edition (DSM-IV-TR) - which gets revised periodically - as a guide for diagnosing all forms of psychiatric and psychological disorders such as mental, emotional, intellectual, developmental, personality, and those related to substance use and dependence. Prior to the release of the current edition efforts were made to reevaluate symptoms and categories of disorders. During this process many revisions were made and several new disorders were proposed, especially related to disorders of personality which are diagnosed only for adults. Anyone who reads the DSM-IV-TR (and I am not suggesting you do so) will find some aspects of their own personalities within its pages. This means nothing more than identifying unhealthy aspects of human nature. Symptoms have to be pervasive and prove to be interfering with healthy functioning to be considered as diagnoses. The fact that personality disorders are assigned only to adults further substantiates my belief in the opportunities we have to help improve the ways kids live their lives. We can do this before their behaviors become more permanent parts of the adult psyche and develop into symptoms of more permanent forms of maladaptive adult functioning and coping styles which constitute personality disorders.

Since I began my studies in psychology I have learned to identify the problematic personality traits exhibited by families presenting with extreme symptoms of dysfunction. The main negative characteristics or traits exhibited by many moms within these families include:

- Experiencing intense changes in mood ranging from relative calm to intense rage;
- Having a limited perception of people as either all good or all bad, with no gray areas;
- Having histories of unstable relationships;
- Showing various forms of manipulation and divisiveness which serve to protect a position of power and control over people and keep them loyal;
- Creating chaos in her life and in the lives of others;
- Being openly hostile and cruel; experiencing only shallow emotions which change
- rapidly;
- Displaying dramatic and over exaggerated emotions when provoked or threatened;
- Having little or no capacity for enjoyment of life;
- Expressing a very negative outlook for present and future situations prior to death;
- Being easily influenced by others;
- Being confrontational;
- Blaming others for her problems;
- Denying responsibility for her actions;
- And, having a preoccupation with being scrutinized and judged by others.

Deep within their souls many mothers possess the capacity to love and have fun. I am not questioning their love, only the capacity to deal effectively with life and those around them. There is generally no conscious ill intent. However, they often hurt themselves and those closest to them by an unwillingness to learn from mistakes and to resolve issues from early childhood on into adulthood. Often they believe the pain and unresolved issues from the past are too frightening to face and then work through effectively and successfully. Many also believe there is no need for improvement and everyone else has problems, but "not me". It is easy for people with maladaptive characteristics and coping styles to switch quickly from being the victim to being the victimizer.

When religion is involved in the mix it is easier to hide behind religion as the only defense against the onslaught of emotions which loom just below the surface. With this influence people sometimes live to die in the sense of believing there is nothing good in this life, only in the next, which can be descriptively visualized from the symbolic teachings of many religious texts and institutions. Because these moms make few efforts to change, children have to deal with many unresolved issues and emotions on into adulthood which could have been eliminated through simple changes in communication, coping styles, and changes in perspective. I believe this to be a very serious and tragic reality within many families. Everyone should be able to look into the faces of deceased parents without regret and resentment, but this is often not the case.

Dads directly involved in families often display some of the same characteristics as the moms within extremely dysfunctional family environments. However, their overall personality and ways of dealing with life can be quite different in the manner in which they are manifested. These characteristics or traits include:

- o   Having feelings of self-importance;
- o   Having a preoccupation with status in the community relative to what others think;
- o   Having a sense of entitlement;
- o   Feeling special and superior;
- o   Displaying arrogance relative to race, women and children;
- o   Using fear and intimidation to control;
- o   Publicly humiliating others;
- o   Being unpredictable with regards to when (not if) extreme rage will be expressed;
- o   Being unnecessarily defensive;
- o   Being intentionally cruel in order to dominate and force others into submission;
- o   Remaining emotionally unavailable and uninvolved;

- o   Taking no responsibility for the pain caused to others;
- o   Possessing no interest in opinions of others which differ from his;
- o   Exhibiting no expression of any emotion which could be interpreted as weakness;
- o   Being physically and emotionally abusive;
- o   Remaining aloof and uninvolved as a way of avoiding conflict;
- o   Seeing himself as the peacemaker with his ability to control by fear;
- o   Demanding respect without regard to respectability;
- o   And, sometimes believing that his role of father includes only responsibilities relative to providing discipline and material needs.

I share all of this information about personalities and parenting styles not only in an effort to understand it better myself, but to help each of you realize that I have come to understand what I teach through all of my personal and professional experiences. I write also with the hope every reader will make efforts to heal relationships in this life before it is too late. Even more importantly, I write to help others recognize and avoid these kinds of mistakes and injustices, and be able to create very positive relationships from the beginning, with only minimal need to correct things in the future.

The Past that Lived in my Present

Unfortunately, the personalities described here represent many of the characteristics of people I knew when I was growing up in the South during the mid-1950's, 60's, and early 70's. My memories especially from age four on are anything but positive, with continuing efforts from my parents to hurt and isolate me. Most prominent are the memories of abuse, which only changed as I got older to be less and less physical, but always and increasingly emotional. Until I was 14 years old, my dad would whip my brother and me with the same belt and in the same manner as he would whip his hunting dogs. He beat them to break their wills and to bring them into submission and control. As with us, when he whipped the dogs for barking or otherwise disobeying, he would yell at them stating how sorry they would be if they ever disobeyed him again. I saw this and heard this on many occasions even though I tried to hide or block the noise while I cried. Even now, just recalling these memories my hands tremble, I feel sick at my stomach, and I have tears in my eyes.

My mother's abuse of us, while oftentimes physical couldn't compare to the abuse from my dad. Mom's abuse was more often emotional, especially in the use of my dad as a way to scare us and to make sure we "got it" when he got home, oftentimes after she had already slapped us around and whipped us herself. She would make us wait and worry anywhere from a few hours to a few days, seeming to enjoy torturing us and watching us try to appease her with the hope she wouldn't tell. The physical abuse toward me stopped at age 14 when I physically challenged both of them. My dad always reminded me after that point not to think I would ever be too big for him to take me down. I believe that the abuse toward me and my brother was their way of physically acting out the conflict between them and within their marriage, and because of their own histories of abuse and victimization.

Can you see how this required relatively little time on their parts, and yet had a very devastating and lasting effect on my brother and me? Their failure to work out their feelings from having been abused as children and their marital conflicts makes this all the more infuriating. Just because they could treat us this way doesn't mean they should have done so. There are no excuses for this, only ways to identify it and try to understand it in an effort of trying to move beyond it. My parents generally did not admit remembering most of what they did, with my mom excusing it as having said and done things when she was angry which she "really didn't mean". Can you feel how insulting that is? My dad on the other hand did acknowledge his part of this a few years ago when I confronted him, but offered no apology. He actually had the nerve to say "but, we had a lot of love in this house." Ironically, people in our community thought we had the perfect family and that my brother and I were very well behaved. They didn't understand the severe consequences we faced for getting out of line.

The result of the kinds of problems created for me by my parents' dysfunction showed up in the form of intense anxiety and self-doubt. The personality characteristics of this "underdog" position took hold and required a lot of work initially to undo and repair the damage. I had no self-confidence and actually came to believe as truth almost all of the negative things said and done to me when I was growing up. For most of my earlier years I lived with a sense of impending doom, believing nothing would ever work out for me. My life during childhood was based in deprivation and an intense fear of unpredictable situations and people. These factors continued to haunt me as an adult. The one thing I take a great deal of credit for is the fact I have never let fear stop me. I have always found the courage to move forward in spite of fear.

I know what I know by experience and by the effort I have put into understanding and resolving my dysfunctional past through my own personal therapy, and through education and job experience within the field of psychology. None of this has come easy for me, and I hope my sharing of these personal details will help others move forward more quickly in their own process of self examination and resolution. This is extremely important both for the sake of individuals and for the sake of children who will be impacted by our adult lives. As we move through the remaining sections of this chapter each of you will see how the negative emotions (FLAGS) develop, and how unfair it is to subject children to our unresolved grief and losses from the past.

Before we move into an open discussion of abuse and victimization, take a few minutes to study another of my many, yet important lists (Appendix H). This one is about Kids Roles and Responsibilities, in the sense of what children are suppose to be able to do. As you read it think about how a perfect world for children would look, compared to the reality of the environments in which many children are raised. It isn't enough for adults to say: "We didn't mean to." There is no justification for not giving children what they need. There are, however, many reasons why children act out their emotion-based anxiety which results from not having the necessary nurturing and modeling to give them a good start in life. One of my main goals is to move people away from their sense of arrogance and entitlement which allows them to seek opportunities to deny responsibility for the problems kids have and to blame kids for everything they, as kids, are doing wrong. As you look over the list think about your childhood relative to your opportunities just to be a kid. Also be aware of how simple the lives of kids are supposed to be from infancy into young adulthood.

Now let's move carefully into the very unpleasant realities of abuse and victimization. There are actually four types of abuse: sexual, physical, emotional, and neglect. My distinction between the first three and the last is that sexual abuse, physical abuse, and emotional abuse are all very active forms of abuse. They constitute an almost unlimited number of bad things done or said to others. Neglect, on the other hand, is very passive in that good things which should be done, said, or provided to others are withheld, either intentionally or unconsciously.

I am not going to spend a great deal of time on sexual and physical abuse. Everyone knows what these are about, and I see no need to relate disturbing details from cases I have had over the years of working with kids and families in the field of psychology. There are, however, a few important observations I would like to share about these two forms of abuse and victimization.

First of all, sexual abuse is by far the most traumatic because it includes all four forms of abuse. It is, of course, always sexual. It also always includes a physical assault and invasion. And, it is always emotionally abusive considering the threats which usually follow, along with the message, whether spoken or unspoken, that the victim is nothing more than an object to which anything can be done. This indicates there really is no sense of you and me, only a sense of you as what I want with no regard to you as an individual thereby neglecting many childhood needs. Adults who sexually abuse children are simply attracted to children as sexual objects regardless of how they may attempt to rationalize this in their minds. Any consideration of sexual orientation is secondary to the child being the stimulus for sexual arousal. Men and women molest children as sexual objects regardless of whether they are gay, straight, or bisexual. In my opinion, adults attracted to children as sexual objects constitute a different categorization without any regard to sexual orientation and more along the lines of children as objects of sexual attraction similar to fetishes. Appropriate labels would be heterosexual, bisexual, or and homosexual predators.

The second category, physical victimization, is, of course, always physical, and is always emotionally abusive as well and, thereby, neglectful. No one who physically abuses others, regardless of age, does so without the result of emotionally scarring the victim. Along with the physical abuse comes a long list of messages that generally are expressed verbally as the physical abuse is being administered. After all, a rational, calm individual never conducts physical abuse. The abuser or victimizer is generally angry or enraged, and out of control, or sometimes mentally or emotionally disturbed. No history of the abuser having been abused excuses an abuser from their deeds, regardless of the form the abuse takes. Clearly, abuse, even in the form of emotional abuse is inexcusable.

Emotional abuse or victimization is the literal act of adding *insult to injury*. Included in my definition of emotional abuse are the other commonly used terms of "mental" and "verbal" abuse. While emotional abuse is only emotional abuse, it is what cuts into the core of how we come to believe who we are relative to issues of self-esteem, self-worth, and self-confidence. When coupled with the other forms of abuse, including neglect, the damage is only intensified on all levels. People, especially those in positions of power and authority, often use emotional abuse as a way of trying to shame others into doing the right things. This of course, never works. It only serves to establish the FLAGS that lead to anxiety/depression, hopelessness/helplessness, and the development of various acting-out behaviors.

Even if the active forms of sexual and physical abuse never occur, the abuse and victimization from being neglected is emotionally damaging as well. Clearly, as a child, my parents provided everything I needed materially with respect to clothes, food and shelter. However, after age four they rarely ever provided any form of emotional support and nurturing I needed to become a psychologically healthy, high-functioning adult. Neglect can also include the failure to provide even the basic emotional/psychological necessities. This is where the element of investing time comes into play, because neglect sends the emotional message that an individual is not worth the time and effort it would take to provide for them relative to all aspects of physical and psychological well being. Neglect, is therefore, emotionally abusive as well, and can be physically abusive if basic physical needs are not being met. Neglect results from individuals who are too self-absorbed or too emotionally or mentally impaired to care for others for whom they are responsible. One of my basic premises in this book is that adults are neglecting the needs of children and often times the needs of other adults with whom they may be connected.

Having addressed all four forms of abuse, I want to really concentrate on emotional abuse (Appendix I) because of the capability emotional victimization has to put the nails in the coffin, so to speak, in the sense of sealing one's fate. For this segment I want you to go back carefully and courageously in time to your childhood and recall the abusive things said to you by other people who played significant roles in your life, and in your subjective history. I want you to see how emotional abuse really reinforces all other negative experiences you have had or may experience in the future. I want you to be aware that we never forget the hurtful things done and said in the past. And I want you to be painfully aware of any emotional abuse you may inflict upon others. Even when people are not resorting to sexual or physical abuse, emotional abuse is now the first effort made in many cases and contexts to bring someone into submission. I see this quite often between adults and kids within all contexts. Again, keep in mind how any form of abuse/victimization fuels the FLAGS, and how little time is involved or invested in such abusive efforts. There is, however, a great deal of wasted energy which could be used more effectively to learn new approaches and deal with unresolved issues. Unfortunately, few people see this as a desirable or even necessary alternative, and continue the attempt to make a process work which is doomed for continued failure and frustration.

Even though there are laws against sexual and physical abuse, and physical neglect, there are no easily enforceable laws against emotional abuse or neglect. Because of this we need to assume and establish some moral and ethical "laws" which will dictate the need to stop the emotional victimization of others as well. Emotional victimization serves no purpose other than to inflict mental or psychological pain upon others. It is used as a means of trying to intimidate and control, and to "challenge" others to do well. Emotional abuse tends to be handed down from one generation to another, often times with us as adults using the same words and phrases upon others we heard as kids from significant adults in our lives.

As you review the next list (Appendix I) think about the three types of abusers/victimizers I have been able to identify. First, there are those who abuse from positions of power and an arrogant sense of entitlement. Then, there are those who are acting out their own FLAGS which exist in the present because they remain unresolved. When drugs and alcohol are added to the mix for this abuser (male or female) the victimization is generally more intense and violent. The third abuser is the one who acts out a history of abuse toward others modeled for them by others and sometimes culturally sanctioned. Included for the victim(s) of this person could be a need to act out their FLAGS resulting from current abuse by victimizing others who are vulnerable to them. This is especially true in situations of domestic violence, and on a more global scale of victimization perpetrated on groups by people in social, political, and religious positions of power and domination.

I have included another list (Appendix J) of just such terms and phrases which are designed to serve any number of negative purposes. Keep in mind that any form of abuse usually occurs during times of intense emotion and is a form of acting out emotion-based anxiety within the abuser. Therefore, the more intense the emotional basis, the more intense the abuse or victimization is likely to be. This can be said of any form of acting out or maladaptive behavior. Again, look for familiar items in the list, and add any items to the list which have not been included to date. Sadly enough this list is the longest one in the entire book.

Generally, there is one question that precedes any abusive statement. That question is: "What's wrong with you?" For me this question was always coupled with the word "boy". As soon as the question is asked, a whole barrage of answers to that question (as indicated in Appendix I) is then thrown at the intended victim. My experience was for these abusive statements to be made to me during the act of physical abuse as well as at other times. It is important to remember that anything said to you abusively is intended only to cause shame and guilt, and should not be looked at as being the truth under those circumstances. The truth is there is *nothing* wrong with you, in the sense of being permanently scarred, which can't be fixed. It is also important to remember that the question in adulthood becomes "What's wrong with _me_?", if you buy into the abuse.

As you looked over the list you may have seen some phrases which didn't sound especially abusive. There are times when some of these statements may actually be a true observation of someone's behavior. Remember the statements are abusive only if they are negative in connotation and context, and/or based in negative emotions. Statements, which are simply expressed as observations based in fact, are not necessarily abusive. However, there is always a fine line within situations that tend to be abusive. Even if someone experiences only emotional abuse the damage to one's self image, self-confidence, and self-esteem can still be extreme.

Emotional abuse is now used as a replacement for physical punishment in many cases. Many adults in varying roles resort to emotional victimization as a means of trying to motivate changes in behavior. Think about the level of disrespect and disregard conveyed to the intended victim of such tactics. Also think of how impossible it would be to respect anyone who is putting you down, especially when the abuse is directed at a child from an adult. Generally, adults will not take abuse from other adults, and children will not take abuse from other children. Why, then, would we expect children to take abuse from adults?

It is important to see the desperation represented by the use of emotional victimization. When adults have failed to give young children the proper guidelines, limits and structure prior to adolescence, many adults engage in open conflict and competition with children and teenagers in an effort to bring them under control. Because kids are too sophisticated to fall for the "old ways", everyone loses in this type of interaction. This endeavor is futile and will only lead to further rifts between adults and kids. Kids may comply, but will likely do so with resentment and hatred toward the adult or even toward any abusive system. After all, please do not limit your application of any of these writings to problems between parents and their children. Open your understanding to include all contexts or settings where abuse and victimization can occur. Also include interactions between many different age groups and levels. The concept of differing contexts will be covered more fully in the next chapter and later chapters as well.

One last consideration in this chapter is that of the purposes of abuse and victimization (Appendix J). If there were no purposes served, then abuse and victimization would be pointless. While I have already addressed such purposes in general terms, please take a few minutes to look over the last list for this chapter which specifically names many of these purposes. As with other lists you may be able to identify a few purposes not listed.

With these ideas in mind of possible purposes served by abuse and victimization, let's now move into the area of contexts where abuse and victimization can occur. I will attempt to connect all of this to the various settings in which people of all ages and considerations are targeted and mistreated. Hopefully, my writings will open up new perspectives and will motivate discussion about how to identify and change current patterns evident within all contexts where human nature and the FLAGS are acted out.

CHAPTER V
Contexts of Abuse and Victimization

In previous chapters I have referred several times to the notion of contexts in which abuse and victimization can occur. In this chapter I want to continue with this idea in an effort to expand on my application of the RFLAGS Model to settings outside of the home/family context which is the first of the six contexts I have identified. Such expansion is a relatively new endeavor in this project, though it has been one of my intentions all along. I have only begun exploring the concept of such applicability during lectures and seminars in recent years. Therefore, at this point in time, my efforts to some extent may be rather tenuous and certainly exploratory in nature. Hopefully I can stir up enough controversy to provoke discussion and further exploration and application of my proposals within all of these other contexts. Nothing within these chapters is intended to offend or single out any specific groups or individuals. My intentions are to identify and resolve misuses of power and authority at all levels and in all settings. Believe me I like a bit of a challenge in life, and I see the taking of certain risks as both exciting and necessary in order to promote growth and stop the abuse and victimization of all those who are vulnerable.

Much of the credibility for some of the statements made in this book is a direct result of the awarenesses I gain through my work with kids and families as they try to navigate successfully through various agencies, institutions, and organizations. This is particularly true from this point on through the end of the text. Because some of my suspicions are difficult to prove I bring them into this writing because if they are accurate, then people, especially in low-income families, are in many cases being unjustly and more frequently targeted. Anytime adults with abusive tendencies are in charge there is always the possibility of victimization rather than assistance. Reflected within this statement is the true nature of such individuals to control and dominate rather than to assist and guide. While suspicions are by nature difficult to prove, they are often worthy of investigation. Children are easy targets for abuse within the contexts outside the home/family. This is not only possible, but is very likely because children are minors and their records in any setting, especially educational and justice related, are protected in many cases more than the kids are protected. What a great way to avoid objective and unbiased outside oversight and scrutiny.

Six Contexts in which Abuse and Victimization Can Occur

The six contexts I have identified relative to my RFLAGS Model in which abuse and victimization can occur are: home/family, school, community, society, politics, and religion. I believe these contexts to be rather universal, and to be inclusive of all possible considerations relative to abuse and victimization. As I attempt to identify their composition remember they are listed in an order of movement away from and outside of the home/family context relative to growth and chronological development. The contexts are also listed ranging from subsystems to larger and more universal systems which have their own sets of subsystems. They move away from the subjective and limited exposure during childhood to a more adult perspective of exposure and later involvement in more complex arenas. "School" refers to the formal educational process that usually ends in late adolescence or early adulthood, and pertains generally to chronological considerations prior to or associated with those ages. It is the only category that is somewhat restricted experientially. The other contexts remain constant categories throughout life, and are to be seen as dynamic and ever changing.

The home/family context is just what it sounds like. It is constant in the sense one generally always has a home/family context in which to live. Certainly, one is always affected by this context even in adulthood by any remnants from the childhood home/family context. As people advance into adulthood and old age, the exact nature or composition of this context changes. It generally expands into our own adult home/family context which we create, then to the expansion of this context into the additional home/family contexts and constellations created by any future generations. One important realization is how the definition of home/family constantly evolves and changes to include previously non-traditional factors relative to composition and newer traditions. Reorganization and redefinition of the home/family context reflects the spiritual evolution of our existence away from arrogance and entitlement to more inclusive viewpoints relative to the diversity found within all aspects of human nature. Such a process moves us away from restriction and closed mindedness into an atmosphere of fewer prejudices and greater opportunities for more rapid spiritual growth by allowing for greater expression of human differences in perspective and lifestyle. The ideal home/family context should be the model for the other contexts with regard to basic well being and positive human interaction.

Clearly the home/family context is the most important context relative to emotional, psychological, and spiritual well being. Relative to size and number, this context is much smaller in scope than the others, but not in its impact on individuals, compared to the other contexts. With regard to impact on individuals, it is extremely important to understand the role of the home/family on preparing people to face the complications present within the other contexts. If the home/family context is not safe and nurturing, then the individuals living within this context will be unprepared to successfully face the larger contexts. After all, it is likely everyone will face some degree of abuse and victimization in the outside world. This fact alone further substantiates the need for adults in the home/family to be effective role models, and the need for the home/family environment to be a safe haven to which we can return when the outside world attacks.

For children, the next context outside of the home/family to which they are forcefully exposed is that of school. With exposure to school comes the rapid exposure to and influences from the other contexts. Generally speaking, prior to starting school, exposure to the other contexts has been somewhat limited and certainly biased and often controlled by the adults immediately present in children's lives. Hopefully, as children venture out into the world they have been given a secure basis within the home/family to give them the ability, confidence, and courage with which to explore the other contexts. Hopefully, too, the home/family context will be a stable environment which models appropriate standards, patterns of interaction and coping strategies for children and for society at large. The ideal of a nurturing, loving, accepting family should be the model for how we treat each other in the world as well. Like the Pointer Sisters sang years ago, "we are family", especially in the sense we are all related on a spiritual level.

Prior to an introduction into the school context, it is likely children will have had some exposure to: societal expectations and realities; adult religious and political beliefs; and to the context of community through general adventures into various community settings, as well as through the media. Some associations relative to the outside world already will have been revealed to children through the experiences of significant adults as children witness, with limited ability to understand, the adult attempts to successfully navigate through the other contexts. This is a major part of the whole concept of being role models. Children learn from our experiences as we display those experiences to them through our actions and attitudes; our biases and prejudices; and certainly through our reactions to and interactions with children in the home/family environment.

One concern I have for school systems in general is possible abuse/victimization in the form of denial of rights to children of low-income families who are viewed and labeled as troublemakers, bad kids, and lost causes. The current trend seems to be that of suspending or expelling these kids from districts for any reason imaginable. I am sure that in all cases these so-labeled kids and their families are not even fully informed about due process. Low-income families, especially from cultures which blindly accept rather than question authority, would be easy targets for this type of victimization when it is occurring. School systems, especially during times of conservative political influence, need to be monitored by independent parties/boards who could objectively scrutinize the implementation of educational policies. This is necessary if kids are to be protected from any misuse of power and authority. If money was reallocated at all levels to intervene in the lives of kids who are troubled, then schools could set up programs to help these kids succeed rather than make efforts to get rid of them. Simply questioning families whose kids get suspended frequently and expelled would likely reveal the misuse of power in a significant number of cases. Closed systems are always dangerous and injurious!

Now let's consider the context of community and the various elements it contains. My definition of community includes the geographic area in which we live, work, play, attend school, and socialize. Communities are composed of various businesses and organizations which help to determine the overall attitude predominant within that area relative to societal, religious, and political views. Many of us even choose our community relative to various factors which we feel will best serve our interests and perceived sense of well being and safety. Generally our community reflects our personal values and our biases; or they reflect our socioeconomic level or social class as the other extreme. Choosing a community for many people is a luxury, and is assumed to be a right to which everyone is entitled. Even within the context of community it is possible to see how the issues and elements of the other contexts impact and define the environment of any given community.

Of extreme concern to me is the existence of separatist kinds of communities which are either chosen by middle and upper classes, or are dealt with as inescapable by those who do not have the luxury of choosing their community and are forced to live in less than desirable areas. The desert region of Southern California in which I lived for nine years was a good example of this kind of dichotomy. There was a clear division between the east and west sides of the Valley. Lines were drawn both relative to ethnicity and culture, and to socioeconomic status. The Valley was littered in the western half with walled communities, which were ever increasing in number. "Locals" and "snow birds" alike inhabited these walled communities. The snow birds were those who "fly" in for the winter months mostly from Canada and the Northwestern and Midwestern states. They were generally retired white couples who usually bring with them all of the prejudices and restrictions from their conservative communities which they sought to recreate there in the desert. Their power was based in their mere numbers and in the very significant part they played in the economic and political considerations in the area.

The eastern half of the valley was primarily composed of people from various Spanish-speaking countries and cultures who generally worked the agricultural and service oriented jobs available to keep the communities in the western region clean and beautiful, and to keep those people comfortable and happy. The west was rapidly creeping into the east as we witnessed a siege of land needed to accommodate the fun-loving and wealthy retirees and tourists. The walled communities within the larger community of the valley only served to separate "us from them". The conservative and frequently bigoted Caucasian people would occasionally come out to enjoy the festivals and cultural events provided by the "others", and then return to their closed-in and sheltered communities.

Even more striking were the differences between groups and communities within the larger cities such as the Los Angeles area. While living there I was shocked to realize that many of the kids I worked with in East Los Angeles had never even been to the Pacific Ocean, no more than ten to fifteen miles away. Community issues are so much harsher in areas where people who are below the poverty level live in overcrowded conditions with very limited options and opportunities. Even transportation can be a serious obstacle for people who want a job, a better job, or more education and job training.

Because obstacles are oftentimes so huge, it is difficult to motivate kids and adults in these low income areas to seek out available opportunities designed to raise their standards of living. Furthermore, because of a number of different fears it is virtually impossible to get a kid to leave the only familiar environment to become a resident at programs such as Job Corps. For kids and adults within impoverished areas these communities often serve as the only reality or sense of worldview they have. These kinds of factors clearly increase the FLAGS for people who are abused and victimized within all six contexts. So many times in areas of limited opportunities survival needs are quite different and the home/family context is generally dysfunctional allowing for no secure basis to face the other contexts. Also, abuse and victimization simply from life circumstances is significant enough to create an almost endless cycle of abuse and victimization within all arenas because limited options increase, perpetuate, and exacerbate vulnerability.

Regardless of race and ethnicity, these considerations are important from a more universal perspective as I look for correlations and connections between abuse and victimization identified in the home/family context and in those contexts beyond this initial environment. I personally believe the arrogance and sense of entitlement exhibited from the privileged toward the underprivileged and disadvantaged in any geographical area is shameful. These factors resemble the same kind of ignorant arrogance and entitlement exhibited by many adults in general relative to children regardless of ethnicity and culture. I also believe the perceived rewards often associated with being an older Caucasian person – and increasingly by people of other races as well – in the United States have perpetuated the arrogance and sense of entitlement we see being defended so desperately by aging Caucasian groups and other conservatives today. This is evident in struggles to end affirmative action programs, and in attempts to deny basic rights to groups of people through proposals such as Proposition 187, an anti-immigration act in California during the mid 1990's. The big issue for the moment is immigration reform and social classes divided according solely to socioeconomic status.

People no longer want to use the terminology used previously to identify "whites" as the "European Americans" we are. Think about the arrogance with which history has been distorted to imply that Anglos discovered America as though it didn't exist until the Europeans arrived. Those throughout history who have fought for "religious freedom" have been much more savage and barbaric than many of the cultures which they have attempted to dominate and destroy in the name of God or some religion. This distortion is one way I see the dynamics of control and arrogance displayed by many adults on more personal levels being played out in the more universal context of society.

Society, the fourth context, is nothing more than a collection of communities and cultures, or subsystems. Each community represents a certain zeitgeist developing from both internal and external factors which help set certain specific community and social values and mores. Societal values of the identified "majority" are not always accepted by everyone; and, conflicts tend to be acted out within the political and religious contexts when such values are challenged or defended by either of the sides involved. Communities often oppose or ignore certain cultural values and norms that may exist as sub-communities or sub-cultures when compared to the larger context of society which generally sets the tone for what is considered both desirable and acceptable. Often times the values and norms of subcultures are not bad or wrong when compared to what are considered to be the "norm". They are just different, and these sub-communities often exist because the majority culture refuses to acknowledge and incorporate their existence. I am also addressing the fact we are still a very classist society, even in most parts of the world. Please don't think I am promoting a return to communism or a redistribution of wealth. I am simply identifying what I perceive to be divisive factors defining our current reality. Today the term "majority" deceptively refers primarily to people in positions of power and authority who set standards, create policy, and make laws, and yet have little to do with actual numbers of people within any given population. Majority is still tied more to race than to other factors. These are the groups with both the wealth and political power needed to sustain their existence and position.

As is true today with kids being too sophisticated to accept previously assumed practices based in arrogance and entitlement, communities and subcultures are fighting against what has been accepted for a long time as the norm. I believe these are the battles currently being fought within the political and religious contexts as those in perceived control seek to retain control - "those" often being various older Caucasian groups. I also believe these battles by the subcultures in this country began in the 1960's during the various human and civil rights movements. No one can argue with the concept of basic human rights. However, people often feel threatened when rights are sought for specifically named groups such as women's rights or gay rights, which are then perceived as asking for some kind of "special rights", rather than basic human and civil rights.

Much of the discussion and controversy I seek to inspire relative to the different contexts lies in the idea of moving away from power struggles based on "color" issues, or based in outdated puritanical dogma which leads to witch hunts and scapegoating all in the name of some form of God. The movement is toward a consideration and appreciation for diversity associated more with cultural implications and differences. Webster's Dictionary defines the adjective "ethnic" as: "of or relating to races or large groups of people classed according to common traits and customs". As an adjective the word "ethnic" is defined as "being a member of an ethnic group who retains the customs, language, and social views of the group". The prefix "ethno-", as in "ethnocentric", is from the Greek "ethnos" referring to "nation or people", and to "neither Christian or Jewish, [rather] heathen or gentile". "Ethno-" is defined as "race, people or cultural group". Even the origins of the word 'ethnicity' seem to be based in an 'us-or-them' kind of categorization of people as being outside of the majority group.

My point is that even though ethnicity is often associated with race, it allows room for an even greater emphasis upon group membership in all of the contexts which is identified by customs, culture, and even language. The shift away from the association of ethnicity and color allows for a better opportunity to appreciate differences based on culture, allowing for the fact many groups are often composed of people from many races anyway. Therefore, I see no need for division along the lines of color which comes in many shades and can so easily be blended into other hues as people seek to further divide and/or connect. Realistically I believe the greatest differences between people in this country today have more to do with class and socioeconomic status than with other factors attributed to historical injustices to which many people still cling. Please note that I do not equate class with standards of living. In other words, people living at a "lower class" level can still have a high standard of living.

For a society to be successful there can be no tolerance for arrogance and entitlement, as there can be no tolerance for people playing the victim role and using their oppression as an excuse to give up and act out emotion-based anxiety. Power based in arrogance and entitlement is gained and maintained at the expense and victimization of others. I believe my approach, along with approaches currently being explored by other people in addressing diversity, will help to dissolve some of the competition for recognition; and, can lead to an open identification of and appreciation for diversity which in most cases has little or nothing to do with color. I also think "European Americans" need to look at their own ignorance and their lofty pursuits at the expense of others, and acknowledge and make amends for mistakes from the past.

Furthermore, I think other groups need to work to clean up their acts and images as well relative to seeking opportunities to better themselves rather than continue blaming others for their plight. One of the best indications of where people are relative to controversial issues of diversity can be found in the comedy shows presented on the various cable channels. Watching such shows is a great way to discover where the different cultural groups are in the process of acceptance and appreciation of the diversity within all of us. If given the freedom to be cruel and abusive, even comedy can be used to victimize others. It can also serve to perpetuate many of the stereotypes and myths born of ignorance and separation. Anglos used this approach for many, many years. People of all ethnicities need to realize that many opportunities in life are lost through bad choices and irresponsible behaviors such as: substance use; promiscuity; poor management of finances and consumer credit; not taking advantage of available opportunities for education and job training; and having a lower standard of living. A standard of living is determined by more factors than just poverty, opportunities and locale. It has to do with pride and self-concept in spite of major obstacles.

Now let's move into the political and fifth context with all of its absurdities, abuses, and lack of ethics and professionalism. The political context has become nothing more than an arena in which to act out special interests relative to power struggles driven by money and the desire to be in control. The single biggest promoter and proponent of this reality is the media which I personally believe share spaces in both the community and societal contexts as they report local, state, national, and international stories. At times the media is as equally without ethical standards as are those within much of the political context. Those in the media are also responsible for the feeding frenzy relative to invasions into personal issues which often times have nothing, or at least very little to do with someone's professional abilities. As fewer numbers of people and groups control corporations, including the media, the special interest groups have the means through which to promote their causes and biases. More and more information is becoming known publicly relative to the kinds of people and groups who head the very sources of information made available to the public. This kind of ownership allows control over the content of what we are told is "truth". Corporate executives give the directives that can facilitate the continuation of biases, misperceptions and erroneous interpretations of relevant issues thereby reducing the degree of objectivity.

As I watch journalists comment on and report events of "interest", I see how they actually represent many of the ways in which the rest of society acts out emotion-based anxiety. I watch them with their seeming sense of being above and beyond accountability and respectability, which again reflects the same kind of arrogance and sense of entitlement I have witnessed in the competition between adults versus kids. Media personnel are often driven strictly by ratings and a need to be on top and the first to report something no matter how damaging or erroneous the details may be either to individuals or to groups they target. Think about the lives of different public figures identified as fair game. Also think about the power struggles between the political "left" and "right", and the stereotyped images perpetuated for many people from various diverse groups which do not fit into the agendas of those perceived, though deceptively so, as being in the majority. In my opinion, many of those in the media as a group personify that which is so blatantly wrong in society - an outright willingness to abuse and victimize to fulfill some self righteous need to act out their own emotion-based anxiety and dissatisfaction with life. In this sense it is possible to identify the competition set up to be "on top", and to be the best for no other reason than to meet some self-serving desire cloaked in the form of rhetoric used to justify injustice. Such people truly represent the emptiness many seek to fill at the expense of others, even if the targets happen to be children, depending upon the need, agenda, availability, and context. All parts of the U.S. Constitution guaranteeing and protecting human rights should be backed by an equally sound set of ethical standards and principles which are practiced and upheld by those who use the Constitution as a justification for and defense of offensive actions.

Consider for a while "Corporate America" which affects us in every context. Corporate America bombards us in our home/family context primarily through the media, especially through television and various technological advances. As I stated earlier much of any community composition is defined and impacted by the businesses within it. Schools often times have certain additional educational and recreational programs funded from grant money supplied through various businesses and corporations to supplement education (this can be a good thing). Even the tobacco companies have supported good causes. Big business certainly plays a huge role in society at large and in politics because money talks, influences, and controls. So many aspects of society seem to come down to a money and numbers game with greed overriding any regard for ethics and the concepts of responsibility and accountability.

Also consider all special interest groups who buy influence in politics simply to give them ever-greater opportunities to make money even when making money leads to the destruction of people's lives and our environment. Think about the lobbying which happens all the time to keep standards of pollution control to low limits regardless of the effect on the environment. Think about how the tobacco companies bought influence in Congress for many years in order to sell a product that is both addictive and deadly. I believe those who represent the states where tobacco is a major cash crop should also be held more accountable for any part they continue to play in perpetuating the fallacy that smoking is not harmful enough to be addressed, controlled, and ultimately eliminated.

Economies based in vulnerability to dependency on oil and the production of or participation in acts that can have detrimental effects on people and the environment can be and need to be redirected. For example, money wasted by government agencies fighting the import and distribution of drugs, along with money spent protecting access to oil could be diverted into programs to assist these economies in setting up industries to develop and utilize alternative energy sources, and to stop environmental destruction. I find it hard to believe there aren't people waiting for funding who are already available with ideas and inventions to change and strengthen unstable economies acting out the FLAGS relative to their own survival and complicating factors. Of considerable interest would be investments in alternative fuel sources. Oil dependent economies, including our own, need inspiration and assistance in making changes. Those economies based in illegal drug trade where terrorism abounds would be forced to seek other economic means of survival if the value of drugs dropped to a level where they are no longer a profitable commodity. In the long run the decriminalization of drugs would not create any more problems than we already have simply because of the reality that drug use is detrimental in a number of ways. Eventually the problem would balance itself out and dealers wouldn't be recruiting new users since the profitability would be gone, especially if monies were diverted toward improving impoverished areas. Based on my professional experiences I would have to say the so-called "war on drugs" is not working anyway.

Having lived years ago in a tobacco producing state where I listened to various media reports and word-of-mouth accounts, I believe the tobacco companies have been (and still are) spreading their lies around the world, especially to developing nations viewed as major international markets. American cigarettes sell very well overseas, especially when coupled with the myth of idealism associated with the American way of life as being the best way of life. They are actually exporting death everywhere. I believe the United States and other industrialized nations should take a very serious position relative to our need to be effective role models to developing nations. This is another opportunity for us to see on a larger scale the role of "parents", or simply as adults and leaders in positions of power and influence within different contexts, providing a healthy example of the most appropriate ways to live and treat others. This cannot be done at the expense of others or to further some cause or hidden agenda. And it should not be done from the arrogant stance of the American way being the only way other than as a consideration and possible example for basic issues of freedom and human rights, and not for the sake of domination or control.

One of the biggest travesties in recent corporate history at several contextual levels is the excessive profit of a few at the expense of many, accomplished through outright lies and deceptions, with many of the culprits having never been criminally prosecuted. It is frightening to think that corporate leaders and government officials, for their own gain, readily finagle business practices through loopholes either created politically within bills signed into laws, or simply without regard for laws and ethics. For example: energy "crises"; insignificant changes in drug formulas allowing for extension of patent rights and market control; the possibility that some diseases are more profitable to maintain than to cure; special interest groups; dirty politics; the underhanded inclusion of provisions within bills signed into law that serve as political extortion. These are only a few of the obvious misuses of power and influence especially prevalent within the United States of America.

Based on statements I have heard from public officials and researched on line, a prime example of deceptive legislation is that of "Homeland Security" and the US Patriot Act. Apparently different law enforcement agencies are bragging about their ability since "9/11" to invade people's privacy more than ever. This is apparently aimed at fighting street crime and gangs, and made possible because of a loophole in the law allowing gangs to be identified as domestic terrorist groups. The general population believes money allocated for "Homeland Security" is being spent on the kinds of terrorist acts associated with the attacks of 9/11/01. Gangs only terrorize each other and not the general population. They are in no way even similar to the concept of global terrorism. Because this is true then an investigation into the deceptive misuse of federal tax dollars needs to conducted relative to the legislation and legislators who made this possible. This would even include the Bush White House and the office of the US Attorney General under George W Bush. This is a tremendous misuse of power and a source of significant abuse and victimization of the American public, and especially of kids in low-income areas. Full disclosure of legislation in a simple easily understood format should be made available to the general public every time a law/bill is proposed at any level of government.

Think about how big business creates a great deal of torment for those at the lower ends of the socioeconomic spectrum. Through all forms of advertising we are told what is best for us in terms of looking good, feeling good, and attaining the highest standard of living. Advertising seems to perpetuate the disparity between those with and those without the things "needed" to make life better. Think about how advertising causes problems between parents and kids when families cannot afford to buy the things kids are told they need in order to fit in with others. Think about how advertisers promote drug use by suggesting there is some pill or potion for anything from which we suffer, including being a few pounds overweight. These kinds of influences in the USA, along with a failed welfare system, have served to perpetuate the societal myth there is always an easy way out. Kids and many adults believe it is possible to get something for nothing, and that people and other systems owe us something. Kids often times have: little or no ability to tolerate frustration; a very poorly defined or nonexistent work ethic; an unrealistic desire to have a good job without doing anything to make that happen; very little willingness to work their way up the ladder of success; and a limited ability and willingness to delay gratification of some desire. In other words people and contexts perpetuate an unrealistic view of the world and life in which people are victimized and exploited.

Many systems operate without a sense of conscience or a sense of responsibility for their actions. This is true of any system not operating or functioning at an optimal ethical level, and without any form of outside scrutiny and accountability. This is clearly a day and age of "buyers beware" because profits are being made through deception disguised as assistance or relief from troubles and pain. Advertisers and promoters are covered by the fine print on paper, on the TV screen, and by disclaimers provided at the end of radio commercials which they know generally go unheeded. Many people and systems seem to have forgotten the concept of "what goes around comes around". My gang kids use this expression frequently and, as I explained in an earlier chapter, can understand what this means relative to flirting with danger and destruction, even if the destruction is of the self. This concept holds true for any system, just as it does for any individual. Everyone and every system creates its own hell so to speak by not being careful of what is set into motion. For every action there is a clear consequence, and those who gamble eventually lose. Think back and become painfully aware of how quickly companies turned 9/11 into a way to make money at the expense of a very vulnerable audience. All of these issues represent a general and unspoken awareness of and abhorrence for problems and deceptions we believe to be real and cannot effectively prove. Many people share with me the same feelings and justifiable paranoia that there is much we suspect and cannot control or influence because of numerous areas of secrecy and privilege. This alone is my justification for many of the statements I make. I watch and listen just like others and wonder where those in positions of power and authority will actually take us next. I am not sure who to trust anymore in any of the contexts outside the home/family environment.

Politics - not much more needs to be said relative to this context. The two dominant political parties in this country have drawn a line between them and each childishly dares the other to cross the line. Everyone on both sides seeks to expose and destroy the other to the point that controversy related to unimportant matters when compared to the common good of the nation takes the forefront in all arenas. People in the conservative arenas have made tremendous efforts to impose their hidden financial and religious agendas, and their need to control and manipulate in an effort to maintain power and position. Beware of the current term "faith-based" as another ploy to retain recognition since the term "religious right" didn't work out so well. The right wing factions are comprised primarily of wealthy European Americans who arrogantly seek to protect their positions of unquestionable authority to which they feel entitled. At the other end of the conservative spectrum are those who often proudly hold conservative religious beliefs based in blind ignorance and allegiance. Fortunately their fundamentalism and prejudices are deceiving fewer and fewer people. Their stance is held without regard to the common good of all other diverse groups. The attempt is to impose the beliefs of a prominent and divisive minority on the rest of society and the world as a way of remaining in positions of power and influence. The improvements of some of these factors within the political context following 9/11 quickly dissolved back into partisan politics as the world began to take it all in stride and move on.

Think about how Washington, DC is used by politicians to maintain the greatest level of influence. It is no longer important for the differing parties to work together for the well being of all. Campaigns and candidates should represent different issues and concerns as related to the well being of this nation and the world without dividing matters along "party lines". Separation of church and state is critical to our survival. The conservative groups are trying to use politics to impose their out-dated morality and values upon those who seek to move ahead and find new approaches to problem solving which need to include some of the basic truths of humanity and spirituality. Such approaches should not be too narrowly defined or dictated by any minority as being what is best for all. These kinds of struggles also tie in very directly to how people and groups within all contexts seek opportunities to act out emotion-based anxiety, rather than face and deal with the emotions which fuel these acts of hopelessness and desperation. So many people today seem to be fighting demons (FLAGS) within themselves by flailing their arms aimlessly at objects and issues outside of themselves. This kind of thinking is the fuel for many acts of terrorism around the world as people react to their own respective internalized FLAGS.

Think about how religion has also become big business with televised evangelism and exploitation. Just like with comedy and diversity I would encourage everyone to tune into the different religious channels, which apparently includes the FOX news channel, as a way of recognizing the ignorance filtering through the conservative religious groups. It is often very hard to find any remnant of spirituality within the messages they present to the listeners. Religion often seeks only to promote its own causes and dogma. Those within any extreme form of religion, in the sense of being defined as self-righteous and arrogant, seek to recruit people to their side and their limited view of the world. People have the right to believe whatever works for them. In my opinion they also have a responsibility to insure that their beliefs are not destructive to themselves or to others.

As you watch the broadcasts on the religious channels, look objectively at the desperation, regardless of religious affiliation, followers use to convince themselves and others that their way is the only way. Look at the limited amount of education audience members and followers often have as exhibited by the ways of expressing themselves, often only parroting what they are told to say and believe. Even those who are educated in other fields are also often heavily educated from within a religious bias that discourages questioning and exploration of alternative ways of seeking and knowing God. People are taught to be afraid of such exploration as being sinful and blasphemous. However, no one in these groups is willing to entertain the possibility such tactics could be interpreted as mind control. Consider those in other countries who kill themselves and others in the name of their God.

These conservative religious groups, here and around the world, seek only to further their various causes and their idea of helping or controlling others only serves to promote their agendas. They truly believe in what they are attempting to do, having successfully deluded themselves as to both the basis and unspoken purposes represented by their actions. However, their beliefs often reflect a desperate need to hold onto something they perceive as being meaningful and necessary. Many of their followers in my opinion also have an unconscious and unhealthy need to be controlled and are easily influenced. Once you are in it is difficult to get out because of the fears of going to hell, not receiving the seventy-two virgins, provoking the wrath of God, and the fear of losing the love from God. Sounds an awful lot like emotional abuse described in chapter four doesn't it? Help comes only in the form of becoming part of "the flock", or accepting some form of domination in many cases. Only those "within the flock" are helped in times of need (to use their terminology).

Outreach to others outside of any particular religious faction is often for the sole purpose of recruiting them into that particular religion, even if this has to be done in some form of deathbed guilt trip, or by teaching their extreme beliefs to children. They are real opportunists looking for any point of vulnerability which can be used to fuel guilt, shame and fear. Even Catholics reserve communion only for those who have been converted officially into "the church", which is also defined as the family of God. This implies that all of those outside of the "church" regardless of the denomination are also outside the family of God. How much more arrogant can anyone get, especially in light of recent "revelations" of sexual abuse and victimization perpetrated against parishioners by clergy and nuns, all of which was covered up for years under the ever popular "code of silence" existing within other contexts as well. The "church" even set itself up as being above the law when it comes to reporting abuse and victimization. As the "Church Lady" from older episodes of Saturday Night Live would say: "Isn't that conveeenient?" What goes around comes round!

Within their struggles it is possible to see how these religious groups are trying to fight against people such as myself who now practice what they refer to as blasphemy and an abomination against God. True spirituality focused on the spiritual evolution of humanity is nothing more than a return to the basics of Spirituality, excluding all of the hidden agendas present in today's religions. I see my work in the field of psychology as a non-religious ministry of outreach, with the difference of not trying to convert anyone to any particular way of thinking. My only goal is to encourage others to seek God in their own way and from within. To look for God outside of oneself is another form of being at the mercy of externals. Spirituality is a way of promoting the development of healthy morals and values, not for the sake of avoiding judgment, damnation and hell; but, simply because pure unadulterated spirituality is the only thing that makes sense. How arrogant it is for religions to teach that their "group" is the only select few who are worthy of God and certain perceived rewards.

Before leaving this segment take some time to examine abusive beliefs and statements associated with people in positions of power and authority outside the home/family context. This list (Appendix K) is similar to the list of abusive statements made by adults to kids generally in one-on-one scenarios. However, this list addresses the arrogance and destructive nature of people encountered on a larger scale in all of the other contexts outside the home/family context. You will be able to recognize how these items apply to the contexts we just covered. Following this list is a list (Appendix L) representing the faulty thinking of victims of larger scale abuse/victimization beyond the home/family context. Understanding the relevance of these lists is critical in understanding how people can be made to feel vulnerability and weakness associated with the FLAGS. Review the list from Chapter 4 (Appendix J) of the purposes of abuse and victimization and apply those items to the next list of abusive statements and beliefs. When you study the list of faulty thinking also compare these items to those in the list in Chapter VI of the results of abuse and victimization. Refer to any of the lists in the appendices at any point throughout your reading for clarification and relevance. Failure to utilize and understand these lists/appendices will reduce your understanding of the applicability of this content within this book.

A model similar to my RFLAGS Model that explains the process of abusive people in positions of power and influence abusing others would probably look something like the model shown below. This model applies more specifically to larger scale abuse and victimization rather than simply day to day kinds of negative interactions any of us are likely to experience. Larger scale abuse and victimization isn't always apparent initially, especially within the societal, political, and religious contexts. Even the ways of acting out I have listed below are different from those associated with more direct and personal experiences identified in the RFLAGS Model (Appendix C). Let's call this model the Roberts Abuse by People in Positions of Power and Authority Model, or RAPPPA. Just kidding! That was the best I could do! Remember the models are cyclical with one stage leading to another, and with the acting-out behaviors only making the FLAGS worse, thereby perpetuating the entire futile process.

ABUSE BY PEOPLE IN POSITIONS OF POWER AND INFLUENCE MODEL

Negative Emotions (FLAGS)	**Conquest & Conquer**	**Complete Selfishness & Disregard**	**Acting-out Behaviors**

ACTING OUT BEHAVIORS

Lying	Deceiving	Cheating
Embezzling	Stealing	Black Mailing
Threatening	Gesturing	Posturing
Grand standing	Molesting	Raping
Pillaging	Plundering	Destroying
Forging	Misrepresenting	Breaking promises
Making false promises	Indulging	Hiding
Running	Ruling	Dominating
Covering up	Creating fear	Intimidating
Physical violence	Abusing/ victimizing	Paying/bribing
Seeking like-minded others	Corrupting	Defeating
Competing	Defying	Denying
Defending	Accusing	Offending
Expecting	Fantasizing	Planning/Scheming
Engaging	Recruiting	Soliciting
Befriending	Winning/gaining	Obsessing

Having explored the six contexts in which victimization and abuse can occur, let's now consider another element necessary in the understanding of my concepts. I have noticed in my dealings with people that there are certain factors, which I refer to as complicating factors or risk factors, which will increase the likelihood of someone being victimized both within the home/family context and in the other contexts as well. A complicating factor is any aspect of being human which makes one vulnerable and sets them apart as different from "the rest". These factors are both personal and environmental.

To give you a better understanding of what complicating factors are,

I have included a list of items (Appendix M) which have been identified to date. This list is *extremely* important since many people in the so-called helping professions, and as educators, and law enforcement fail to take these factors into account. It is impossible to work effectively with low income, disadvantaged kids and families if people do not understand all of the realities present in their lives. For anyone to work with any population and not understand the realities in their lives is the highest form of incompetence, and a major violation of established professional ethics. As you review this list I again encourage you to try and identify other elements which have not yet been identified. Also look very carefully at identifying any complicating factors present in your life currently or historically.

The Past that Lived in My Present

Having included the list of complicating factors, I come to another one of those parts of this book where I feel I should reveal to you more of my own history. In other words I want to give each of you an opportunity to understand how my set of complicating factors increased my likelihood of being victimized within all six of the contexts. This is intended to be a forum only for sharing and understanding so each reader can understand how I know what I know. Again this book is not about me, but it does come from within me based on both my subjective personal and professional experiences. Hopefully my words will challenge everyone to examine their prejudices and to open their minds to learning about the factors present in everyone's lives which make each of us unique. Each person has their own very personalized set of issues and complicating factors which shape us, and which influence the way we view others and the world. Remember this book is all about honesty, reality, and self-examination for the purpose of changing human interaction and lifting it to a higher spiritual level.

My set of complicating factors can be summed up rather simply and quickly, and even though you have already read about some of them, I will recap them briefly in this segment and then add to them at the same time. It goes like this.

I was born in 1954 during the post World War II era, to middle class parents, each of whom came from very dysfunctional backgrounds. Neither of them ever worked through their own sets of complicating factors which then impacted my life in a very negative way, especially after the tragic deaths of my mother's family members in 1958. I was born in Alabama, and began the first grade in September 1960 at an elementary school in the suburban city which billed itself as "the all white city" until at least the late 1960's. This is an important factor for later as we consider the impact of the civil rights movement.

School was a very frightening environment for me, primarily because my home/family context was so unstable. I was sent into the world with no self-confidence and with very low self-esteem. Because my home/family context became so abusive, it is easy to understand my fear of the world. I started school filled primarily with fear, loneliness, anger (which was buried very deep within), guilt, and shame. The FLAGS were waving and I had no resources from which I could seek help and understanding. Furthermore, people in general didn't give much credence to emotional/psychological issues at that time in history, especially relative to a child's perspective.

The FLAGS became my internal guides of how to respond to the other contexts. Because the FLAGS are negative rather than positive, every experience I had was faced with dread. I hated to get up in the mornings because of my fear of what the day would hold relative to its unpredictability and my perceived lack of control over probable events. All of this was based in being deprived of the emotional strength and stability I should have been armed with prior to starting school. This is a clear example of the emotional neglect I described in a previous chapter. The only so-called '*tool*' I was given was an extremely distorted image of God who was to be feared rather than viewed as a source of comfort and aid. Thanks to my parents and the local Southern Baptist Church and its minister at that time, even God served as a source for the FLAGS. I had the wrath from God and from my parents to worry about, along with the belief taught to me by those who "loved" me that if you had a problem, you simply had to pray about it and it would go away if your faith was strong. That approach never worked and made me feel like an even bigger failure given the fact even my "faith" was faulty!

The only early memories I had of attending church are those of my dad taking me outside to whip me with his belt on the sidewalk for not sitting still during church services. After the whipping I was given no time to regain my composure, being told to "dry it up or I'll give it to you again". I was then brought back into the church sniffling, fighting hard not to cry, and feeling like everyone in the church was looking at me. After all, I had been told they were looking at me, and that I was a shame and a disgrace to my parents for embarrassing them like I had done. I was no more than three or four years old, possibly younger because my parents started taking me into the church building rather than leaving me in the nursery. This was another one of my dad's control freak tactics he used to teach me a lesson

I was never allowed to dance because dancing was sinful, even for first graders. My mother caught me dancing at a birthday party once with my first grade friends. When she arrived to pick me up she saw me dancing, and ordered me to the car after I was met with a slap across my face in front of all of my friends. I guess I was a little slow in understanding the concept of sin. However, I learned the concept of the FLAGS very early on. Needless to say, I was never invited back to this friend's house. This experience and others served as major complicating factors which impeded any opportunity to learn effective social skills as a child. To further complicate socialization I was allowed to visit only one friend a week for one hour. My parents told me they did not want me to be a "nuisance" in the neighborhood. Most of the rest of my time was spent at home alone and working in the yard which I had to maintain, along with help from my brother, from a very early age. Keeping up the yard allowed Daddy to "piddle around" and work on his projects, and also allowed him to spend more time away from home hunting and fishing. I always felt like an unpaid hired hand as a kid.

I was always made to look different because of my parents' conservative ways of dressing me and cutting my hair. My dad cut my hair until I turned 16 and could afford to pay for my own hair cuts after I began working my first real job. Even at age 16 my haircut, this simple act of asserting my independence, was taken as an act of defiance. The standard retort when I complained about looking different was: "if everyone else jumped off the bridge I guess you would jump too." In addition to limiting my socialization, all of these tactics proved to be complicating factors as well because they were intended to squelch my individuality and to impose strict external control for no other reason than to break my will.

To make matters even worse relative to school my vision was so bad I couldn't see well at all and didn't realize it until the fifth grade. My grades were bad and my parents were forever punishing me for this because teachers told them I was intelligent, but that I was not living up to my potential due to laziness and not applying myself. When I say I didn't realize I couldn't see, I guess I mean I didn't make the connection between not being able to read the eye chart and my low grades. I already felt so much like a nerd I didn't want the added injury of having to wear glasses; so, I memorized the first five lines of the eye chart. In the fourth grade I tried to tell my parents I needed glasses, but they accused me of lying and wanting attention. They went to the school and the teacher told them I had read the chart successfully. Because of my fear of getting in trouble for having memorized the eye chart, I took the punishment they doled out with their belief I had lied and had also embarrassed them yet again. In the fifth grade I broke down and cried when the teacher tested my eyes, telling her I could not even see the big letter "E" at the top of the chart. I begged her to call my parents for me so they would know I wasn't lying and would take me to the eye doctor. After I got my glasses my grades improved to the level of A's and B's, and in the sixth grade I received an achievement award. However the damage to my self-esteem had already been done. It took me until my mid thirties to finally get to the point where I could wholeheartedly believe in myself.

Things got worse when my younger brother started school making all A's and was able to skip the second grade. I was always compared to him both academically and relative to his athletic ability. Comparing me to him further set me up to hate him and to seek out any opportunity I could find to fight with him. Only in recent years have we been able to get completely beyond feeling distant from each other because of the dynamics our parents set up between us. Even as Dr. Roberts I have received very little respect from my family members due to other complicating factors primarily related to major differences in religious, political and social beliefs.

Much of the distance between my family and me was always justified using religious reasons. However, this was not the true reason as the real reasons were based in a fear of what others think relative to what my parents perceived as a life of sin primarily because I am outside of the church and their way of thinking and believing. Because I came out to them when I was 29, I was completely disowned for nearly 18 years. This act of being orphaned as an adult through no fault of my own set the stage for me to finally embrace and accept every aspect of my total identity. Believe me, I gained much more that I ever lost. I have a letter from my mother I received while in graduate school in 1991 telling me I am from the devil, and telling me she and my dad didn't know why I was ever born. It took me getting a BA degree, two master's degrees, and a Ph.D. to finally convince myself I am not what they told me I was. Believe me, my RFLAGS Model comes to you from my heart and from my own difficult life experiences. And, we are not finished yet. Obviously I grew up knowing that I was "different" from the other boys.

Rather than being given a natural athletic ability (and good vision) like my brother, I was given the complicating factor of musical ability. I was such a disgrace to my parents. I couldn't play sports and I wasn't interested in hunting, so the distance between my father and me continued to grow, as did my jealousy toward my brother. Because of looking like a nerd and because of my lack of athletic ability I was the target of much abuse and ridicule by other kids at school.

These factors continued to plague me throughout my entire school experience even into college. Fortunately, my college experience was somewhat less traumatic simply because people tend to become a little less cruel as they get older. If someone had taken the time to teach me I really believe I could have played some sports. I was a very good swimmer and learned to water ski, both of which I enjoyed tremendously. In an adult education program I attended during my junior and senior years of high school I actually ran a touchdown while playing football. No one in this program knew my history of being "sports-less", so I had a chance to try some new things. I can also see how my lack of self-esteem and self-confidence served as complicating factors for me as well. Believe me all of these factors are connected and interrelated.

My sense of shame in my abilities was amplified by my dad's reluctance to attend any of my recitals or other musical performances. He very readily and eagerly attended all of my brother's sports events. My mother even had to insist my dad attend my first college graduation. No one in my family has ever attended any of my graduation ceremonies for the different graduate programs. I am their oldest son and one of the few people in the family to have ever graduated from college, and the only one in the family, both immediate and extended, with a Ph.D. All of these experiences caused a great deal of emotional, mental, and spiritual damage that took me years to identify and then overcome. This is true in varying degrees for virtually anyone if you will only be honest about your past. While my story isn't as bad as some, it was bad enough. I can't imagine how I would have survived if additional external complicating factors had been thrown into the mix.

Let me summarize by reminding you I grew up in a strict Southern Baptist environment in the "Deep South" just prior to and during the civil rights movement. I can remember all of the factors of discrimination such as the white and colored water fountains and bathrooms, as well as dining areas and waiting rooms. Not only did I watch the news accounts of then Governor George Wallace and the problems in Birmingham, I lived through some of the horror created by "white people" and supported by my own parents in response to integration and change. This was a disgraceful time to be white and I am amazed at how recently it all happened.

I became a high school dropout in the eleventh grade because of the violence in the county school district where I lived. I completed my junior and senior years in an adult education program rather than stay in the middle of the chaos and violence where no one was learning anything productive. I made this choice rather than attend one of the little private "Christian" schools which popped up all over the area. My high school was on national news during the 1969-70 school year - my tenth grade year - because of riots and bomb threats resulting from the forced integration and rezoning of schools. The Southern Baptist Church I attended even had men stationed outside to keep African Americans from trying to attend the church services on Sundays, all in the name of God and based on arrogance and entitlement.

In addition there was the hippie movement and all the drugs and music which went along with that culture. It was a time of drastic changes.

Fortunately I never bought into any of the bigotry and prejudice I was exposed to during my childhood. I remember watching on TV all of the disgraceful acts committed by whites (who, more often than not, also claimed to be Christian) against blacks. At the same time I had to listen to my parents' commentary on and justification of the horrible and shameful acts of abuse and victimization. With the utmost respect and sincerity I look up to Rosa Parks as one of my role models because of her one act of defiance that changed history forever. As I grew into an age when I could question all of this I had to do so secretly and internally. When I challenged my parents' beliefs and use of racial and ethnic slurs I was met with insults and an occasional slap across my face for being a defiant, disrespectful, and uppity "n----r lover". Imagine what would have happened to me if they had known that I was secretly harboring the reality that I was gay - at least by my early to mid teens. This reality almost ended with me committing suicide if not for the intervention of a college professor when I was 18. My attempt to change my sexual orientation by marrying proved to be a major disaster, with the exception of having fathered a wonderful daughter who has given me six beautiful grandchildren over the years. If anyone could have changed this complicating factor it would have been me. I am amazed that I survived my childhood, especially in light of this major secretive life I had to hide and try to bury, almost literally. No child should ever have to live like this.

The other big issues at that time, especially in the Deep South, were the Beetles; men with long hair; the "shameful and defiant acts of those hippies"; and men identified as "fags, queers, and perverts". Any human behaviors and ideas that didn't meet the standards and approval of "Christian white folk" were fair game for ridicule and scorn. Only as an adult did I finally have the opportunities to really gain contact with groups outside of the closed, conservative, religious and ignorant white culture. My home/family history of abuse and victimization coupled with chaos and turmoil in the world and within _all_ of the other contexts made growing up very difficult. Also important to the time were the constant threats of a nuclear war; being drafted into the war in Vietnam; and all of the religious extremists predicting the sure and eminent end of the world. Thank God for my maternal grandmother; for the relatives and neighbors who occasionally addressed how mean my dad was; and for the misfit professor at a private Baptist college who opened my heart and mind to unimaginable realities and potential. Other than these factors, along with some degree of intelligence and a desire to rise above all of this and learn from these experiences, I have no other explanation for my qualities of resilience, transcendence, and determination. Keep in mind that

I had only an extremely distorted version of God as any source of spiritual guidance. Obviously that has changed as I moved forward and away from all of this negativity and falsehoods.

Many people have complicating factors and secrets they drag with them from childhood into adulthood. Secrets of any kind further complicate other complicating factors. Remember, too, I had help along the way as I entered adulthood, so I didn't have to face my past realities alone. I sought professional help as an adult and always looked for opportunities to learn how to deal with the remnants from the past more effectively. Furthermore, I continuously seek out new people and resources that help me to grow and learn. I see my life as an ongoing process rather than as a means to an end, and I look forward to whatever lies ahead simply because I will always be able to learn something which will both advance the growth of my soul and will be worth sharing with others.

Also remember this account of my past is my reality. As I said before I am not completely sure of the accuracy of the details of some of the very early instances. However I am painfully certain of the emotions connected to these events, and of the scars, some of which may never heal completely. Even though taking control of my life cost me my family for many of my adult years, this loss is nothing compared to all I have gained. The chances are I would never have done most of what I have pursued simply because I would have still been under their control, foolishly and pointlessly living my life to please others at my own expense. I allow no one to impose unreasonable limits on my life and am a stronger and more spiritual man for having tried and succeeded. Ironically, abuse and victimization can make people stronger if they learn to recover from the damage. Remember from Chapter I there is no opportunity to fail, only opportunities to learn and grow.

I am often amazed that as a "white" man I am able to work with gang kids and juvenile offenders without them having any idea of the ways I can relate to and understand them as underdogs. I tell them that I know how bad it feels to feel bad, and I encourage them to never do that to another human being. Because they too know how bad it feels to feel bad, they are able to connect with me without a need to know how I can look beyond what they do and be able to see their souls. These kids represent my heart and soul, and couldn't even begin to understand how working with them has helped me to get through my own issues and insecurities. I tell them all the time (without being able to explain why) that I never ask them to do anything I haven't had to do in some form in my own life. Somehow they just know on a professional level that I am for real and that I care.

Chapter VI

Results and Losses Associated With Abuse and Victimization

Having looked at abuse and victimization, and at the contexts and complicating factors, let's turn now to the results and losses associated with victimization. In this chapter we will identify and describe possible factors of unresolved grief associated with losses. We will see how losses arise from the results of being victimized, with loss being one of the results. We will also look at how loss and grief are acted out in the varying contexts as well as on an individual level. In addition we will look at how these unresolved losses get passed down from generation to generation through different personality types and patterns of negative interaction and perception.

Abuse and victimization leave a lasting imprint upon the psyche of the victim. The duration of the victimization and its intensity determine the depth of the imprint or wound. Quite often these wounds go unhealed for an entire lifetime. As with all significant wounds, even though healing may occur, there will be a scar to serve as a reminder of the past, with the prominence of the scar equal to the severity of the injury. Open wounds are those which cannot heal due to infection and inattention.

If an individual had a very healthy home/family context as a child, the chances are that individual will be able to face any form of victimization experienced in adulthood in a much more appropriate and healthy manner.

Even life can seem to be a source of victimization as we face uncertainty and loss throughout our entire lifespan. Given a solid psychological foundation from which to face negative situations we will not only survive, but also gain strength to prepare for any other negative event which is almost inevitable in the ever-revolving cycles of life. No one stays on top or at the bottom forever.

This book and especially the material covered in this chapter are directed at those of us who did not have a solid basis from which to grow as a child. It is also written for those of us who had to deal with various complicating factors that made the world outside of our home/family (and sometimes inside our home/family) an unsafe and frightening place as well. Our ability to cope generally depends upon the dysfunction and trauma from the past - the open wounds and the prominent scars. Hopefully by now each of you is beginning to see how the Fear, Loneliness, Anger, Guilt, and Shame (FLAGS) originate from the deprivation and unpredictability we experienced as children.

As you have seen from my own life, even a good start can go horribly wrong if traumatic events occur prior to the development of a strong ability to cope with such events. This is intensified even more when the adults involved in our childhood did nothing to resolve the issues related to their own dysfunctional backgrounds. The ability to function in adulthood is even more chaotic and problematic when, from the very beginning of life, an individual was abused and victimized, and forced to experience other complicating factors with little or no period of positive influences and opportunities. Abuse and victimization are inexcusable. Negative life events and experiences we are sure to face are not the problems. The problems lie within our ability to cope with these elements as determined by our upbringing and the emotional states of the adults within all contexts who were responsible for teaching us and giving us the things we needed in order to grow and function at optimal levels. In other words, the problems arise from the numerous negative results and losses associated with abuse and victimization, remembering that abuse also includes neglect, perhaps better described as deprivation.

In my professional and personal experiences I have become aware of the concept of unresolved grief which can either be active and chronic, or can lie dormant on an unconscious level until triggered in adulthood by some negative life event. This is what I believe is meant by complicated bereavement, meaning grief extending beyond some reasonable time period or healthy emotional reaction. From my observations and experiences I also believe unresolved grief is particularly likely in the midst of multiple losses whether these are obvious losses as with death and dying, or are more abstract and subtle as in losses of childhood, innocence, and hope associated with victimization and various complicating factors.

The Past that Lived in My Present

I believe this concept of unresolved grief is what happened in my own family for both of my parents. Their lives were likely somewhat dysfunctional even in early adulthood prior to their meeting and getting married. It is also likely the first six years of their marriage were relatively okay, with less significantly damaging conflicts occurring than those that would come later. My mother's marriage to, and subsequent divorce from, a very abusive older man also served as a major source of distress and guilt. She got married at 18 because of a pregnancy which resulted in a miscarriage due to extensive domestic violence, no details of which came out until after her death in 2000. This was a major missing piece in all of my past as well. So it is fair to say the unresolved grief and emotions from the past were probably simmering on an unconscious level in both of them. My dad demanded that my mother keep her previous marriage a secret which she was to have taken to her grave.

As the years progressed and my parents tried to deal with the differences between them relative to characteristics of individual differences, the unresolved factors continued to heat up. The final trigger for them probably started with all of the changes I delineated earlier just after I reached my fourth birthday, culminating in the tragic deaths of my grandfather and my uncles. Unfortunately none of the unresolved issues were allowed to become conscious. However, both of my parents began vigorously acting out the emotion-based anxiety that was already present from the past and never dealt with. My dad even tried to murder my mother when I was seven or eight years old due to the fact her previous marriage had to be revealed. He had been nominated to become a deacon in the Baptist church I mentioned previously. Because he was married to a divorced woman he had to disqualify himself and explain why to the board of deacons. The conflict over this event led to months of tension which culminated into him strangling her over the kitchen sink in front of me and my younger brother. If my grandmother had not heard the commotion and rescued my mother, she would clearly have died right in front of me. Talk about reinforcing my fear of my dad. None of the reasons for this were revealed to me until after my mom's death and my dad was never held accountable for attempted murder. This will become a topic of family secrets at a later point in this book.

The main reason I still have so much trouble respecting my parents is because their discipline toward me was very confusing, and only intended to impose external control simply for the sake of control and compliance to their way of thinking. Their approaches to "mold my character" allowed for no recognition of or respect for my own individuality. Their abuse toward me gave them an opportunity to act out their own frustrations and conflicts. These abusive actions also facilitated their need to break my will and force me into compliance through fear and intimidation. I also believe they sensed my resilience, which they interpreted as being hateful, strong willed, and defiant, when I was still quite young. As a result they felt the need to mold me in such a way as to protect their needs for control and compliance. All of these factors created for me the many negative personal and emotional results and losses I have had to face and deal with in adulthood. This was true for me in all of the contexts I have identified in a previous chapter. My parents needed to blame outside sources for all of the mistakes they made. This approach allowed them to rationalize their actions according to their religious beliefs in the external influences of Satan and evil. In their minds they were fighting what they saw as sin and as defined by the context of religion to which they desperately ascribed until the end.

It is obvious to me that, while much of what I am saying is purely speculation relative to dynamics within the members of my family, my interpretation of their emotional states makes sense. Clearly life events can further complicate and exacerbate unresolved grief and emotions from the past by adding to them. Experts on grief indicate an individual can only grieve one loss at a time. However, that is not to say the collective unresolved grief from previous losses doesn't complicate and extend the current grief reaction. My mother could not stand to talk about the deaths of her relatives ever in her lifetime. Neither their deaths nor the collective emotions from the past were ever identified and resolved. For her, as well as for my dad, the FLAGS existed in extremely intense forms which may be a good way of understanding the intensity of factors or symptoms associated with the various personality and psychiatric disorders identified in the DSM-IV-TR, including alcohol and drug abuse/dependence.

As I mentioned earlier, the process of dysfunction tends to be handed down from one generation to another. Even though neither of my parents had alcohol or drug problems, they perpetuated the dysfunction from their respective pasts to my siblings and me through their intense physical and emotional abuse. Murray Bowen, a well-known family systems therapist, identified this "multigenerational process" and used "genograms" as a means of tracking such trends and behaviors. A genogram is basically a family tree display used to identify significant people and events from the past which served as exacerbating factors and/or triggers, intensifying the dysfunction and insuring the likelihood of it continuing and being passed on to the next generation. Anyone reared in a dysfunctional environment, even relative to complicating factors and victimization in other dysfunctional contexts outside of the home/family context, will pass the dysfunction along unless they identify it and work to stop it. Even as a child I told myself I would never do the same things which were done to me by my parents to my own child or children. I believe my ability to see the problems during my childhood resulted from the unconditional love given to me by my maternal grandmother. I also had the opportunities to observe the contrasts between my family and other families in the neighborhood to see those like my own or worse, against those which seemed to function on a more appropriate level. I am certain that much of my resilience and defiance were fueled by these environmental influences.

The determining factor in whether or not dysfunction gets passed along to future generations lies in the conscious awareness of the abuse, victimization, and neglect/deprivation from the past. As in my life, I had the opportunity to consciously compare my family to others, and I knew how genuine love felt and sounded from "Granny". She was a wonderful woman - not perfect, but wonderful – who lived to be 100 years old. For others the process of problem identification can begin simply through positive interaction with an effective, non-arrogant role model; someone who looks beyond the behaviors of a kid and sees the kid behind those behaviors. As a psychologist I always look for a little piece of heart in the kids I serve, which I then seek to nurture by creating a safe and mutually respectful atmosphere in which we can explore the soul and psyche of each kid and family. I lightheartedly refer to this approach as the philosophy of 'Psyche-Soul-ology', a term I coined myself which is the title of my second book, and a companion to this book. It is amazing how much difference, even in my own life, one person can make when they appear at just the right time and with just the right skills. The only way to avoid the continuation of the multigenerational process is for each individual to identify and work through her or his own unresolved issues always resulting from victimization and neglect/deprivation.

Please allow me to share a little about my research with any mental health professionals and other interested parties in my reading audience. For both my Master's thesis and my dissertation (both works are also included within my third book *ProKids, Inc.: The Message and The Movement; A Guide for Parents and Professionals* – www.createspace.com/3526148) I conducted research to develop the Roberts Grief and Loss Analysis Scale (RGLAS), an instrument designed to detect such unresolved grief and related issues in adults and as addressed in this chapter. I believe with further research the RGLAS could also be used to detect the same factors in adolescents from about age 12 and up. The intent is to measure grief associated with losses from dysfunctional backgrounds rather than from grief relative to traditional associations with death and dying. Test scores reveal indications of current levels of dysfunction and coping skills. While additional research needs to be done to further establish its reliability and validity, the results to date indicate the RGLAS is measuring something more than just depression and anxiety. No other professional involved in the supervision or review of my research has ever questioned its face validity, a further indication of the correctness of my perception of adult dysfunction being based in unresolved grief and emotions from the past. At the risk of sounding too technical, the RGLAS is intended for use within therapeutic settings as an assessment tool in conjunction with other assessment instruments and techniques, to include assessment/intake interviews.

Based upon my experience and upon my research and education, I also believe much of what is diagnosed as depression among people in general is simply unresolved grief which results from deprivation and unpredictability associated with abuse and victimization, including neglect, in childhood. Unresolved grief will always include elements of depression and/or anxiety, which are based in negative (in the sense of being unpleasant) and yet appropriate emotions - the FLAGS. (Parenthetically and relative to the FLAGS, let me say that when I refer to the FLAGS as negative, I do not intend to imply they are inappropriate. I wish only to convey the necessity of correctly identifying the negative emotions in an effort to control them rather than be controlled by them in the sense of learning from the resulting anxiety and depression.) Deprivation is easily understood as neglect regardless of the form it takes. At the beginning of my graduate training as I began to think about the nature of emotional states, I thought of them being based less in thought and perception, and more in the FLAGS. Rather than emotional or psychological states being created by irrational thoughts as suggested by researchers such as Aaron Beck, I believe the psychological states of depression and anxiety create the irrational thoughts which then serve to establish hopelessness and lead to the destructive acting out behaviors we have already discussed.

Furthermore, I believe the states of depression and anxiety, especially anxious depression, unless physiologically generated, are better described as emotional states rather than as psychological states because of the negative emotional bases from which they are generated. I believe even depression associated with grief is purely emotion-based, with hopelessness resulting from the negative or irrational thoughts generated from the emotional state, not vice versa. Negative and irrational thoughts will not result and take hold if the individual is able to successfully identify and face the emotions associated with any negative event. Even with positive emotions such as joy and contentment, emotional states of over zealousness and reckless abandonment will not result if these emotions are also identified and dealt with in the sense of keeping things in perspective.

This distinction is necessary in order to give people the accurate perception of being able to face and resolve their grief from the past. To say depression and anxiety are based in irrational thinking ignores the more logical sequence of: events or experiences creating emotions which then lead to an emotional state resulting in hopelessness and the need to act out emotion-based anxiety to avoid bringing the emotions to, or experiencing them at, a conscious level. If the events and emotions are positive, the emotional state will be that of some degree of happiness, contentment, or even temporary euphoria. However, if the events and emotions are negative, the resulting emotional state will be that of depression and/or anxiety. If depression is emotionally based rather than physiologically based as with chemical imbalances in the brain associated with major depression and bipolar disorders, I believe it will likely be mixed with anxiety. This mix makes it a more active emotional state, in the sense it is likely to be acted out if it is not faced and dealt with from an emotional perspective. Depression alone, as with physiological depression, tends to be more passive and can be quite debilitating. One could even argue that the act of giving up and withdrawing is a way of acting out depression. However this kind of withdrawing tends to be without intention or purpose, and often originates in the debilitating effects of the chemical imbalances in the brain associated with depression.

Both depression and anxious depression result in hopelessness as one tries unsuccessfully to act out the emotional state as a way of avoiding the physical state they create. When people experience an emotionally based state of anxious depression, they talk about the way they feel. I believe the feelings they are referring to are physical rather than psychological in nature relative to their manifestation and conscious awareness. People will often think of depression and anxiety as feelings that should be listed on a chart. To successfully identify the associated emotions, an individual must first check their physical sensations, or remember how they felt physically at the time the emotions were experienced. This is my way of distinguishing between a feeling and an emotional state. For instance a feeling of love can result in an emotional state of joyous abandonment and excitement which are experienced as physical sensations. Actually, and as mentioned in Chapter II, there is very little difference in the physical manifestation of anxiety and the physical manifestation of excitement. For example, I can feel both excited and anxious at the same time about a public presentation of my workshop materials. I can only make the distinction through conscious effort. Both sensations are emotional states manifested in physiological arousal based in emotions. The difference lies in the perception of one state as positive and pleasant, and the other as negative and unpleasant. However, both are based in the autonomic nervous system which creates the fight or flight sensations.

In order to keep people from becoming confused I need to distinguish in more detail the difference between emotions and physical manifestations of those emotions. When we ask someone to identify a feeling - as with the use of a "feelings" chart - we are actually asking them to check their physical state, as an indicator of their emotional state, in the sense of using the physical state as a spring board for free association. The person is actually identifying the first word(s) which come to mind as associated with and manifested by the physical state. I teach kids and families to use their physical bodies and sensations as indicators of their current emotional state. I encourage people to learn to identify the physical signs of emotions and use these as a gauge to literally regulate the emotional pressure building up inside. Because adults and kids are generally cut off from the awareness of emotions this process requires a great deal of conscious effort at first. Many individuals will move rapidly into a stage of acting out before they even realize they are being controlled by their emotions. I am not referring to control in the sense of stifling emotions; rather, in the sense of learning to identify and deal with emotions before they take over and serve as the controlling factor which then determines an individual's behavior. This inability to recognize and deal with emotions is taught to us during childhood within many of the six contexts relative to the denial of and suppression of emotions as actual reactions and experiences of children. Children are often taught to deny their emotions rather than being taught to develop appropriate coping mechanisms and appropriate expression of emotions.

Many of my kids (clients) will tell me they hit walls and throw things as a means of releasing their anger. My response is to encourage them to identify their anger before it reaches a point where it needs to be acted out. As stated previously I often tell kids and adults: "just because you can ..., doesn't mean you should." In other words just because you can hit a wall, drink or use, beat your spouse or partner, victimize a child or adult, or act out some form of prejudice, etc., doesn't mean you should. If children are not allowed as early as possible to learn the proper expression of and identification of emotions, they will learn to either turn their anger inward and upon themselves, and/or throw it outward toward others. By teaching children and adults to see their bodies as a tank with a pressure gauge attached, people can literally learn to regulate emotions before the emotions progress to a point of dominating the individual's thoughts and actions. This is accomplished by becoming aware of one's breathing patterns; level of arousal; heart rate; blood pressure; body posture; body language, including gesturing; energy level; degree of agitation; tone and volume of voice; sweating; dry mouth; tears; difficulty speaking; rate of speech; etc.

When I mention the issues associated with unresolved grief, I am basically referring to two different categories - the results or outcome of victimization (Appendix N), and the losses associated with victimization (Appendix O). This of course means it is time for two more of my crucial lists. I make the distinction between results and losses associated with victimization as losses being one of the results requiring further delineation. My goal is to help each of you recognize the connections between the Fear, Loneliness, Anger, Guilt, and Shame, and the results and losses associated with abuse and victimization. As you look at the respective appendices which follow you will be able to see how these two categories of results and losses differ. You will also be able to see how losses need to be identified, acknowledged, and resolved through an appropriate grief process. This way adults can be effective role models and can avoid creating unhealthy environments and contexts for children we are given charge of in different capacities throughout our lives. At this point in the book we are only exploring and identifying issues and elements related to ineffective adult behaviors negatively impacting children. Efforts will be made in a later chapter to identify solutions and alternative ways of dealing with these components. Keep this in mind especially as you review the lists and find some of the results and losses to be difficult to face. In other words, keep reading and remember there is nothing wrong with you. There are simply things which may be wrong in your life, and these can be corrected.

After studying these lists, and identifying those factors which apply to your own life, give some thought to how these factors can result from victimization and neglect within contexts outside of the home/family as well. Also think about the reality of how difficult life is without the safety provided within a healthy home/family environment. Furthermore, try and connect results and losses to the development of the FLAGS. Keep in mind that many of the problems we experience in adulthood relative to the appropriate expression of emotions result from the inability to properly identify and express these emotions in childhood. If someone is raised in an unhealthy home/family environment the expression of emotions is stifled either through emotional victimization, or through the denial from adults that kids even have emotions other than anger, which should be repressed and controlled rather than expressed.

As emotions are stifled children basically learn their emotions are not real or are insignificant when compared to those of adults. We are often taught unintentionally (in the sense of there being no other recognized alternatives) by the adults from our past to act out emotions rather than identify and resolve them. This is the reason we move into hopelessness and develop irrational thoughts, and resort to acting out rather than backing up to deal with the origins of the emotion-based anxiety and/or depression. As this process of acting out continues we further complicate our lives and the lives of those around us always asking the question: "What's wrong with me?" The more accurate questions should be: "What's wrong with where I came from and what I've been through; and how can I resolve the FLAGS from the past?"

This is probably a good point at which to explore personality types and parenting styles which set up the abuse and victimization and resulting complications. I believe the single most important element relative to victimization, next to the unresolved issues and grief from the past, is arrogance. I cannot express this strongly enough. Arrogance is defined in Webster's as an expression of an exaggerated sense of one's own worth or importance in an overbearing manner. It is further defined as a feeling of superiority, and as presumptuousness. Along with arrogance comes the sense of entitlement I have mentioned in a previous chapter. In both my personal and professional experiences I encounter arrogance exhibited by adults on a regular basis – in the community, in the workplace, in the schools, in different religious settings, in the justice and law enforcement systems, in government and politics, etc. Nothing makes me angrier than to see anyone defend their position of arrogance and entitlement toward any other human being, especially toward children and adolescents.

People who are arrogant are often control freaks and are generally very defensive (as well as offensive) and insecure. They choose from a number of tactics which include: playing games; being passive/aggressive; competing to be right or on top; playing the victim and/or victimizer according to their needs and purpose; retaliating; back stabbing; judging; being territorial; being vicious and cruel; being sarcastic; being deceptive and blatantly dishonest; etc. Arrogant people generally are very threatened if their positions of superiority and power are not acknowledged, or if they are challenged. Religious leaders, politicians, people who espouse bigotry and prejudices, parents, teachers and other school staff, and people in the law enforcement and justice fields present prime examples of people with such characteristics when working with kids of all ages. Many times arrogant people are acting out their own FLAGS and emotion-based anxiety in an effort to compensate for their lack of positive self image and self perception which never developed in childhood. Quite often they are acting out all of the FLAGS in ways modeled for them by improper role models when they were growing up. For others the sense of arrogance and entitlement comes from a position of perceived status and importance which may have originated in childhood as well by growing up within a home/family environment of privilege. These are people who as kids were taught that they were more special than everyone else – the prince and princess complexes.

A major problem relative to arrogance lies within the concept of strength in numbers. A few good examples are religious leaders, teachers, politicians, and law enforcement – so-called "peace officers", all of which often exist within closed groups in which membership status is perceived as being above and beyond that of the ordinary citizens. This is not true for all people within these groups, and while I am not sure what the actual percentages would be of effective to ineffective, I believe the percentage in the negative group would be rather alarming if kids and adults impacted by these groups were polled. Adults within all of these roles need to realize they are no better than, or more important than any other groups involved in the lives of kids. The scary fact is people in these groups can do considerable damage if they function from an arrogant stance and sense of entitlement, both based in power struggles (competition), and a need to control others and situations. Many in these groups want their jobs to be respected, and to be respected personally and professionally regardless of their respectability. I am talking about respectability relative to how they interact with and feel toward others, especially toward children.

For example, I have had the experiences of teaching these very principles to teachers and school staff. Afterwards I was able to observe them in their respective jobs creating all of the FLAGS within children through emotional abuse by using the same abusive verbal statements we had just covered in a workshop and as identified in a previous chapter in this book. This represents an intense form of denial of, and resistance to the possibility these adults may have some issues to resolve, or have some need to do their own honest self examination/assessment. This is the kind of arrogance, coupled with ignorance which sets up children to fail and then get blamed for their own failures. The really sad fact is that many of these adults actually mean well. They are just not willing to examine and change their approaches to kids in order to have a positive impact on the kids' lives and futures. Shame and guilt only lead to very poor self-images and are very prominent components of the fear, loneliness and anger identified in the RFLAGS Model. As we begin to understand the results from abuse and victimization, we also begin to resolve and eliminate guilt and shame from the FLAGS mix by recognizing all of the hurtful messages we were given as kids as the lies they really were. These ineffective and inappropriate approaches will continue to exist until the multigenerational cycles of abuse and victimization are acknowledged and broken by everyone. I have been able to break these cycles in my life, and so can you!

It is important to know that the very adults who often make the negative headlines in the news are likely living out and acting out their emotion-based anxiety which resulted from emotionally unhealthy experiences within the home/family context. My proposals are presented only as realistic explanations of destructive patterns, not as excuses for or justifications of them. Also important are the influences from the other contexts in which abuse and victimization occur against kids by adults who do not make the headlines or get the negative publicity they deserve. These adults include: abusive, ineffective teachers or school staff; self-serving politicians; an abusive police officer, who along with a partner beats up a kid who runs, and/or plants evidence or exaggerates and creates information to make sure that charges will stick; or religious leaders who are just as human as everyone else yet preaching that others are worthless, evil beings; etc. All of these people perpetuate the victimization that any given kid may be experiencing within the home/family context. This is what I mean when I talk about complicating factors which open anyone to further abuse because of the fact kids generally cannot control what is done to them in any context. This is what I mean by arrogance relative to kids being the targets of many injustices based on an adult's need to be right and in control.

The kids we are raising today will be the very ones in the headlines tomorrow if we do not deal with our own issues and then dedicate ourselves to raising healthy kids; or deal with our unresolved issues before we ever bring kids into our lives. Anyone who becomes a parent or works directly with kids, regardless of their role, needs to take an oath and recognize the seriousness of such associations. Any formal connection between an adult and a kid should be thought of as a marriage in the sense of a matching or union for the sake of establishing a nurturing, spiritual bond, the length of which is defined by the circumstances and situation surrounding the association. The oath for each union between adult and child, as parent, guardian, or professional, should take the form of some solemn vow such as this:

An Oath to Children

At this moment I choose to take you into my life. I do so either by creating you as a parent would; or by willingly accepting the fact our paths have crossed through no design of your own. I have chosen this role as part of my own journey through life. Because the crossing of our paths is the result of my own choices I will take very seriously the responsibility of providing for you in every way. My responsibilities will be limited only by the role I will now play in your life. Therefore, I promise to know myself at the deepest level possible. In an effort to be the most positively effective role model I can possibly be for you, I will seek to resolve every negative element from my past. I will give you the acceptance and respect you deserve, and I will seek to correct very quickly any mistakes I *will* make along the way. I am here to meet your needs, and ask only that you apply yourself to the fullest level of your potential. I seek not to make you, but only to nurture you into the exciting discovery of your true nature relative to who you can become. I want only to set the potential into motion, and then applaud as you learn to create the motion for yourself. This is my solemn and heartfelt commitment to you in recognition of the wonder of your uniqueness.

This kind of oath, even taught to adolescents before they choose to become sexually active and risk becoming parents, should be posted on the walls, notebooks, refrigerators and bulletin boards in every adolescent and adult environment as a constant reminder of our spiritual obligation as caregivers for children. The continuous reminder of this obligation would help to establish it for everyone from an early age on relative to the development of personal morals and values. Adults are the building blocks for the future relative to the world of possibilities and hazards we create for the generations of kids to follow. Each successive generation should work very diligently to advance the spiritual evolution of the world and mankind relative to our position in the universe, moving ever closer to existing as the image of God according to original intention. The Source that is God is the ultimate example of the perfect adult/leader who gives us everything we need to grow into eventual perfection. All we have to do is listen to the "whisperings of our souls" and seek guidance from effective role models who will guide us and then let go as we learn and grow, creating the motion for ourselves. I firmly believe that the energy that *is* us is God *within* us.

Chapter VII

KIDS

I have decided to call this chapter simply "KIDS" – not good kids, bad kids, at-risk kids, problem kids, or gang kids – just "KIDS". In an earlier chapter I addressed the issue of our tendency to label kids and place them in certain categories. As you will remember, one of my main points was to emphasize how our use of labels and categories directs our thinking toward and interaction with kids. The labels also clearly reflect our biases and prejudices, and allow us to fall into the pit of ineffectiveness, no matter how honorable and altruistic our intentions may be. While to this point my focus has been on adults and the mistakes we make, the most important element in writing this book is for each reader to understand how what we do as adults affects the kids for whom we are directly and indirectly responsible.

My role as father to my now adult daughter Melissa is the best role I have ever played in this drama we call life. As she was growing up I always managed to separate what she was doing from who she was at any given moment. As her father I marveled at her imagination as I watched her play. I spent time with her lying on the floor and listening to music. Outside we would sit and feel the wind on our faces and we would watch the clouds as they formed and changed. I tried to give her at least a good start in life. In later years all of the groundwork paid off as I have watched her struggle with many obstacles and heartaches in her life. Melissa is an incredible poet and I hope each of you will have the opportunity in the future to hear her story chronicled through her own creativity. Her life also confirms my belief in the importance of at least having a good beginning, especially relative to the development of resiliency and the ability to transcend negative experiences.

Even though Melissa's mother and I were divorced since Melissa was three years of age I remained a very active and consistent part of her life in spite of the fact Melissa and I were separated by distance. I always paid my child support and I always made arrangements for her to spend summers and Christmas vacation with me. Divorce is certainly not ideal, but it doesn't have to be totally devastating for the kids involved. Melissa always knew beyond the shadow of a doubt that I continued to love her with all of my heart. She has never had to question this fact in spite of the regrets common for kids whose parents are divorced or separated. Giving up my day to day physical presence in her life was one of the hardest things I have ever done. Rather than seeing the divorce as an end to my role as Melissa's father, I was able to see my role as having only changed. I grieved the loss of my direct presence in her life and worked very hard to create something new by making my somewhat indirect presence in her life work for both of us regardless of many obstacles and much opposition.

From a very early age I always taught Melissa to separate who she is from what she did. Once, in an attempt to insult me, my mother said: "That child doesn't know the difference between you as her father and you as her friend." For me this was quite a compliment and my reply was simply: "She knows the difference." With my daughter I could be both, but always making sure my role as her father remained the more predominant role of the two. Kids need to know through adolescence that their parents will be consistent in the parental role if they are to feel safe. They count on our consistency to nurture and guide them in the right manner and in the right directions. When we fail to play our part effectively by trying to be their friends kids get lost in the confusion of being kids and in the confusion of needing, and not having the proper role models to successfully lead them into becoming high functioning, independent adults.

In the example above of my mother's commentary on my parenting skills, she was actually making a reflective statement on her definition of the parental role. In her mind, kids are to only recognize the authority of parents as she and my dad had so clearly demanded from me. What she was commenting on was the fact Melissa and I could have fun together. What my mother failed to see prior to her statement was the proper balance I always maintained between the two different aspects of my roles, with the greatest emphasis always on my role as father. When Melissa was growing up my role included all of the factors I identified in the chapter about adult roles and responsibilities. In that list I identified many different hats we need to wear relative to our connections with kids. The point I failed to emphasize is how much more responsibility we have as parents. In comparison to other adult role models, parents *must* make sure all of these required obligations are carried out, balanced with the need to also enjoy being a parent, and to enjoy being an observer and active participant in the wonder of each kid's uniqueness.

Let me clarify my definition of the role of parents as friends to kids. A friend for any of us is someone we see as an ally and an equal. Friends are loyal, trustworthy, and can be counted on to provide support and guidance in times of need. However, the relationships between friends tend to be somewhat fragile, and are subject to being dissolved due to any number of factors including differences of opinion, betrayal, and separation by distance. It is possible to bring in new friends to either replace the old ones or to simply add to the list. Friends also tend to see each other as equals in the sense of choosing to be friends, and in the sense of having things in common relative to similarities and common interests. Unlike friends, it is not possible to replace family – believe me, I know. The significant difference is the connection by "blood" which exists within families and not with friends. This connection clearly implies an unspoken obligation to be loyal and to stay together in appropriate ways. Parents who seek primarily to be friends with their child or children are likely acting out unresolved issues from their respective pasts. This will result in at least some degree of ineffectiveness which will deprive their children of opportunities to learn from adults who are adults – not from adults who still need to see themselves as kids.

Parents, on the other hand, bring children into this world either by choice or by accident. It is very important to recognize the fact that in families there are many different personalities involved. I believe reality suggests that in some cases we would not necessarily choose to associate with the people in our families if not for the simple fact we are together as family. Look at how people within families do not always get along or even like each other in some cases. Before parents create a child some thought should be given to the lifelong commitment needed to love, accept, and nurture any child regardless of whether or not they meet our own expectations. As parents our goal should be to simply raise a child to be the best they can be, making sure they have the resiliency and ability to transcend any losses; also making sure as parents we are not the ones creating such losses.

Kids born into families have no say in the matter. Always remember that no child ever asks to be conceived or born! An infant is created and a soul fills that body. As parents we do not get to choose from a list of desirable characteristics we want a child to possess, and in that sense we, too, are the victims of chance. It is simply a happenstance union of egg and sperm which determines the outcome relative to genetic possibilities. While males have millions of sperm present to fertilize the available egg, there is a tremendous factor of chance in the particular egg present at the moment of conception given the number of eggs available in the female's body. Children can be wanted and intended, wanted (after the fact) and unintended, or are completely unwanted. There simply are no other possible combinations associated with bringing kids into this world. Sometimes kids can be "wanted" for the wrong reasons. These include the ideas of having something to love, saving or keeping a relationship, or receiving a government check. Once the reality sets in that the child did not solve the problems, quite often the child then becomes an unwanted nuisance and hindrance.

In addition to the factor of chance relative to genetic possibilities, there are numerous random factors coming into play relative to the physical development of the fetus, and also of the child once they are born. The result of all random factors is the uniqueness of each child – those parts of each of us which serve to identify who we are physically, as well as the potential for personality development, and personal growth and achievement. Who we become as an individual relative to the physical and genetic characteristics is impacted and determined significantly by the environments in which we are raised. Other factors include the people in those environments who are responsible for our care, along with our own resiliency and ability to transcend heartache and hardship if our external components and contexts are not favorable.

As you can see, the home/family context is crucial. This is the only context we as parents can directly and willfully control. It is the one factor in the lives of kids which determines how they will experience and survive the contexts outside of the home/family environment. Because of the randomicity of so many chance factors, it is also possible to see how easily complicating factors for kids can develop. Randomness sometimes results in extremes. Without an opportunity to balance out the extremes created through no intention of our own as individuals relative to the creation of our physical identity, factors which complicate our lives tend to dominate our lives and serve as the fuel which feeds our emotion-based anxiety.

I see these elements among my friends and among the kids and families with whom I work. For example, Susan, one of my closest and dearest friends was born with spina bifida. This left her with numerous complicating factors relative to her physical abilities and appearance, and relative to how her family and the world reacted to and interacted with her. Susan was old enough to have been born prior to the recognition of the rights of those with handicaps and disabilities. There were also a number of environmental factors which served to further complicate her life even into adulthood. She was not able to go to college, and was denied many of the opportunities for personal growth and development most of us take for granted. However, in spite of her complicating factors both inside and outside of her home/family context, Susan used her resilient spirit to transcend many of the obstacles which potentially could have impeded and further handicapped her. Though her body was deformed, she was blessed with physical beauty, and an incredible mind and spirit which allowed her to fight against and beat many of the odds she had to face.

Think carefully about how this one physical factor complicated Susan's life in all of the contexts I have identified. The context in which she found the most comfort was that of religion, which for her focused more on spirituality than on outdated edicts and dogma. She was lucky someone didn't decide at birth that she shouldn't be allowed to live. Her contributions to my life and to this world would never have happened, and her uniqueness would never have been celebrated. Susan was who she was by conscious intent, determination, and purpose, allowing her to take control of the external factors which sought to destroy her and keep her down within virtually every context of her existence. Fortunately, laws have been enacted within the other contexts which ultimately gave her the protection and some of the acceptance she deserved. Susan lived to be 63 and was truly an inspiration to all who knew and loved her.

Another example of resiliency and the ability to transcend is that of Charlie, my childhood friend I have known since first grade. Charlie always had to struggle with learning difficulties concerning math and reading. Looking back it is clear to me that he had, and still has ADHD. He was given a very creative mind and a loving and supportive family. His mother made sure he had whatever help he needed in order to be successful. Fortunately his parents never put him down through emotional or physical abuse. Instead they always encouraged him, steering him in the direction of college and the career of his choice. This is a good example of how the home/family context helped him to overcome the obstacles and to face the outside contexts which had the potential to disable him. He is now a very successful architect working overseas under contract with a major American-based company. Even as a child I envied the loving environment relative to Charlie's family, and I respect so much his determination to succeed, even if he has had to learn a few lessons in humility and caring for and about others along the way.

Having given you some examples from the lives of my daughter and two friends who have had to deal with complicating factors, let me now turn to the kids I encounter within the context of my profession as a psychologist and as a psychoeducational instructor. With wholehearted enthusiasm I dedicate my entire focus professionally toward the kids who are labeled by the rest of society as troubled, bad, undesirable, delinquent, incorrigible, the problem, deviant, dangerous, etc. Also within this focus I am able to work with the adults, including parents and family members, who directly impact the lives of these kids. It is important for each of you to know that the kids I work with come from all walks of life, and come in all sizes and cultures imaginable. These kids are generally victimized within all of the contexts because of arrogant and ignorant adults who perpetuate their sense of exaggerated self importance and sense of separation, thereby not taking any direct responsibility for helping to create the environments in which these kids are raised. This is true both from within families and outside the home/family context.

In this chapter and throughout other parts of this book I want to share with you my perspective relative to working with any population of kids who have problems, make bad choices, and do bad things. As I stated in an earlier chapter, I know my role as a psychologist is very different with kids compared to the roles of people in settings where more control over situations and environments is necessary. However, as I also stated earlier, once control is established relative to providing a safe environment, optimum benefits and opportunities to the kids within any setting, the issue of control and domination needs to take a leap backwards and out of the way. Adults in any role need only enough authority and respect necessary to effectively perform their roles for the kids they have vowed to serve.

My first step in dealing with kids referred to me from various settings within the community including community based agencies, schools, social service programs, and justice related organizations, is to establish rapport and an environment of mutual regard and respect. My primary goal is to create an environment which will facilitate the opportunity to know and understand any kid in order to better identify and meet their needs. My first statements to kids serve as indications that I am likely different from many of the adults they have encountered in the past. I assure them I have no need to control them, which would be a pointless intention anyway. The last thing I want is for a kid to feel any expectation from me of needing to bow down to my authority. I make sure to never convey any sense of arrogance or sense of being entitled to receive respect from them. After all, we have just met and they do not know if I deserve their respect. I clearly recognize the need to earn their respect, and I avoid any form of competition relative to power struggles or perceptions. I am not offended by language and I do not make the use of words an issue as my goal is for kids to speak freely and not be on guard. My only limitation relative to language is that words not be thrown at me as weapons and out of disrespect. Because I am respectful I ask for and get this consideration in return. Only one kid has ever threatened me and did so on two different occasions. Both times I literally stood up and told him not to continue any further with his threats, indicating that I didn't deserve to be treated like this. Both times he sat back down and later told me the only reason he trusted and respected me was due to the fact that I was not afraid of him. This kid was one of the most out of control clients I have ever had. Once I proved myself to him by standing up to him our professional association improved completely.

My first interview with a kid is conducted with the kid alone. The only exception is if they are below the age of 7 or 8, or if they are somehow unable to adequately speak for and represent themselves. This will usually limit the time a younger kid is willing to spend with me, making the encounter somewhat brief, and will then include more parent/guardian participation than I have with older kids. The initial goal is to get a clear picture of the kid's perspective and sense of reality as to why he is seeing me professionally. Many kids don't always know the facts associated with their lives, but can always tell you what they think are the facts when asked in the absence of adults. In fact, in many cases I never work with or meet the parents or guardians as oftentimes the kid is referred to me as a requirement of probation. This was especially true when I worked in California. Because I worked in a community-based clinic the financial paperwork needed to set up a case was handled prior to my first actual appointment. Quite frequently the parents of the kids I generally work with couldn't care less about family therapy and only want me to "fix" the kid without involving them in the process. In some cases the insistence on including family therapy is actually absurd and can be detrimental to the goals of helping the kid. This is especially true if the family is extremely dysfunctional and/or the kid is at least sixteen or older.

Ironically, and contrary to many professionally recognized theories or interventions, success with a kid and without family involvement is not only possible, but at times in the kid's best interest. Virtually all of the kids I see appreciate the opportunity to meet alone with me because historically meetings about the kid with adults outside the family have been unfair and upsetting to the kid. In these kinds of meetings the kid sits there being talked about as if they weren't even in the room. More often than not, the kid listens to a long list of "what's wrong" with them, with the adults not being honest about their own flaws and inappropriate behaviors which increase the kid's motivation to act out. I have learned that adults only tell a fraction of the truth relative to the ways they act out inappropriately with their kids and in their homes. Generally adults are quite surprised when I ask them in front of the kid "what do you do that contributes to the chaos in your lives?" I assure them that while I do not know the truth, I am aware that both of them do and I can only hope they are giving me an accurate account of the problems they experience. Even then I know I am only seeing or hearing a relatively small part of the total reality.

When I have the opportunity to do so, I explain my therapeutic approaches to the family member(s). I stress that my main focus will be on the well being of the kid, with an effort to uncomplicate the kid's life, which in turn will benefit everyone involved. Furthermore, I stress the parents' or guardians' need to respect the kid's right to a reasonable amount of privacy, having already explained to the kid the limits on confidentially prior to this exchange with the adults. Other than issues required by law, I only report things I think put the kid at serious risk of unusual or extreme harm to themselves based on risky behaviors or faulty thinking. Even then I always give the kid the chance to talk to the adults first or allow me to do it for them and hopefully in the presence of the kid. A kid will not talk to anyone they can't trust, and I believe in most situations it is better that they talk to someone rather than to no one.

In many cases families are accustomed to being blamed and judged for the problems existing within their lives. I very quickly address this by establishing that my job is to make observations and then be honest about what I see, not out of a need to be right, and with a willingness to make adjustments as we go along. If they have a history of what I call "therapist jumping" I suggest they jump before we even get started given the fact they won't always like what I have to say. I also set limits by telling them I won't allow them at any point to turn on me and blame me for problems existing before they ever walked into my office. I have had no more than 5 families get angry with me since I began providing therapy in 1990. Even then, with the exception of one case, I was able to work with the kid in spite of the unwillingness of family members to cooperate and participate in the process. Also in those cases the family members continued to keep me up to date on the issues they felt still needed to be addressed. One case in particular was successfully closed when the kid finished high school, an accomplishment that no one in his family ever expected to see.

From the start I stress to the kid my desire to try and help by getting to know them, treating them with respect and fairness, and acknowledging my inability to assist without their permission and cooperation. I always validate their perceptions and observations of people in their lives once I believe their perceptions to be accurate, even if this means agreeing that a person(s) or situation(s) is extremely difficult to deal with or face. From there I help them identify ways of facing and dealing with the realities of people and situations in such a way as to avoid further complications for themselves. I stress that unfortunately in many cases I have to teach them to survive and grow in spite of people and factors which are frequently unchangeable. By giving any kid the opportunity to objectively identify reality it is possible to get them to learn to respond rather than react to situations where they simply cannot win, even if they are justified in wanting to do so. They can clearly see that taking care of themselves is not the same thing as giving in and letting an adult win. It is only a matter of protecting *their* butts without kissing the butts of others. It is possible to get this point across by giving them examples of situations in which I, as an adult, still have to use this approach, also acknowledging that it is much more difficult for them than it is for me given the fact that kids are automatically at a disadvantage. Kids appreciate my style and candor.

As much as possible, and as it is appropriate, I try to make the encounters with kids relaxed, and occasionally fun and comical. When I feel resistance to an issue I leave it for awhile as there are usually many other things to address. Once mutual respect and regard are established effectively it is possible to laugh with kids at their own absurdities and extremes. From the moment I take on a case I assure the kid they are now "one of my kids". I then pledge to do all I can reasonably do professionally to help, guide, and back them up as long as I know I can trust them to be honest with me. Regardless of challenges to the contrary by other professionals and adults, I believe that most kids are very honest and open with me, especially after I explain to them that I am required by law to protect their privacy, given certain fully explained limits relative to confidentiality.

Every once in a while I get fooled and I don't hold back my own sense of disappointment, betrayal, and anger, especially when the dishonesty led me to defend them against adults in positions of authority over them. I have also learned not to stick my neck out too far until I am as sure as I can possibly be that it is the right thing to do. This kind of betrayal has happened to an extreme in only two situations out of literally hundreds of cases. Both times I made the kid very aware of how I felt, pointed out their need to feel shame and guilt, asked for and received an apology, as well as a promise not to be deceptive with me again. I believe it is important to be real with kids when their words and behaviors affect you either negatively or positively. Through these approaches kids learn it is possible to trust, respect and regard another person to such an extent that the kids feel badly when they feel they may have jeopardized a connection with someone who genuinely cares for and about them. Don't get me wrong, I am never punitive with a kid, only real. Anything more would make it personal and unprofessional, a fine line which must always be regarded and never crossed.

My main focus with kids is on the reality of how their choices are complicating their lives. In this sense my only goal is to help them figure out how to uncomplicate things for their sake alone. There is no threat in this. I do not pretend to have all the answers, nor do I pretend to know everything that would be best for them. Also, I try to understand the reality of their lives and the perceptions they have of their respective reality before I try to proceed with problem resolution. Always, I attempt to undo any damage I perceive to have been done by others through the process of labeling created within the contexts outside of my office. I simply model for the kids the way adults in all roles are suppose to treat them, with the balance of influence directly related to the role and experience of each adult involved.

As stated previously my role as a father to my daughter has been the best and most rewarding role and identity I have ever assumed. Within the parameters of reasonable professional limits, I play this same kind of role in the lives of the kids with whom I work. I have even found that many single moms will bring their kids to me as a male therapist for this very reason. The role of being a single mom is a very difficult one, especially with regard to raising sons. I do not mean in any way to sound chauvinistic in this position. Most of the single moms and their kids would agree with my statement as well. I have even had kids jokingly refer to me as "Dad", and even though they laugh it off I acknowledge their perception and put it into perspective for them. Keep in mind that many of the kids I work with have no dad immediately present in their lives. Even the ones who do have fathers or father figures present in their lives use me as a measure of what a good father should be. This is very useful when working with the entire family in therapy. I use my role as therapist to model the proper interactions which should take place between parents and their kids, always working not to get caught in the middle of parent/child conflicts.

I believe the single most significant factor missing in the lives of kids is balance. I am not sure kids have ever had much balance in their lives at any time throughout history. Hopefully as a result of the spiritual, not religious, evolution of the world this concept is beginning to surface as a major item of focus needing to be addressed to better the lives and futures of children. In relationships between adults and kids, regardless of the role of the adult, the scales should always be incredibly out of balance, and always tipped in favor of the kids. As adults we have an obligation to meet the needs of kids, even if we have to do so at the expense of our own needs at times. I am not saying we have to sacrifice ourselves 100% of the time. After all, we need to give to ourselves first if we are to be effective for others. However, our needs should never take precedence over the urgent and essential needs of kids, especially within professional interactions. Sometimes the needs of kids can be put on hold if they are not urgent and significant enough to be taken care of immediately. The reverse cannot be true of our needs being met at the expense of kids. No matter how urgent our needs are we still have an obligation to see that the needs of kids are met at least temporarily through some other source until we can return our focus to them. Parenting is a full-time job until kids become self sufficient and independent. Other adult roles are more confined relative to time and situation.

What does balance in the life of a child look like? To me balance does not come in the form of compromise in terms of this *or* that, rather, in the form of this *and* that. Love and regard for any kid cannot be measured in terms of balance. These elements should always be to the fullest level possible and free of conditions. Balance looks like proper amounts and degrees of: freedom and limits; responsibility and leisure; self exploration and guidance; creativity and structure; individuality and connectedness; praise and constructive observation (rather than criticism which is judgmental); self expression and respect for others; spirituality/intuition and freedom to think; morals/values and rights of others; self focus and other focus; expression of emotion and self control; self support and support from others; and ability to soothe oneself and the need to be soothed by others. These are only a few aspects of what likely could be another of my long lists.

The kids I work with have very little balance in their lives, which means most of their lives are lived out in the extremes, and at the mercy of external factors. In many instances single parents will cling to their children in times when their own emotional needs are out of balance, only to discard the kids when life gets better or they meet someone new who replaces the kids relative to their role as provider of care and emotional support. It is quite common for many adults to see kids relative to the benefit kids can provide to them. Even more frightening is the fact that some people have children and/or assume other roles to interact with kids without any forethought to the needs of kids who will be left in their charge. This means that in many cases kids are brought into the lives of adults for the primary purpose of meeting needs and filling emotional deficits of the adults. The only goal for creating children and for working with children should be the expressed desire to experience the enrichment of life associated with nurturing and guiding children into adulthood. Children should never be accidental and unwanted. Nor should anyone enter into any association with children with their own agendas and needs at the forefront of their motivation. Sometimes motivation and needs fulfillment can be dominant and unconscious, especially when there are issues of loss and unresolved grief present in the adult. This is why honest self-examination is so crucial for all adults.

Effectiveness is much more important than intention relative to associations with children. As I have said, people with the very best of intentions can sometimes do the most harm. After all, kids are judged according to the behaviors they display. These behaviors often indicate how effective adults have been in giving kids the balance they need, not how bad, undesirable, or problematic a child is. Balance means a kid is in control intrinsically rather than extrinsically through fear and intimidation which lead to compliance and broken wills. External controls also result in emotions which are way out of balance and which have been created for kids by adults. Extreme examples of personality characteristics can cover a wide range. The opposite ends of the spectrum go from being spoiled and arrogant relative to feeling more special than they really are, to being out of control and acting out in undesirable and unacceptable ways. In many cases kids know what they are doing is wrong, but do not know how, or at times even want to control their actions. The balance between these extremes manifests as a child who becomes a high functioning adult with incredible regard for self and others relative to conscious awareness of the interconnectedness between and among all elements of the universe.

Now let's focus on balance and what this involves for adults. Remember my belief is in the responsibility all adults have for the world we create for ourselves and for children both in the present and in the future. As I indicated earlier I believe the world has been and is going through a balancing act relative to all of the changes in perspective that have occurred since the end of World War II. From much of what I hear and read I believe people are focusing more on our respective selves and our place in the universe relative to spirituality and relative to our spiritual obligations to be effective role models for kids. The focus turns more and more to the need for loving, nurturing families and support for both adults and kids if balance is to be achieved.

Balance has quite a different meaning today than it did during the times of ancient societies and civilizations. I believe my writings reflect the zeitgeist of the current day and age as did the writings from the past. Even though the contextual factors may change relative to the need for balancing, the basic spiritual truths in my writings and the writings of others will remain constant. It is the evolving Truth which is literal relative to inspiration, not the transitory historical details. We must seek only to present and promote a universal Truth of unconditional love and acceptance, with no room for judgment, discrimination, or inequality within any of the contexts addressed herein. We must seek only to celebrate diversity among kids and adults and focus on the spiritual evolution happening in the world today as a means of balancing relationships between adults and kids. It is the Truth heard in our hearts, from within any truly inspired writings, upon which we are to focus. This is the kind of balance adults need to be seeking and passing along to children.

Factors in the lives of adults which need to be in balance include: professional and personal roles; time for self and others; work and "re-creation";

aspirations and reality; secularism and spirituality; focus on self and altruism; loving and being loved; learning and teaching; liberalism and conservatism; individuality and connectedness; emotionality and rationality. Again, these are but a few of the endless combinations of opposing issues and extremes in our lives. However, this should establish a good basis for each of you to generate more subjective examples.

With regard to some issues and extremes there is no room for balancing, only for eliminating the negative extremes in any pair. For instance, there can be no balancing between: love and hatred; acceptance and intolerance; knowledge and ignorance; understanding and bigotry; peace and violence; spirituality and prejudice; love for children and victimization or neglect; reciprocity and selfishness; positive regard and disregard. This list, too, is virtually endless, with the point being there are simply some things that need to be eliminated rather than balanced.

Imbalances and misunderstandings always result from arrogance, ignorance, separation, feelings of threat relative to position and status, and a lack of willingness to open oneself to other possibilities and perspectives. I believe the unwillingness to be open is based in fear. Furthermore, I believe the unwillingness to remain separated out is based in loneliness and anger. Shame and guilt exist on both sides of any separated groups where one group is perceived to be dominant or in control. On the "up" side, guilt and shame are often conscious processes based in the repressed awareness that to dominate is wrong. From the perspective of the "down" side, guilt and shame also exist on an unconscious level. This is from the perspective of being made to feel inferior, when in fact the very actions establishing and perpetuating the perception of domination are nothing but lies based in arrogance, ignorance, and victimization. As I stated earlier, guilt and shame are acquired emotions and can be eliminated as long as there is nothing upon which to base these emotions. On the "up" side, guilt and shame sometimes result from things done to and withheld from others; whereas, on the "down" side the feelings of those targeted are based in what has been done to and withheld from them. Through a process of eliminating the negatives and balancing the other factors, it is possible for both sides to move toward positions of acceptance and understanding.

In the next chapter I will begin to connect more closely how each of us fits into the RFLAGS Model. Hopefully, each of you already has a better understanding of the ways we act out emotion-based anxiety upon ourselves and upon others. We will look at how and why kids make the choices they make relative to our own responsibility as adults for creating the opportunity and need to make such choices.

CHAPTER VIII
Balancing the Scales

I want to focus again on the concept of arrogance. This time the focus will concentrate more on how some segments of society have fought actively against arrogance since the 1960's with the whole Civil Rights Movement, the hippie generation, and with the efforts of every equal rights group, even through today, joining in the fight for change. Everyone was basically fighting against those identified as part of the "establishment" who held onto and forced their perceived positions of authority and power as the norm since the so-called "discovery of America". European American males dominated within every context based upon the biblical and religious precept of a male godhead ruling the universe and having the church as the obedient, submissive bride of Christ within the Christian religions. Men, and especially white men, saw themselves as the "great providers" for their families and for everyone else in the world. European American women and children submitted to this notion based on traditional values and morals from the past, partly for status, and partly because this was accepted as the norm. Other groups were held at bay by the negative emotions (FLAGS) associated with abuse and victimization.

Even the government of this country was founded upon the notion of religious freedom for the benefit of European immigrants, and was modeled after the governmental structure of the Church of England. (Remember the "P" in WASP stands for 'protest-ants'.) Many of the early settlers from Europe saw this as an opportunity to promote and preserve their own limited views of the world relative to religious beliefs and doctrine. What actually resulted from much of this was the beginning of a tremendous experiment of various religious groups attempting to peacefully coexist with each other at the expense of the people already living on this continent. The land, people, and cultures were conquered on the pretense of saving the souls of its inhabitants, using the name of God to mask greed for both materialism and power. I believe the establishment of a democratic society was somehow part of the overall plan for the spiritual evolution of the world. However it got thrown off track by ego-based flaws of the originators of "justice".

Don't get me wrong. I do support the freedom associated with living in a democratic society. However, I think the decades since the 1950's have sought to balance out the flaws which have remained in effect almost from the beginning. Many of those flaws are directly related to the imbalance of power established by and for European American males. In this day and age where so many people are fighting to keep out the illegal immigrants, we have allowed arrogance to blind us to the reality that unless people in this country are Native American we were all immigrants here at some point in our respective ancestral histories. No one is better than anyone else! Better *off* doesn't mean better *than*.

As an optimist I personally believe (hope?) the pendulum is currently seeking to settle more into a moderate position where the recognition of equality for all people ultimately becomes the norm. The realist in me recognizes we have a long way to go to accomplish this balance. A position of moderation and acceptance of all undeniable forms of diversity will keep a limit upon the possibility of our society becoming a decadent and immoral one. This will be achieved through a sense of balance within each individual in any society as each of us recognizes our responsibility and need for self-examination and self-rectification; and also by a general shift in focus from differences to commonalities.

Furthermore, a true recognition and acceptance of unchangeable diversity will also be necessary for this balance to be achieved. Diversity has much more to do with who we are than with what we do relative to observable behaviors. It is necessary for each individual to temper their behaviors relative to their own personal balance and to some degree to the balance of society. This is not to take away the right for some to fight conformity. It simply comes back to my belief in an individual's right to be and do as long as these things do not hurt other people. I am not referring to people being hurt in the sense of being offended from an arrogant perspective of judging others as wrong according to their own rigid sets of standards. I simply believe the ways we define morality and values are also becoming more balanced, moving away from a puritanical, Victorian era viewpoint, toward a more realistic recognition of and appreciation for diversity. It is only within these kinds of parameters that it will be possible for people to each possess their own beliefs with a more prominent focus on spirituality rather than upon the self deceptive notions of control and a limited view of God and God's purpose.

Arrogance, a sense of entitlement, and a misinterpretation and misuse of the word respect are all associated with people who perceive themselves as being in positions of authority and dominance over others. Experience and common sense teach me that arrogance, coupled with ignorance, is the great offender and destroyer of justice and balance. Any position of authority should be seen as a position of leadership rather than one of rule. People can only be ruled through compliance and submission. Therefore, anyone in a position as a ruler is actually in a position of power, which should not be confused with respect.

For example, I will respect a leader who truly represents the people being lead, as in developing nations where people need a credible teacher to lead them out of deprivation. However I will not respect a person in a position of power who seeks only to rule and dominate. Haven't we learned anything from history, including recent and current historical injustices and outright bad decisions and policies? In a situation of being ruled, there may be no choice immediately available for me to do anything but submit, with submission being mixed with resentment and anger. The only times I would submit to a ruler is when I am afraid not to, or when there is some advantage in it for me relative to job and advancement in any personal and professional areas of my life. However, my submission will only be temporary, as I will seek to remove myself from this position of being dominated and controlled as quickly as possible once the benefit to me no longer exists, or when I can find some reasonable means of escape. As an adult I can play this game only when it is necessary in order to advance my causes, and only because I know I have the ability and freedom to make choices. I also have the ability to make decisions and learn from my mistakes. In addition I have the determination never to be dominated or controlled by anyone or by any abusive situation.

On the other hand, I will follow a leader when the leader is worthy of my consideration, and I will gladly be a team player as long as the goals of the team match my own goals which I seek to balance between my welfare and the welfare of others. While by nature I am now much more of a leader than a follower, I recognize my need to learn by example in many situations in life where I can respectfully submit to someone who knows more than I do. Or I can submit to someone from whom I wish to learn as a result of the respect I feel toward them. Furthermore, I want to be appreciated for who I am and for what I already know in the sense of what I have to contribute, believing the relationship between leaders and followers, or rather between teachers and students, is reciprocal. Each of us has something to teach and at the same time something to learn from the experience. Depending upon the circumstances of the situation, hopefully the teacher has more knowledge to impart. If not, the teacher is in a serious state of denial and position of arrogance, and should therefore step down and assume the role of student. A ruler can either talk to a captured audience, or switch roles to that of a leader/teacher and experience the reciprocity of such an exchange of information and the generation of new ideas and different perspectives. In life we all need to assume different roles ranging from student to equal participant to teacher.

In this sense a leader is basically a teacher, which means the role of teacher is temporary and transitory. In other words the role of leader should exist only when it is necessary to reach a common goal and the common good, and only until those being lead or taught have also learned how to lead or teach. In reality and ideally, shouldn't all of us be able to change roles from teacher to student at the drop of a hat relative to our own personal and spiritual growth and that of others? In light of these concepts, is it any wonder why Anglos, and particularly European American males, have fought so hard in the last four or five decades to retain their positions of power? Is it any wonder why the various conservative religious groups have also fought within all contexts, especially within the social and political contexts, to remain in control relative to the rigid, self serving moral standards they seek to force upon society? Because they believe in a punitive, arrogant God many religious people live their lives in fear and submission, rather than serving a God who loves and teaches us by example to accept all diversity without evaluative judgment which seeks only to divide people into groups of us versus them. Think about how the Bible has been used to justify white supremacy, even to this day. Look at how those who participate in hate group activities carry banners proclaiming their "Christianity", and verbally proclaim many of the extreme views and beliefs of fundamental religious groups. As a student of psychology I believe there is serious impairment for anyone or any group afraid of new ideas and perspectives. This is especially true when thinking outside the boxes can lead each of us more rapidly through the process of Spiritual evolution, and toward the resolution of issues which only fuel the FLAGS and our need to act out.

Much of this country was founded upon the need to escape from persecution and domination, only to re-establish much the same principles and experiences against others for centuries in this country. In my opinion many people have lost sight of spirituality which cannot be limited within the confines of outdated religious dogma and doctrines. Spirituality is progressive and dynamic, rather than traditional and static. I believe very much in the spiritual evolution of the world and its inhabitants which includes all living things, each with its own position of importance and relativity. I believe we will see the death of arrogance and the birth of balance within a reasonable period of time as the older generations die out and take with them many of their biases and prejudices which they hold onto as an acceptable way of living and thinking. After all, when something ends, something new always begins,

Balance will only be achieved when each of us is willing to give up our selfish needs to be on top, so to speak; and only when each of us is willing to be both teacher and student, lover and beloved. Jesus of Nazareth and many other historical spiritual leaders – all of whom are sons and daughters of God – acknowledged themselves as teachers and as messengers from God. None of them meant or asked to be worshipped; they only meant to be copied. As teachers each of them came to teach us as students to see ourselves as the sons and daughters of God. From there human nature and our ego-based needs to dominate and control (which are based in the Fear, Loneliness, Anger, Guilt, and Shame in my RFLAGS Model) have sought to turn spiritual teachings into divisive religious sects. By doing so, people have bastardized the original intention, relative to the messages from God of unconditional love and acceptance. Coupled with this is the need for balance between our explicit responsibility to self and others.

Many people seem to have their heads buried in the sand relative to righting wrongs and protecting kids. Not long ago I saw a news report that attributed the increasing number of deaths of law enforcement officials in the late 1990's to a decline in respect for these individuals. Immediately I recognized the arrogance and absurdity of such an explanation. It is like I have stated earlier, kids and adults are too sophisticated to give respect to those in positions of power without considering the respectability of these individuals. When people speak of defiance of authority, which I hear all the time relative to kids, I believe they are actually referring to a defiance of arrogance which can finally be acknowledged and addressed in recent years due to changes in perception and perspective sparked in recent decades. No one will continually disrespect someone or some reality that is respectable. Many law enforcement officials may in reality be dying in the line of duty as a direct result of the actions of those who still seek to abuse and victimize others relative to law enforcement's demand for unchallenged respect and submission. This possibility is especially true relative to the injustices and secrecy established and perpetrated under the guise of Homeland Security and the U.S. Patriot Act.

Think about the last time you may have been stopped by a law enforcement official for suspicion of some violation such as speeding, failing to yield, or jay walking. Initially my reaction, and the reaction of many others in such circumstances, is one of fear. My voice sounds shaky, and my hands are trembling as I try to find my driver's license and automobile registration. This reaction is based in my fear of what the officer may do to me relative to some kind of power play, expecting me to humble myself and submit to his or her perceived position of domination over me. For me this feels too much like the past that lived in my present for many years. I deeply resent this feeling in spite of the fact I may actually have broken the law. Even though I may get angry for having gotten caught, I will be able to accept that fact and face my consequences more readily if the officer treats me with respect. What kinds of needs are met for officers who need to victimize the offender who is not out of control, oppositional, or threatening?

I am not seeking to diminish the role law enforcement officials play in any society; however, and as everyone knows, a few bad apples can spoil the image of the whole bunch. Think about the kinds of atrocious acts peace officers have to commit to even draw attention beyond their own "Internal Affairs" departments. The point I am trying to make is that respect has to be earned. It cannot be demanded or legislated. Because some positions of authority are necessary for the public welfare, it is important for people in those positions to resolve and balance any aspects of their personalities creating a need to abuse and victimize. If anyone complies with the expectations of an abusive individual, it is out of fear, not out of respect. Many people in society today have these two concepts very confused! Every profession needs to create, publicize and enforce a rigid set of ethical principles and standards. I would bet that such ethics actually exist in theory within the groups I am addressing, but are simply ignored rather than upheld and enforced.

My constant focus on religion, politics, community leaders, public servants, and society are reinforced by all of the chaos and terrorism (abuse/victimization) present and predominant around the world. 9/11 only brought home to the United States the harsh realities many people in other countries have lived with currently and throughout long periods of history. Everyone in positions of power and authority should be as altruistic and honorable as those public servants and private citizens who died while engaged in heroic efforts to save and assist others during the aftermath of 9/11.

American arrogance is a good example of how foolish it is to believe we can't be vulnerable, or to expect that everyone will like and respect us because of our prosperity and grandstanding. It is time to look back historically to see how and why other great nations and civilizations have crumbled throughout time. I think about the people in the United States who suddenly displayed flags in many public places to heighten visibility. Where were these symbols of patriotism prior to 9/11, and what criteria will people use to determine the time when it is appropriate to take down the flags and put them away?

Flag waving only in the face of a crisis is nothing more than a divisive and arrogant act to prove that "might makes right", all cloaked in a deceptive cover of patriotism and unification. Think about how many of those flags after 9/11 were also flown along with the confederate flag, clearly supporting my suspicions. Flag waving occurs all of the time in other countries as a way of separating themselves from us and showing disrespect, disregard, and hatred toward the arrogance of both American leaders and for the American people. Patriotism based in any stance of us against them, with "us" seeing ourselves as better than "them", can only serve to cause further division between the us/them groups rather than serving to unite people.

A prime example exists in our efforts immediately following 9/11 to solicit support from other nations. Most of the world leaders outside of the United States were at first reluctant to join what appeared to be "our cause" rather than join what should have been promoted even prior to 9/11 as a united "worldwide cause" against terrorism. Even the rhetoric initially used by political figures following 9/11 literally paralleled the very thinking and jargon we attack and punish in kids who promote and commit acts of violence as a way of acting out the same FLAGS created for them due to forms of social injustice. Because of my job as a psychologist I was shocked at the extent of hypocrisy and ignorance exhibited by such reactions from political leaders. Only when these reactions became more thoughtout responses were we able to begin effectively addressing terrorism and join as a team member with other nations in a unified effort to identify, stop, punish, and block perpetrators of abuse and victimization. Then along came the whole issue of Iraq and the need to make a show of force to let the world know not to mess with the USA. This again left us standing alone with looks of shock and despair (not "shock and awe") on our faces when this didn't work out as promised. Notice I didn't say as planned. And we wonder where kids learn to think and act the way they do!

By focusing on these issues, I am attempting to establish some credence for the perspective of how each of us should recognize our respective roles as opportunities to be teacher and student, giver and receiver, even antagonist or promoter. I want us to now turn our attention to our adult roles and responsibilities relative to the children directly and indirectly in our charge. In this section I want us to redefine the home/family context relative to the concept of balancing and the roles we play at any given point.

Let's start with what a family would look like where the lives of the adults are balanced. Remember, one of my biggest points relative to the contexts in which abuse and victimization can occur is the importance of a healthy home/family environment as far as establishing a strong foundation for kids before venturing out to face the other contexts. For adults to have balance in their own lives adults would have already started a process of honest self-examination and self-rectification. Notice I used the word process, indicating self-examination as a life long effort, with the intensity of the effort ideally declining in the future through an increase in insight, wisdom, and self-awareness. Hopefully this process started before the adults became parents. However, it is better late than never. I genuinely believe if adolescents were taught these concepts concerning adult roles and responsibilities, and the need for self examination even during the middle school and high school years, then parenting could be taken on more effectively and hopefully not until adulthood.

In order to understand adult roles and responsibilities adults first need to identify the goals of raising children. One of the primary reasons for having children should be to enrich the lives of the parents. Their enrichment should come in the form of an intense desire to successfully raise kids to be healthy adults. In this sense parents should not take on the role of ruler. Instead, the role of leader and teacher is the only effective stance to take. Remember, the imbalance of parent to child should always be to the benefit of the child. In other words the scale should only be tipped for the parents to assume the dominant position of role model for the purpose of then nurturing a kid's own ability and need to balance both internal and external processes. The scales should never be tipped in favor of a parent's need to dominate and control simply for the sake of ruling. How many of you have ever heard the expression "I rule the roost around here"? This should never come out of the mouths of parents and adults in any roles or settings. It is necessary for kids to follow rules, but not from the perspective of being ruled. Think back about the statement made to me by my mother about my daughter not knowing the difference between me as her friend, or me as her father. What my mother was actually commenting on was the sense of balance I had with respect to my relationship to my daughter. The relationship was balanced, even though at times I had to assume my role as father/teacher for her to understand her need to learn appropriate behaviors relative to herself and others. Balance, as it pertains to the roles we play in kids' lives, is always between love, acceptance, and nurturing, and the elements of teaching and guiding. Anything less is not in the best interest of kids.

The balanced home/family context would also include an adult's ability to balance personal and professional considerations, as well as a balance between personal goals and objectives and the goals and objectives of being a parent. As long as kids are under our care we owe them the consideration they deserve.

No decisions directly or indirectly affecting the lives of children should ever be made without the full consideration of the impact our decisions will have on their lives. Failure to give such consideration is based in the arrogant position that kids will adjust and simply get over it. Like it or not we as adults have a major responsibility to serve kids, not the other way around. Until adults are ready to accept this reality, no significant roles and associations with kids should be established. Adolescents need the opportunity to fully understand the seriousness of becoming parents before they engage in any sexual activity that could produce a child. They also need to identify what is missing in their own home/family context and seek to either correct it or establish the determination they will not continue the dysfunction from their childhood into the lives of the next generation.

Also, the balanced family would focus on respect for individuality and the good of the child relative to what each kid wants and needs out of life. I believe if kids are given a solid basis in the first 4 to 6 years, parents can relax a little as children reach adolescence. If kids are taught balance and self control from the beginning of life as intrinsic qualities and characteristics, the chances are they will be able to utilize these values as they venture out on their own in an effort to explore and establish their own sense of self. After all, by the time a kid reaches adolescence we as parents can only hope we have given them the skills needed to navigate and negotiate their way through the many issues they will face. Trying to impose control externally simply for the sake of control during adolescence is pointless. Control placed upon kids who are out of control must be tempered with the appeal for kids to uncomplicate their own existence for their sake alone by learning internal self control which they were never taught. I have seen this approach work time after time with the kids who are referred to me for therapy. To impose control for the sake only of compliance and control results in anger and resentment, thereby teaching kids that control is only necessary when someone is watching. This seems to be a very viable explanation of impulsive behavior, especially in the cases of families rooted in extreme religious beliefs; and families that include people from the military and law enforcement arenas. Kids from these families often revolt and get into as much trouble as other groups of "at risk youth". To me the term "at risk" applies to kids who come from home/family environments at both ends of the spectrum where there is either neglect, or the atmosphere of extreme control and domination.

As I work with kids and their families in my role as psychologist, I see many parents from various backgrounds and environments coming in with the attitude of simply "fix my kid". They will openly lie and minimize the part they often play in creating the problematic behaviors they are asking me to fix. They will even become very defensive when I turn to them and suggest, strictly as an observation, that the choices they have made in their own lives have helped to create the problems their kids are now experiencing for themselves. Parents often times like to play the victim, asking "why me?" followed by the statement, "I/we did the best we could." Parents sometimes have a strong sense of guilt and awareness of the responsibility they bear for the downfall of their kids. However, they seldom admit their mistakes and push this awareness to the back of their minds. The other adults involved directly and indirectly in the lives of any kids also need to own up to the responsibility they share as well. No one is without responsibility for the world we have created which makes it possible for kids to take guns to school to kill others for the wrongs existing in their own lives. I am not seeking to blame anyone in this case in the sense of pointing a finger. I seek only to reveal what I consider to be the truth about mistakes we have made for many years. Even in the Old Testament we are warned about "the sins of the fathers". Arrogance keeps us as adults from claiming our part for the trauma kids experience and then create for others as a way of acting out their own emotion-based anxiety.

When it comes to the consideration of blame, I know this serves no purpose. I am constantly amazed how people are so accustomed to being abused and victimized (which is what I believe blaming and criticizing to be) they are almost always on the defensive. One of the most difficult parts of my job is to get people to actually listen and hear what I am trying to say. At the same time, the most rewarding aspect of my job is when parents and adults can actually hear and understand my words for the help and support they offer. I have no need to victimize anyone by making them feel worse than they already do. I must try to help them deal with their own sense of shame and guilt, as well as with the other FLAGS of fear, loneliness, and anger. I know when a parent tells me they have done the best they knew how to do, they are actually telling the truth. People often do not know what to do and seldom ever think about the need for self examination and rectification in order to successfully transcend their respective pasts and provide the elements needed by children to grow up healthy in all respects. After all, very few people recognize their need for professional help much less actually ask for it.

A parent's feeling of shame generally comes from the fear of what others are thinking about their effectiveness as a parent. I have already addressed this issue earlier of how we are taught at very early ages to falsely believe the whole world is watching us and cares about what we are doing. For instance, the issues within my family really are no one else's business unless I choose to share them as a means of teaching my concepts. No one has the right to judge my family or me for any of the mistakes that have been made. I dare anyone to sit in judgment of my family or me for all we have been through. We are all good people who have simply made mistakes and bad choices. In this sense we are no different than anyone else. This kind of thinking allows me to hold my head up high and encourage others to look beyond their own arrogant need to judge rather than face these same and other problems within their own families. I can only hope those of us in my family, along with other people and their families, can work out our differences before it is too late in this lifetime for ourselves and for future generations.

It is also very easy for others involved in a child's life to avoid facing their failures by blaming kids for their ineffectiveness. Some teachers are very good at this in many situations. Oftentimes teachers allow their arrogance to keep them from seeing the need to approach some children differently, recognizing their own personal limits and tendencies to victimize in some cases which impede their ability to help. As I have said with families, if something is not working relative to problem solving efforts, it probably never will. Therefore, why not try something different? No one is above this kind of scrutiny. I acknowledge that the challenges for teachers and other professionals to work effectively with youth at risk are often enormous. However, these challenges require well thoughtout responses toward the goal of meeting the needs of these kids. There isn't a single profession associated with kids which doesn't require extra effort, skills, and a higher level of commitment and ethics.

I am glad to hear through the media of people wanting to hold teachers and other school personnel accountable for their performance and abilities. I will be glad someday to see the same standards applied to those who work within the juvenile justice systems, including district attorneys, public defenders, judges, probation officers, and all staff who work in youth placement facilities and juvenile detention centers. It is a known fact that certain kinds of jobs attract people with specific abusive personality profiles, with an intense need to control, belittle, and dominate. People with such tendencies should be screened out rather than hired in positions of authority over kids. The approach of judging kids solely based on what is recorded on pieces of paper or computer records is wrong. Every kid deserves the opportunity to spend time with someone neutral like myself and other effective caring professionals who can get to know who a kid really is on the inside and make recommendations relative to their future. It is wrong to depend solely on the often inaccurate accounts which are used as evidence to convict kids of crimes. Judges, attorneys and staff in various settings often discount the opinions of professionals such as me as representing the ideals and philosophies of "bleeding heart liberals" who are out of touch with reality. Years ago I actually had a probation officer tell me this to my face. People like this should be encouraged to listen to those of us who are trying to redirect the lives of kids rather than to simply punish and control them.

I even find some within my own profession who take such an uninformed and unintelligent approach to dealing with kids at risk. Locking kids up without making sure each kid gets the help they need and deserve is again an arrogant and ignorant position of dominance and submission for the sole purpose of control. When people are saying there aren't enough resources, those in positions of power and authority should be less politically motivated and less concerned with their popularity and ability to maintain their positions, and more motivated to serve the good of kids involved. It is too easy for others to sit and judge from the sidelines about what causes kids to act out and what needs to be done about it. For some reason at this point in history the tendency is to get rid of kids as though they are the problem. This is obviously much easier than expecting changes from those who arrogantly believe they have played no part in kids' lives relative to having contributed to the negative choices made by kids. Even corporate America is willing to do anything it takes to make a buck off of kids, no matter what the potential consequences may be. It is time to hold everyone accountable for the mistakes we are making, not in the sense of blaming, rather in the sense of finding solutions which we all must generate and participate in if things are to be better for future generations. The only way such solutions will be found is for everyone to undergo some process of self-examination and rectification.

Now let's consider how unbalanced families look relative to some very basic formulas or profiles. Keep in mind my RFLAGS Model and how people of all ages tend to act out emotion-based anxiety. Always look for connections between the past and the present relative to the emotions fueling the anxiety and the tendency to act out. We will look first at a family where both parents are together. Next we will examine blended families where parents are separated/divorced and remarried. Finally we will look at single parent families. Much of this will be familiar to many of you, so we will not spend a great deal of time on these topics. I simply want to help make the connections between the past and who we are in the present.

Generally, when families are together with the biological parents and all of their offspring living under the same roof, there are fewer problems for the kids. However, there is often at least one kid who exhibits problematic behaviors and is considered to be the one acting out the emotion-based anxiety of the family as a system if the family structure and patterns of interaction are out of balance. These kinds of families can range from being overly involved to being significantly underinvolved. Also remember there is no such thing as the perfect family, and that all families fall somewhere short of this ideal. Family compositions can range from totally dysfunctional to nearly perfect, with all families falling somewhere within the range. However, when thinking about families and balance the range is more of a curve, with balanced families falling exactly in the middle of the range from extremely under-involved to extremely over-involved. My personal belief is that many of today's families are more toward the tails of the curve rather than in the middle, making the curve inverted rather than bell-shaped. The more balanced families become the more positive the curve becomes, with families shifting away from the extremes toward the mid-range of a pendulum which is well-balanced and keeping perfect time.

Families who are overly involved can range from families where one or both parents are control freaks, to families where there are no real boundaries relative to where I end and you begin. The control freaks are the parents who rule rather than lead and teach, and they do so through fear, intimidation, and humiliation. Families with no real boundaries are also into control and are those who are over protective, and who have no respect for privacy and individuality. According to my education and experiences the strange result from both of these extremes is they produce dependent children who clearly exhibit all of the FLAGS, along with many unresolved grief issues on into adulthood. The children in these families are victimized and abused at least emotionally by never being given the opportunity to learn to be self sufficient with a strong awareness of who they are and what they are capable of accomplishing.

Those kids whose parents are overly involved grow up confused, resentful, and unsure of themselves. These kids tend to make many mistakes during adolescence and in adulthood through defiance of arrogance because they were never given the opportunities to learn appropriate skills which would help them function at optimal levels as adults. Anytime families fail to give kids what they need in order to be healthy in all respects are guilty of neglect and deprivation, which we identified earlier as passive forms of abuse and victimization. Arrogance and ignorance come into the picture relative to parents' beliefs there is nothing wrong with their parenting skills, and therefore, convince themselves there is no need for self-examination and rectification. Parents need to look at the issues fueling their own needs to act out their unresolved emotions and anxiety from the past upon each other and upon their children.

Keep in mind also how each of these patterns of parental ineffectiveness creates complicating factors which make the world outside of the home/ family context even more threatening, and more of an opportunity to act out when kids think no one is looking. Some kids will act out as a result of peer pressure. However, I think it is important to look at the extent of acting out and the kinds of acting-out behaviors chosen. Plain and simple, if a kid takes a gun to school and kills his classmates, even if this is the first offense, either this kid has serious mental problems which should have been identified and attended to by family members and professionals, or he is acting out all of the FLAGS which have built up as a result of various forms of abuse and neglect. Neglect can also include a lack of much needed monitoring and supervision of kids, their friends, and their activities. Kids who kill frequently come from homes where there is either serious over involvement or serious under involvement. In either case, parents of these kids must be in a serious state of denial, and are the very parents you see in the media playing the victims. I base this observation in the simple reality that kids do not just wake up one morning and decide to kill without some prior history of evidence indicating this potential for extreme violence. Adults are not as innocent as they want us to believe they are. Furthermore, adults are not as innocent as they need to believe they are either.

Now let's shift focus to the idea of blended families where parents are separated/divorced and have remarried. Often times these adults bring other children into the picture from previous marriages, and they then have one or more children together. In my opinion there are two very big mistakes made by adults who become romantically involved following separation/divorce. First, many adults tend to jump into rebound relationships because they are unable to deal with the emotion-based anxiety which probably created the first bad marriage, and served as the motivation to marry again without working on the unresolved issues.

Secondly, adults fail to consider how the presence of someone else will effect the kids involved, especially when the motivation is for "all of us to be a family again". This is actually an adult fantasy need imposed upon the kids as a way of trying to make kids embrace advantages, existing primarily for the adults involved. Divorce and separation only reinforce the reality that intimate relationships are fragile as opposed to the parental connection which is permanent even when ignored and abandoned. Parents are entitled to happiness and they need adult companionship; however, an adult's *first* responsibility is to their children and their well being until the kids are old enough to live on their own. Many adults expect kids to love the new partner as though they were their biological father or mother. This is too great a demand to make of kids. Adults should be satisfied if the new spouse and the kids can simply agree to peacefully coexist. If more than this is possible, then great. However, this should not be an expectation as expectations limit the range of possible responses.

It is extremely important for all adults to remember that kids generally have no say in decisions adults make, even though the decisions will greatly impact the lives of kids as well. Adults expect kids to accept changes without any complaining and with total acceptance and compliance. This is adult arrogance and ignorance at its best. As long as we are happy, kids should be happy too. As far as I am concerned, parents forfeit their right to make any rash decisions which can potentially have an adverse impact on the lives of kids simply by virtue of being parents. I am not saying adults should allow kids to dictate and rule the lives of the parents; rather, that adults need to take their time to communicate effectively with all involved before moving forward. This approach keeps kids from acting out their emotion-based anxiety which will surely develop from separation/divorce situations.

Adults who are separating or divorcing have a responsibility to work out their issues appropriately and not at the expense of the children who are often used as pawns, with kids feeling they have to choose between parents relative to love and loyalty. This is almost criminal and certainly immoral. I am glad to see some communities now requiring counseling and negotiation with respect to settling marital issues of property and custody. Kids of separated/divorced parents are scarred for life; whereas, the lives of the adults tend to mend and move forward, except in those cases where people continue repeating the same mistakes by not recognizing the need for honest self examination and rectification.

Again, the defiance of kids in blended families is a defiance of arrogance resulting in the lack of consideration given kids relative to their feelings, desires, and needs. Kids resent being treated with less respect than is demanded from them, and they will act this out by openly challenging the role of the stepparent. Rather than seek to mend the wounds which have resulted from the lack of consideration and regard, parents and parental figures usually set up the competition of you will do as I say, rather than admit the mistakes, apologize, and seek forgiveness. This represents true respect for kids. I am amazed at how healing the words "I'm sorry" can be when spoken from the heart by a parent or other adults. After all why should a kid forgive us if we cannot or will not admit the wrongs we have done to them? To have a parent look you in the face and tell you "there was a lot of love in this home", when you know in your heart and soul this is a lie, is a very insulting experience.

While parents may mean well, there is no greater hurt than the denial of how what adults do effects kids. When love is expressed properly it doesn't hurt or leave open wounds which sometimes never heal. This is especially true when kids are dealing with complicating factors such as sexual orientation, or some form of handicap/disability, which makes them feel less than others anyway relative to self esteem issues. Homosexuality can be a form of handicap, not in the same sense of some type of physical impairment, but in the sense of the resulting discrimination and bigotry. This is forced upon those who are gay from families and society which often times arrogantly holds onto its need to believe that people (especially males) who are anything less than heterosexual are deviant and evil. Some of you reading this book at this very moment have a homosexual or bisexual child living in your home. Hopefully, you will seek the information necessary from such organizations as Parents and Friends of Lesbians and Gays (PFLAG) (not to be confused with my RFLAGS) with many local chapters nationwide, before it is too late. There are increasing indications that many unexplained adolescent suicides are due to FLAGS related to sexual orientation. Homosexual and bisexual individuals are truly at the mercy of external factors, as they are handicapped not because of themselves, but because of the limits society, politics, and religion tries to place on them.

In my experience I have found single-parent families to be the most problematic and chaotic, especially when a single mom is the head of the household. Like it or not, there are basic differences between men and women, even if these are perceived rather than actual differences relative to parental roles. I have made this statement to many single moms, all of whom agree with me. Kids miss the presence of a father or at least the presence of a positive father figure. I also believe boys have a much more difficult time dealing with this than the girls do. Quite often boys feel they become the "man of the house", and believe mom cannot tell them what to do. This is made even worse when moms look to their oldest son to take on the adult role, as what is referred to as the parentified child. Many moms make the mistake of becoming dependent upon their children, especially their sons, for emotional support following separation/divorce. This mistake becomes very problematic as the kids get older and feel like no one can set limits with them. This results when parents allow the roles to become reversed – a mistake that should be avoided at all costs. Parents need to always be firmly in the role of parents no matter what the circumstances are. When they feel unable to fulfill their roles as parents, it is extremely important for them to seek adult, if not professional support to help them through whatever transition is occurring. Both males and females should carefully choose who will be the stepparent of their kids for the sake of all involved.

The roles between parents and kids should never become reversed or confused. When this occurs the scales are way out of balance, and adults are expecting more from kids than they have a right to expect. In times of trouble families need to pull together and support each other; however, the roles cannot be reversed without dire consequences in the future. When a child is given the role of an adult, they feel they are in control of the situation. Because kids have no idea how to be an adult, especially if there are no effective role models in their lives, kids will fail miserably and jeopardize their own futures.

This will result because they were never taught self-control, effective decision-making skills, anger management, responsibility for actions, respect for self or others, or the ability to tolerate frustration. These skills which are lacking result from the fact kids have had to take on adult roles and responsibilities without any period of training relative to successfully acquiring and executing these traits. These deficits also result from ineffective and inappropriate role models both within the home/family context and outside in the other contexts as well. Boys always agree with the observation that many times they are cheated out of an opportunity just to be a kid because of the need they feel to protect moms who still present themselves as victims in many divorce/separations situations.

When the scales are out of balance in single parent families, kids pay a high price for the imbalance. This kind of profile sets kids up to be fully at risk for failure and the need to act out. The problem for parents at this point is the lack of effectiveness at attempts to impose control. Kids who have never been taught control from within are simply not going to accept control from the outside in the sense of being able to take it in. They will bitterly fight against such attempts with open defiance of arrogance, even if the arrogance exists on an unconscious level within the lives of both adults and kids. This is where I see many battles raging in many settings between adults and adolescents who are in competition with each other for positions of power and domination. Kids will actually fight arrogance with arrogance. That should come as no surprise, since this is what they have encountered throughout much of their lives. In this kind of competition of wills, everyone loses, especially the kids who will grow up to have lives equally as complicated and chaotic as the lives of the adults who were responsible for their care.

The only approach with adolescents at this point is to appeal to their own sense of self preservation and get them to see how their decisions and actions are complicating their lives more than the lives of the adults involved. It is only fair for adults to hope an adolescent can do something for their own survival rather than for the survival of others in their lives. This is also the time to provide kids with effective role models outside of the family who can then guide and nurture kids in the right direction as a neutral party with no hidden agendas; i.e. no need to control or dominate, compete or win. As any kid learns self control and survival skills the adults in their lives will also benefit from the changes. Unfortunately many adults will very arrogantly have the need to take credit for any positive changes kids make. While on the other hand, they readily blame kids for anything the kids do wrong. Arrogance! Arrogance! Arrogance!

CHAPTER IX

In Defense of the Underdogs:
Those Truly at the Mercy of Externals

This chapter is dedicated to the nearly 3200 kids I have worked with since 1990, as well as to the kids I will work with in the future. The kids I am referring to as underdogs are the outcasts and throwaways from society, who by their own often unconscious choices for survival have set themselves up to be hated and rejected by most everyone they meet. These are the kids who are the by-products of the world we as adults have created, and they are the ones we seek to scapegoat as the dregs of society who should all be locked up and forgotten. These are the kids who frequently are motivated from an unconscious level to consciously choose to become criminals, drug addicts, alcoholics, gang members, punks, runaways, taggers, freaks, devil worshippers, goths, head bangers, etc. These are the kids who frighten us as we walk down the streets and inside the malls of most any city; the ones whom we fear will rob us or kill us if they need or want something we have. These are the kids in our communities who, motivated by rage fantasies and revenge, walk into school settings and kill classmates and school staff, after having killed their parents at home. They represent kids who futilely cried out for help many times before they got to the point of being so obviously impaired relative to emotional, intellectual, and psychological functioning. As children they have grown up under the most adverse conditions of abuse, deprivation, and numerous complicating factors from within all of the possible contexts. These are the very kids I work with in different settings, trying to reach out to them when others write them off as lost causes. They reflect what is wrong in our society and in our world. We are the ones who have created the world making all of this possible, and we are responsible initially for the choices they make.

More and more adults among us are beginning to wake up and see our responsibility for these lives in peril. Some among us are finally coming to realize the answers are not found in building more detention centers, or in strengthening the laws to treat these kids as though they are adults or urban terrorists under the U.S. Patriot Act and Homeland Security. Rather the answers are to begin assisting kids at risk much earlier in their lives before they begin entering the juvenile justice systems, or become runaways living on the streets of impoverished communities and larger cities. Somehow the world has never offered them the hope of success or even of life beyond a certain very young age. When these kids say "I don't care", they really mean, "Why should I care? No one else does!" This is the true hallmark of feeling both helpless and hopeless.

From my heart I believe these kids are in part and in some cases the result of many years of debilitating public assistance programs which have taught adults and kids it is possible to get something for nothing. They are also the result of the numerous societal changes, including a breakdown in previously acceptable family systems, which have taken place over the last 3 to 4 decades. The welfare system, which is finally under some degree of reform, has taken away a sense of pride for many people who receive rather than work for material possessions and personal gains. This along with disability programs failing to properly monitor true need for such assistance only allow for more abuse and victimization by fostering dependency and limited awareness of opportunities, many of which still need to be developed. People of all ages and cultural groups, regardless of race, have been given the sense of easy come easy go, allowing kids to believe there will always be something or someone to bail them out of any kind of trouble. Some parents of kids growing up below the poverty level have forsaken their kids and have shown them the world is not a reliable or safe place in which to live. Many of these parents have taught their kids it is okay to break the law, and that you only get in trouble because you were dumb enough to get caught, not because you did something wrong. While some families truly need help, there are many others who fraudulently milk the systems for all they can get, even viewing their kids as sources of income.

Kids and many adults, regardless of socioeconomic status, have little or no sense of delayed gratification. Some kids and adults living in extreme poverty situations will take what belongs to others out of a sense of entitlement, with no regard for the value of human life and the rights of others. Adults and kids alike in these situations often do not care, or sometimes do not see the criminal nature of their actions. This is currently referred to as "pro-criminality" or "pro-criminal thinking". These are kids who, in many cases, have been dumped on since the day they were born, and who exhibit behaviors which have been modeled for them by adults within the contexts and environments in which they were raised. Sometimes even adults outside of the home/family context model and spark negative behavior because of our tendencies to approach these kids with prejudices and extreme misperceptions. How arrogant and ignorant of us to expect them to consider and accept better ways of thinking and living if we fail to approach them with the respect they deserve as human beings first and foremost. Then and only then can we begin to address the behaviors which make kids so threatening even to themselves and to society.

I am basing these observations about families, who are considered to be of lower socioeconomic status, upon my experiences of working primarily with families who fall into this category. Please keep in mind that in this chapter I am using examples of kids who comprise a very small percentage out of all the kids in this country. Understand, too, I blame the systems providing the opportunities for dependency and fraud for some of the problems I am identifying, and not the people participating in the programs. Therefore, within the population of kids and families I work with I have seen many more extreme instances of abuse/victimization and neglect. There are much higher percentages within this relatively small percentage of the total population of all forms of dysfunction, including people who have kids just to receive more assistance from government and community agencies. It is much more likely kids in this category will have been born as a result of carelessness, and quite often are unwanted or at least unwelcomed. More adults in the lives of kids in this group are likely to have criminal histories and extensive histories of drug addiction and alcoholism, often times coupled with serious mental and emotional problems. It is also probable that kids born into this level of poverty and hardship may not have received good health care and nutrition either during pregnancy or after birth. Furthermore, more females in this category are likely to have used alcohol, drugs, and tobacco during pregnancy, and are more likely not to receive adequate prenatal care and guidance. Please understand I am not saying everyone who has received assistance from welfare and other programs has failed to provide loving and safe environments for their kids. The above factors, however, unfortunately play significant roles in the lives of many of the kids I work with professionally. Keep in mind that the kids from "functional" home/family environments generally don't end up in mental health clinics or the juvenile justice systems. Living below the poverty level and within low-income areas doesn't guarantee broken lives and unproductive futures. However, these conditions do considerably increase the probability of such outcomes.

If you will notice, European American kids committed many of the recent acts of extreme violence reported in recent years through the media. My experience tells me more acts of violence committed by European American kids would be reported if the media weren't so quick to point the finger at other ethnic and cultural groups. As I pass through the waiting area outside of any juvenile courtroom, I generally see kids from every cultural and ethnic group except European Americans. My own speculation as to the explanation for this is related to prejudice on the parts of law enforcement officials and systems, and to the fact parents of European American kids are often better able to afford attorneys who keep kids out of court and detention. It is also possible that not as many European American kids get into trouble on a higher percentage basis because of their positions of perceived privilege and opportunity, never being as fully exposed to all of the complicating factors of being below the poverty level and being "non-white". I believe European American kids resort more to hate crimes and forms of physical violence associated with membership in extremist white supremacy groups, hard rock cultures, and satanic cults. I also believe that a significant number of European American kids who commit crimes are spoiled, arrogant brats who have little or no regard for the rights of others or any greater sensitivity to the value of human life than kids from other cultural groups. Nowadays more European kids are drawn into groups, including gangs, which previously were associated with different minority groups. While there are many factors to consider in determining possible outcomes, they do not foretell with certainty any results.

Again, I believe society is also responsible for this reality as evidenced by a higher percentage of people from groups other than European Americans being below the poverty level, with higher concentrations of lower SES groups in inner cities where they receive more negative publicity. I also believe in areas where criminal acts are committed by European Americans living below the poverty level, other European Americans are in such a majority - as in parts of the Southeast and Midwest - these acts do not get much attention and are probably under reported. These are the areas where white men still reign supreme and the "good ol' boy networks" are still alive and well. After all, who pays any real attention relative to crime and lower SES issues in Midwestern states and backwoods Alabama, Mississippi, Tennessee, Arkansas, Georgia, Kentucky, North and South Carolina, Virginia, and West Virginia? Some militia and white supremacy groups in these areas may be watched and monitored by government officials. However, they don't get much media coverage unless they are ranting and raving in the streets and on the Internet about white power, the desire to overthrow the government, or bombing federal buildings, churches, and abortion clinics. Perhaps war should have been declared on the terrorist groups and individuals that are comprised of European Americans and other American citizens after the Oklahoma City bombing of the federal building, an act based in hatred and extremism. This was no different than the attacks of 9/11, with virtually all acts of terrorism in this country prior to 9/11 being perpetrated by "whites" for centuries.

Another major area of concern to me that tremendously impacts the lives of the "underdogs" is the actions of politicians with opportunities to circumvent the democratic process. They often pass legislation that was either voted down by the people or blocked in the courts when presented on ballots in the form of initiatives, referendums, and propositions. One of the best examples of this was the famous California Proposition 187 in the mid 1990's that sought to drastically change immigration laws and procedures generally as they applied only to people from different Spanish-speaking countries. This proposition has not really been heard of since it got blocked in the courts until the California recall election in 2003. While Proposition 187 was voted in by the public, it was successfully blocked in the courts. However, many of the laws and rights relative to immigrants have been affected by legislation quietly and deceptively shuffled through state and federal systems disguised by such movements as Welfare Reform, Healthcare Reform, and changes in immigration policies which had nothing to do with protection against terrorism.

I personally believe we need to limit the flow of people into this country, a practice common in many countries around the world. However, I also believe we need to help those who are already here regardless of legal status, who have established themselves in this country, working the jobs most American citizens do not want to work. Furthermore, I believe we need to continue working with the governments of Mexico and Central and South America to improve their economic situations, thereby making it less attractive for people from these countries to migrate to North America. Most of these people who live in this country do so under extremely deplorable conditions just to survive. It is sad to realize how bad things must be in their own countries that make hardship in this country look like the fulfillment of a dream.

It is also time to stop focusing exclusively on people from Spanish-speaking countries as though they are the only ones living in this country illegally. There are many others from around the world doing the same thing without gaining much media focus, at least prior to 9/11. Probably the U.S. sees the political ties with countries in other parts of the world as being more important than the political ties to the developing nations south of our border. It is also probable that we see the countries south of our border as being less of a threat relative to our economic well being, with the only exception being illegal immigration. Hopefully the people in the southern half of this hemisphere are not regarded as less desirable relative to their usefulness to further our selfish North American pursuits of prosperity and materialism often at the expense of others. After all these people existed historically within the Americas before our European ancestors left Europe to come to North America.

All of these elements from the community, social, and political contexts are experienced inside the home/family context and beyond as factors which give kids cause to act out their emotion-based anxiety. The families and kids I work with are often the victims of many of the reforms currently taking place. Non-Hispanic/Latino people I spoke with in Los Angeles actually voted for Prop. 187 foolishly believing we would be able to end gang violence by sending all of the people primarily from Spanish-speaking countries back to Mexico. Political rhetoric attached to such measures is usually inflammatory and misleading. These actions and beliefs still continue through present day views and sentiments. After all, many ethnic groups in the western states believe anyone who speaks Spanish or has a Spanish accent is automatically from Mexico. In my work with gang kids, I have found the greatest majority of them to be U.S. citizens who are entitled to the same rights afforded to all other Americans. Furthermore, Spanish-speaking people come from a number of different countries other than Mexico. Some of the most dangerous are from El Salvador.

I use these examples to point out the arrogance and ignorance of people in power who are making decisions and laws which then become complicating factors for others. In many cases this is often done without a real sense of reality or responsibility. Politicians and voters are sometimes too far removed from the truth to be able to make unbiased decisions without creating undue hardship for those groups targeted as threats to position and power. Politicians are so interested in being elected and re-elected they will cower to the demands of any group they believe will get them into "office" which is nothing more than a deceptive term for a position of power. The George W. Bush administration and conservative present day politicians are prime examples of this.

I believe it is a huge mistake for any of us to think that government officials will always represent the people when it comes to sensitive issues such as human rights and other considerations related to social injustices. Politicians are so interested in promoting the causes of special interest groups which got them elected they lose sight of the overriding principles of spirituality upon which this nation was founded – principles such as life, liberty, the pursuit of happiness, equality under the law, and justice for all. God forbid anyone should fall into a category of being undesirable and outside the protection of these principles simply because of unchangeable differences which are perceived as threatening to groups of people (such as ultra conservatives) who are actually in minority status, and yet hold positions of power. Everyone needs to wake up and join forces against any groups of extremists who seek to keep the scales out of balance in this and other parts of the world. Remember with balance there are no extreme positions which result in gains for some at the expense of others. Arrogance and ignorance exist in all contexts and must be identified and eliminated by replacing it with acceptance and appreciation for diversity and the parts all of us play in creating a better way of life. This represents idealism and moderation at their best, huh? If you really think critically about the ideas I present they reflect a moderate position of fairness and equality for all which should be considered by every politician. This might even help end bipartisan political views as we know them today.

Obviously I am by nature a thinker. I am also an observer, a teacher, and a healer. And, you are right I am using this book as an opportunity to scream out some of my views. Even though I am "white", I have experienced numerous forms of heartache and challenge in my own life. Through all of this I have gained the strength and courage I need in order to face whatever lies ahead. I have also learned to appreciate and defend those who are in positions of being the underdog, this through an acquired ability to learn about and appreciate their struggles. Most important of all, I have learned from all of those whose paths have crossed my own regardless of their ethnic/cultural origins or other forms of diversity. For all of my challenges and experiences I am a better person and I am more spiritually grounded than I have ever been. I am grateful for all I have gained and most of all for the opportunity to work with targeted underdogs who need guidance and support. In every experience there is an opportunity to learn something. Hopefully, each of you will see my ideas and experiences in this book as an opportunity for you to learn something as well. Nothing shared within these pages is done with malice or ill intent, only with the hope of sparking enough controversy to initiate productive discussions leading to changes in perspectives, and changes in myths disguised as reality and truth.

With the preceding paragraphs as an introduction, allow me to share with you my experiences of working with society's underdog kids. Within each of my kids it is possible to find a piece of heart I can then work with to help them find themselves in spite of the heartache and hardship in their own lives. By occasionally sharing limited and appropriate parts of my own personal issues with my kids, I allow them to become aware of my ability to recognize many of their struggles by giving them the respect they deserve and need from others. By example I show them the kind of respect I want in return, and I have never had a kid completely turn on me. I have had kids who get angry, but not with me. After establishing rapport and trust, and because I treat them with respect I can say virtually anything I want to them relative to my observations of and perspective of truth and reality in their lives. For many of these kids this is the first time any adult has treated them in this manner.

Success is hard to judge in this population of kids so labeled as "bad kids", "problem children", "troubled youth", "at risk youth", "undesirable elements", "incorrigibles", etc. This makes it especially difficult for anyone to work with these kids if they need to see instant and measurable results. The results can only be measured with time in the span of years, for much of what I do is to plant seeds for future growth when the conditions are right. I never enter into a competition with these kids, nor do I have any need to be right, although at times I do insist that I know what I am talking about even if they choose to dismiss it for the time being. I trust my instincts and intuition, as well as the ability of each kid to take things in regardless of occasional outward protest and resistance.

My days at work are always challenging and sometimes frustrating, especially when I get bogged down in the same caseload for extended periods of time. This happens as kids and families keep getting into trouble and don't seem to be making as much progress as I would like to see. I have to recognize their right to make mistakes and be very careful not to take things personally. Furthermore, I have to recognize that these kids continue to struggle for survival within the very contexts which have given them cause to act out their FLAGS and resulting emotion-based anxiety. I care about these kids and they know that, but sometimes I have to let them go if they are not ready to work on their issues. Amazingly, many of them come looking for me as they get older and need further guidance or assistance. I can let them go because I trust my ability to have planted seeds which will likely begin to grow someday, even if I am not there to see this happen.

The greatest joy for me is to be the very first person to effectively connect with a kid who is believed to be particularly difficult. This is what keeps me going as afar as rewards from my job. To watch a kid relax and let go of that tough exterior as they realize I am not a threat is truly exciting and humbling. To then experience the establishment of mutual trust and respect is even better. All of my kids will tell me their gang moniker, and I use this as an indication of the level of trust we have established, occasionally reminding and reassuring them of confidentiality. This also indicates they have allowed me to enter their world as a friendly observer, with some kids even referring to me as "homie, homes, or dog" which are the names they use to refer to their fellow gang members and friends. These terms represent an acceptance rather than an insult as many people tend to think. All of this is proof to me that it is impossible to inspire others if we, ourselves, are not inspired. Our professional associations with this population of kids must be met with a high degree of both passion and compassion.

The biggest threats to their success in treatment are the extent of their substance abuse and the extreme negative conditions of their families and communities. Drugs, alcohol, and dysfunctional environments are very difficult factors with which to compete. Many of the kids are drug addicts and alcoholics by the time they are referred to me. Most of the families are too uninvolved in the lives of their kids to be aware of the extent to which their kids drink and use, with most families seeing the gang as being the biggest and only competitor against them. The families are not usually aware to what extent they are also competing with drugs and alcohol. Sometimes this is also true because of the family's lack of knowledge relative to substance abuse, and because of the fact some kids are really good at deception. The other reality is the extent of drug and alcohol use in many of the homes and in the communities. Parents often allow kids to drink and use drugs at home convincing themselves it is better than kids being under the influence out in the streets. Wow, does this ever send the wrong message!

Remember joining a gang is simply another way kids act out their emotion-based anxiety. As they become more involved in the gang lifestyle, which is truly a choice, they get caught up more and more in the negative elements associated with this identity. Realistically gangs exist for the sole purpose of establishing and protecting a territory in which to conduct illegal activity to include the selling of illegal drugs and weapons. The larger a gang is the more organized it will be and will likely be involved in more criminal activities in addition to weapons and drugs, and with more extensive national and international networks. The older gang members, even from within the prison systems, will often use the younger kids referred to as "youngsters" to do the "dirty work" so they can avoid the likelihood of facing three strikes and life in prison. This kind of attention appeals to the younger kids who feel they need to prove themselves to someone, especially to receive the acceptance, attention and praise from positive adult role models they so desperately lack and yet crave in their lives. The answer to this is not to establish laws to increase already harsh consequences applicable to kids. The best alternative is to put money into prevention and early intervention, not into incarceration which serves only to ease the minds of those who are uninformed and sitting judgingly, arrogantly, and ignorantly on the sidelines pretending to have all the solutions. However, it all comes down to politics, biased and incorrect societal views, and to money and numbers games for existing law enforcement agencies and organizations, all of which are very difficult factors to change or even impact.

Gangs, hate groups, satanic cults, hard rock cultures, and white power/supremacy groups - which arguably are gangs as well - serve to unite kids for a common cause which can only be achieved through loyalty, mutual trust, respect, and support. This also sounds a little like churches and various civic and political organizations doesn't it? People within these groups unite for the same reasons, but generally with less detrimental consequences. Keep in mind there are many different kinds of gangs to which many of us belong, sometimes for the same reasons as the "gang members". Take a little time to review the following lists of what the families of these kids have to offer compared to what the gangs have to offer. Picture a kid standing in the middle of these two lists and try to understand how easy it is for many kids to turn to gangs as the only alternative and hope for what limited future they believe they can count on anyway. Pay particular attention to the numerous factors in the "family" list (Appendix P) which are based outside of the home/family context. Then pay attention to the appeal of a gang subculture (Appendix Q) relative to the open defiance of arrogance and ignorance, not authority, and see how drastically the scales are tipped against the kids from these kinds of environments and with these kinds of complicating factors.

Within these lists I have tried to include factors that are relative to kids from any level of socioeconomic status. I think at times people arrogantly and ignorantly believe many of the factors on the "family" side of the list only apply to those from the lower socioeconomic levels of society. Furthermore, I think kids act out differently relative to their class status, if for no other reason than the simple fact that money plays an important part in the choices they make. Kids from all levels/classes drink and use drugs, while kids from higher income levels are less likely to steal in order to drink and use, unless they do so just for the "rush". Also kids with more money available to them are likely to have cars and better clothes, as well as better living conditions all the way around. Therefore, the issues for middle to upper class kids relative to acting out are more likely to be from a self-indulgent stance of privilege and reckless abandon, especially when the adults in a kid's immediate environment are not very involved in the life of the kid.

Two of the most significant factors for kids who act out are the lack of parental supervision, and the lack of various positive things to do. This again, is especially true for kids from lower socioeconomic levels. Families in higher socioeconomic levels can provide a greater variety of activities, but may not provide any better supervision or involvement in the lives of kids than families at other levels. In other words, money and privilege are very significant factors in determining both the ways kids act out, and the motivation to act out.

Ironically, one of the most positive aspects of my childhood years was the role the church played in providing activities. While I do not agree with the religious beliefs I was taught along with the activities, I am very grateful for the fact I had something to do as a kid. The church we went to had numerous music programs, recreational and social activities, and weekend retreats. However, the church was so far removed from reality and so afraid of losing control over its members, especially the younger ones, by having us exposed to the temptations from the devil/world (interchangeable terms). Because of these factors as I grew older I found no value in many of the lessons I was taught and left the church because of its very narrow minded perspective. However, as a child I am grateful for the opportunity to have been privy to the privileges associated with group membership. In my job I am reluctant to refer kids to churches because of my fear of the damage which can be done in the name of God to an already abused kid. This is the reason for my appeal to churches and religious organizations to focus more on common Spirituality than on particular religious dogma arrogantly and deceptively based in a need to control the minds and lives of members.

One other positive experience for me was my membership in Boy Scouts of America. I was very active in a scout troop, reaching the rank of Eagle Scout and becoming a member of the Order of the Arrow. This organization also provided me with many opportunities to participate in activities which would not have been available to me otherwise. God knows my family didn't do much together constituting anything fun or pleasant. I looked forward each year to summer camp and to the weekend camping trips we would take to various sites. Actually I have many fond memories of my years as a Boy Scout. It is too bad kids nowadays think of such associations as being for nerds and schoolboys.

Another tremendous factor for me during my childhood was the fact my siblings and I always had adult supervision. My mother didn't work and my maternal grandmother lived with us and was usually around to cover when our parents were unavailable. Often times the supervision by my parents was too strict and amounted to control simply for the sake of control. However, it limited our opportunities to get into trouble. I know I would have acted out more than I did if I had not been so closely monitored. The same was true for other kids in my neighborhood who had the same or similar types of supervision. The ones who didn't have this factor were known as the troublemakers in the area.

Probably the only other valuable life lesson I learned as a child was the sense of a work ethic, along with an appreciation and respect for the things I worked to obtain with regards to both material gains and to other kinds of goals and aspirations. My dad always made it very clear that no one owes us anything, and that anything worth having is worth working for and waiting for with respect to short term vs. long term gains. Looking back I can see how my dad believed a family works together and shares the responsibility for making things work out. After all, he grew up in a fairly large family, with everyone working together to run a small farm and fight against poverty and hardship due to the times and to irresponsibility on the part of their father. I only wish my dad could have tempered and balanced these principles with a sense of fairness and gentleness which he lacked. Perhaps I could have appreciated him more as my father if he had worked through, rather than acted out, his unresolved issues from the past.

I am emphasizing here the important elements from an era which has passed – along with a few positive elements such as opportunity, togetherness, and values. I see these factors missing for all of the kids with whom I work as a result of the changes occurring during the past fifty plus years. Many of these changes have been very positive, and I would never even suggest a return to the past. I am simply waiting and hoping for people to find a way to incorporate the good elements from the past with the reality of today's world and people. I sometimes wonder where we would be today if the focus in the past had not been so out of balance relative to perspectives on power and domination. If the focus continues to shift more to equality and appreciation for diversity, we will likely begin to incorporate more of the positive aspects from the past without actually returning to or holding onto the past as many conservative groups would have us do as a society. This would only be a repetition of the previous mistakes, and would serve to indicate very clearly our inability to learn from our historical errors.

I firmly believe the kids who fall into the underdog category act out in reaction to emotion-based anxiety created by the FLAGS. At the other extreme of the spectrum from privileged to "privilege-less", I believe those kids who fall into the former category act out based in arrogance and ignorance. The higher each of us moves up on the scale, the more difficulty we have relating to the struggles of those behind us. We tend to forget what it feels like to feel bad, at least until we begin to recognize the empty existence we created with our exclusive pursuit of material happiness. At that point we as adults often begin to act out our own emotion-based anxiety which results from the FLAGS created by our own greed and failure to accomplish those things which are truly important. At the other extreme are those adults who never really try to accomplish anything positive, dragging the past with them every step of the way. These are the ones who seek to bring everyone around them down to the same level of misery and hopelessness. These are the ones who play the role of victim or victimizer, or some combination of both. If nothing else, I hope this book will help each of us pinpoint where we are within these lists and spectrums. I hope each of us will then seek the solutions we need to resolve the unfinished business from the past, and work to heal the relationships to ourselves and to others which have suffered and/or have been destroyed as a result.

One of the most significant aspects in the lives of kids who are actually underdogs is the concept of survival. When kids lack appropriate role models they are left to their own devices relative to figuring out how to negotiate their journey through life. Because these kids are also acting out their emotion-based anxiety created by and within all of the contexts in which abuse and victimization can occur, they are going to make many seriously negative unconscious choices – unconscious in the sense they are unaware of the motivation (FLAGS) fueling these choices. For those sitting on the sidelines who do not know or understand the need simply to survive on a day to day basis, we have no right to judge or even make decisions or suggestions relative to what should be done with these kids. Talk with and listen to people like me who work in the trenches so to speak and have a good read on realities as they exist in the lives of many.

Let's go back for a moment to my belief in the transient opportunity to help kids turn their lives around. Remember my explanation of the behaviors of kids being more temporary compared to the behaviors of adults which tend to be more permanent and more truly a representation of whom they are. It is much more difficult to separate what adults do from who they are as people relative to personality characteristics. Even the kids I work with are able to recognize the differences between themselves and the adults they see. I agree with the need for strict penalties for adults who are serious repeat offenders of violent crimes relative to issues of parole and early release programs. Again I base this position in my belief it is much more difficult for adults to change habitual behaviors than it is for kids. Ironically two of my kids who are serving lengthy prison sentences write to me about their desire to learn and grow in prison. This clearly reflects the work we did together with them telling me they wish they had really taken my efforts and words to heart. Both of these guys are studying to become psychologists in prison and plan to make a difference within institutional settings in the lives of fellow inmates. My influence is even passed on and into higher levels of confinement. This is why it is so important for us to pour all of our efforts into giving young offenders the opportunities which will help them to avoid creating permanent ways of acting out. If kids must be confined they must also receive very positive and effective attention and interventions from adults who understand, and who lack hidden agendas, and who will give them the insight they need into the principles I am writing about in this book. Too many adults within juvenile justice agencies follow the "might-makes-right" approach of control, domination, and the breaking of wills and spirits.

Survival refers to our ability to exist on the planet and to fend for ourselves. For most of us as children we took for granted there would be those around us to provide for our survival needs. Kids who grow up in contexts where neglect, deprivation, and unpredictability are commonplace will not be able to take such things for granted. One of the saddest things for me is to hear a kid locked up in juvenile hall talk about how much better he or she feels compared to living in a destructive home/family environment, and/or out on the streets. For many kids confinement is a reprieve from the daily hassles and uncertainties of trying to survive in an unsafe and unfriendly world. They talk of the fact that while being confined everything, including structure, is provided for them.

I know that in many cases it is necessary to confine kids who break laws and are dangerous to themselves and to others from a criminal perspective. However, I do not see the merit in using this strictly as an opportunity to punish without also seizing the opportunity to teach and divert or redirect energy and effort. This can only be accomplished by fully incorporating effective and appropriate mental health services and interventions into the mix delivered only by well-trained professionals knowledgeable and successful in working with this population. For now the lack of properly screened and trained staff are the biggest tragedies and travesties within juvenile detention facilities, placement facilities, and departments of juvenile probation and parole. When my kids get locked up, for many of them it is the first time in a long time they have felt reasonably safe. It also may be the first time they have been able to get clean and sober from all substances. All of these factors together create an incredible opportunity to do some very intensive work to resolve the FLAGS, and to teach kids self control by modeling and teaching appropriate means of coping with and facing life.

Unfortunately the kids in these settings encounter more of the same kinds of ignorant arrogance and need to control from staff members and various legal system staff which they experienced at the hands of family members and adults in other contexts. Therefore, the opportunity to help many of these kids is lost because of the lack of awareness of the real needs and issues of these kids. As I visit with the kids in juvenile hall who are referred to me prior to being locked up, I have other kids who will ask who I am and why they are not allowed to talk with me as well. It is hard for me to explain to them the reality that the "system" is not set up to accommodate them and meet that need. I believe there is not a single juvenile offender who doesn't need and wouldn't benefit from an opportunity to speak with a qualified, well-trained mental health professional, unless of course a kid is severely impaired either mentally or developmentally. Kids are starved for positive interaction with caring adults.

Unfortunately, those in positions of political and social power and authority are more concerned about pleasing their constituents than with the real need of helping kids turn their lives around. People on the outside see kids according to the labels they use to define and identify them. This is clearly another example of arrogance and imbalance at the expense of the kids who need our help and attention. These people tend to be older, arrogant European Americans who have money and who also hold onto the outdated views of kids simply needing to be controlled and taught a lesson. When will people learn that to teach a lesson requires compassion and unconditional regard not further abuse and victimization? When will adults, especially older adults, take responsibility for the selfish and destructive choices they have made which have created the environments leading to such destruction? When will adults realize the need for honest self-examination and rectification relative to improving the dynamics and levels of dysfunction existing at all levels and in all contexts? Until these changes are made and the ignorance, arrogance and selfishness are acknowledged and eliminated none of the needed changes will take place quickly enough to stop the loss of kids to ever increasing apathy and misunderstanding.

I even agree to some extent with proposals being presented to decriminalize drugs, consensual sex, gambling, and any other currently identified criminal act which causes little or no harm to others. I believe we need laws that protect others, especially kids, from being victimized by irresponsible acts committed against them. However, I do not agree at all with the attempts to legislate morality. Again, these are issues based in politics and money. Think about how much money is wasted on investigating, prosecuting, and punishing offenders of victimless crimes. These are issues which get politicians elected and provide jobs for people who feel the need to control and dictate how others should live their lives. The monies in the budgets of agencies fighting victimless crimes could be spent more effectively and less wastefully through prevention and diversion programs other than confinement and incarceration. Redirection and support services should be critical components of any programs related to juvenile and young adult offenders. Programs could be developed even using my RFLAGS Model and related concepts to teach the need for internal control based in self-respect, mutual regard, and higher standards of living for both juvenile and adult offenders.

While we are in the process of trying to balance the scales with personal responsibility, open and honest self-examination, and rectification, why not throw everything possible into the pot that needs to be balanced. Laws do not stop people who engage in behaviors where there are no victims. If anything, the laws create many more opportunities to break other laws and increase criminal activity where there are victims as in illegal drug trade and its associated violence. It would be better in my opinion to use the money spent fighting victimless crimes to teach people the art of balancing their choices in connection with the lives of everyone else.

I am surprised how many of my former beliefs and opinions have changed having now witnessed firsthand the problems facing people who fall into the categories of kids with whom I work professionally. Gangs and other criminal factions will only be diminished when the scales in all contexts are finally balanced and tempered with mutual respect, unconditional regard and a true awareness of the interconnectedness of each of us relative to our places in the world. By coming to understand the survival needs of most of the kids I identify as underdogs I have been able to open my heart and mind to alternative ways of viewing and interpreting the world and the people in it. I no longer feel contempt for others except as it relates to ignorant arrogance people take pride in, and any mistreatment of people and especially of kids. Hopefully the day is coming where others like me will take a stand against the so-called norms and fight to correct the wrongs being perpetuated. The only victims of many behaviors are the persons acting out the FLAGS - those who truly learn to perpetuate their history of victimization acted out upon them from external sources and turning it inward and against themselves rather than resolving the issues from the past.

CHAPTER X

Pairing and Parenting: The Basics

I want to spend a little more time in this chapter focusing on the changes which have taken place in the last 50+ years. Beginning with World War II let's consider how the "family" constellation has changed from the standard two parents model- working dad and homemaker mom - to an almost total lack of definition and clarity at this point in time. Remember to think of societal changes as represented by a swinging pendulum that only keeps perfect time when it swings in balance – not too far to the left or to the right. The significance of these changes is extremely important relative to the concepts of pairing and parenting.

You can also picture this idea of a pendulum in what is referred to in statistics as the bell-shaped curve which is exactly what it sounds like. This concept was also identified previously. When graphing statistical data the middle 64% represents whatever is considered to be "normal" for the population or group being studied. From there and out to both the right and the left are areas referred to as the tails of the curve. This simply means that the more people move out from the middle and toward the curves representing the extremes, the more they deviate or stray from the norm. Some degree of deviation is always expected, and even hoped for and useful, depending on the population being studied. The mid range is considered to be the mean or the average, with the lower end of the curve generally representing the less favorable range; and the higher end the most favorable. A good example would be graphed indications of intelligence or IQ.

When thinking in terms of societal standards and conditions it is better to think of the tails or the full range of motion for the pendulum as simply being extremes, with any extremes generally being negative and a clear indication of a lack of adequate balance relative to change. For a clock to run accurately the pendulum must swing to both the right and the left and cannot stay simply in the middle. However if the range of motion is too wide the timing will be off. The same is true in thinking about change on any level regarding the six contexts of home/family, school, community, society, politics, and religion.

Through most of my life I have heard that during World War II women for the first time were literally pulled out of their homes and put to work in factories to support the war effort. Because so many of the men were involved in different military roles, the labor force in this country apparently was reduced to such a low level that women were the only solution. At the end of the war many of these women were sent back into the homes as the men returned to take over the jobs in the factories. In my opinion this exposure to the workplace set the stage for the ultimate struggle by women for equality and recognition which occurred in the 1960's and 1970's. Women were given a chance to see themselves as more than just wives and mothers and I believe many of them returned to their previous roles reluctantly and with a degree of resentment.

With all of the social unrest in the 60's and 70's people realized that the those traditions previously established and taken for granted as reality not only needed to be challenged, but needed to be changed. This was a time of extremes when the pendulum was swinging away from conservative thinking toward much more liberal thinking initially resulting in chaos and confusion often accompanying times of tremendous change. While there have been other times of extreme change throughout history, I believe recent decades to be the most pertinent in the United States to the issues we are still struggling with today. At the same time that many good things came out of the uproar, there were many issues of adjustment, redefining, and acceptance which are still occurring today in the sense of still looking for balance and something representing an agreeable composition of factors.

Along with tremendous improvements in the recognition of basic human rights for all came the fight from conservatives to maintain the status quo. After all, what man wants to give up his position in what was previously a male dominated existence, with all of the privileges associated with being on top as a figure of speech? Suddenly women were burning their bras in public and demanding that they were not only equal to men, they were exactly the same as men. Even some women fought this kind of thinking which today seems to have settled into the range of equality relative to ability and competence, rather than to the idea that men have to stop being men and women have to stop being women. There are differences, associated with gender, which I think are recognized as reality. However, these are limited to more obvious physical characteristics than to any other aspects. Men fought against the ideas of having to become part of all aspects of family life, including sharing roles previously defined as being female. There was an even bigger adjustment to the ideas of having to share the workplace and jobs of leadership and management with what was literally referred to as the "weaker sex".

Having lived in the South during these times of change even into my early adult years, I watched and had to adjust as well to the breakdown of assumed male roles, particularly that of white male privilege. My first job outside of the business world which I left in 1988 was as the only male member of a 16-member crisis evaluation team at a private psychiatric hospital in Georgia. I found out very quickly that these women, including the female supervisor, really weren't interested in giving me my previously assumed birthright of being listened to just by virtue of being white and male. With some time I was able to adjust not only to being a team member rather than the boss, but also to the fact that women generally have different and effective ways of accomplishing established goals. This job also gave me my first opportunity to work closely with African Americans who shared the 11 to 7 night shift with me. Because we worked the night shifts we had a lot of time to sit around and talk when things were quiet on the units. I quickly learned how ignorant I was relative to historical issues for black people, many of which both shocked and shamed me as a white male.

What an incredible time to be alive and become part of a struggle to right the historical wrongs existing in this country for centuries. All of this means that if a poll was conducted today to determine what are considered to be the standards representing the "norms" of today, the issues included in the 64% mid range would be quite different than those of the 1940's and 1950's. All of the wrongs in this country until the current changes were based completely in white European (WASP) arrogance and extremism. It is possible to see how the dominant segment of society during those years did a very poor job of nurturing the healthy development of a new civilization, much the same as parents and other adults are responsible for nurturing the healthy development of children. This again ties into my RFLAGS Model which can also be used to identify how the FLAGS were created for the "underdogs" of the times – and believe me there have been many different "underdog" groups throughout the founding and development of what became the United States of America. The RFLAGS Model also helps to identify and explain how these groups who were abused and victimized for so long developed the FLAGS which created the emotion-based anxiety still being acted out today as the pendulum continues to search for the balanced range of motion.

One of the most serious results of the social unrest of the 60's and 70's was the breakdown of a traditional family structure, but with nothing to replace it that could insure the stability of families for the sake of kids and adults alike. For the first time, however, there were laws enacted making child abuse illegal, thereby giving kids the first opportunity to even speak out and seek protection for themselves. Also, in recent years there have been new laws enacted against domestic violence and elder/dependent abuse. However, nationally there are no consistently enforced laws to guard against domestic violence, with the only known deterrent to on going abuse seemingly being the incarceration of the abuser, which can be both male and female.

Many times I have had male/female couples in my office talking about issues of domestic violence. There is still a desire on the part of some women to be seen as victims in order to gain sympathy and control, especially in circumstances of divorce/separation, and domestic violence. However, more and more I am seeing trends where the females are the perpetrators of the violence and the cause of the breakdown of relationships, and yet only focus on how they are still being victimized by playing the "weaker sex" card.

In one particular case a woman came into my office with a bruise on her face. Her tearful telling of the story of her victimization stopped when her 13-year-old son told her to tell me how she was the one who always attacked his dad first. The kid went on to tell me of mom's history of hitting, kicking, biting, ripping dad's clothing, insulting his masculinity, pushing, and cussing toward dad with this being the only time dad ever got mad and hit her. Mom got really angry with her son and with me as I confronted her on her behaviors. I assured her it is equally as wrong for women to become violent as it is for men. It is often more dangerous for women given the fact men in general are physically stronger than most women; but it is also wrong for women to provoke rage in others. I told her I was surprised this was the first time in their 20 year marriage he ever got physical with her given her history of assaulting him repeatedly and regularly. She was rather insulted and indignant about all of this, trying hard to hold onto the fact I should see her as a victim. I simply told her that in her case of domestic violence the process would likely stop if she would stop provoking her husband's rage.

I met with her husband the next week and listened to him cry about how bad he felt about hitting her. While I let him know that I do not condone his act of violence, I assured him that I hold everyone to that standard regardless of gender or age. He told me his wife had refused to come with him that week and he thought it was funny when I told him how I had confronted her on her history of assaulting him. He felt like he got support and could see that his self-restraint had actually lasted longer than it might have for most. Both parents reported later that the violence had stopped, with mom able to see how she had actually provoked it over the years. They clearly understood that I was against the actions of both of them. If her son hadn't been sitting there to speak up in defense of his dad, I would likely have never known the truth as the dad admitted being embarrassed about being attacked by his wife and probably would not have told me.

The chances are that many of the cases of domestic violence against men and perpetrated by women go unreported or are under reported. I know of times when both parties were equally responsible for the situation of domestic violence and only the man was arrested in spite of his obvious injuries. Women and men both need to press charges against abusive partners and stick by their right to do so, especially if they have no intention of ending the relationship. Domestic violence is one of the most frustrating issues to deal with professionally as women generally won't leave abusive relationships, sometimes for a number of valid reasons. However, even with tremendous sources of support they still refuse to see the reality that such abuse is likely going to continue. Perhaps laws should change so that any parties involved in domestic violence are arrested and prosecuted equally, with incarceration seeming to be the only deterrent to continued violence. When I left the state of California at the end of 2004, efforts were being made to make domestic violence reportable if there are kids in the home. Soon this is likely to be added nationwide to the list of mandated reports already dealing with other forms of abuse and victimization.

It is important to tie all of these issues to the reality that probably all of these adults are acting out emotion-based anxiety created by the FLAGS. With a history of previous abuse/victimization the current levels of violence are likely as bad as or worse than in the past. This is where it is possible to see how someone who has been abused can continue to be a victim or become a victimizer as well, if not toward the one abusing them, then toward others including children in their care. Sometimes abusive experiences can create FLAGS which never existed from the past. However, people who were not abused during childhood are much less likely to take abuse, or allow it to continue with someone in adulthood.

With the tremendous rise in the divorce rate since the 1970's came a huge number of other issues way beyond the scope and intent of this book. So at this point I only want to address the changes in relationships and in our reasons for trying to pair up with another. A huge motivator for pairing is the reality of loneliness no one wants to feel. However, the reasons for getting and staying married have changed from historical survival issues to really trying to pair up based on romantic love and some sense of mutual purpose in life.

I am not sure where the term TLC (Tender Loving Care) originated, but I find it useful in trying to identify factors which could at least increase the probability of successful pairings between consenting adults. In my search for meaningful and useful ways to teach different concepts I have come up with what I call the "TLC's" representing at least some of the minimum requirements before anyone should even consider a relationship as long-term. Obviously in my use of these letters the two most important elements are Trust and Love. From there I am amazed at how many of the other elements all start with the letter "C". My list includes:

Compatibility	Consideration	Communication
Commitment	Compromise	Competence
Compassion	Concern	Comfort
Connection	Caressing	Caring
Coping	Control (self)	Commonalities
Continuity	Companionship	Comradery
Change	Choices	Consistency
Contingency	Character	Charm

While there are others, such as respect, which start with different letters of the alphabet, these are a good place to begin, especially with the concept of compatibility. One of the biggest mistakes I think many people make today is to start out a new relationship sexually, before the two people have a chance to really know about other equally important aspects. Oftentimes, when the sex is good people quickly assume this means we must be in love. It is all too easy to use the "L" word when people are sexually aroused, only to regret it after the lustful passion has again subsided. Love must develop, even if it appears to be a love-at-first-sight experience. While I do believe love-at-first-sight is possible, it doesn't guarantee any hint of success or longevity until the two people have a chance to really get to know each other on all levels.

Perhaps one of the most important indicators of compatibility is the ability to communicate effectively and comfortably. Frequently in the early stages of relationship development couples are able to talk about non-emotional issues presented more as factual and historical information, giving each person a chance to learn personal data and details one about the other. This is a very good time to look for personality characteristics, one of the "C's" I failed to list. The kinds of things you look for through communication, both verbal and non-verbal are issues of reciprocity and goodness of fit relative to the pairing. Look for things like: attentiveness, interest, understanding, appreciation, respect, courtesy (another "C"), comfort level, openness, quirks, emotionality, degree and depth of mutual exchange, intimacy, passion, and all of the other "C's" listed above.

If the communication patterns aren't compatible then nothing else is worth pursuing if looking for intimacy and longevity. One critical factor is the opportunity for each person to be open and honest about thoughts, feelings, desires, and observations. With each of these timing is everything, especially avoiding situations already emotionally charged. Expression of deeper levels of personal aspects should be attempted in such a way as to encourage reciprocal communication and not used as a game to set someone up or try to trap them. If games are the only way you can try to communicate then you really should look at the need to review dynamics from the past and to become aware of the presence of the FLAGS you might be ignoring.

When expressing thoughts, feelings, desires, or observations the use of "I" statements is critical. If the word "you" comes out of your mouth as a primary part of any sentence then you, as the speaker, have set up an offensive situation in which your partner will feel the need to be defensive. This is the pattern most people in all situations use and expect to encounter, so the use of proper communication skills will take some time to adjust to, but should be practiced and maintained. As long as you are only saying what "I" think, feel, want, or see then any defensiveness from the other person will clearly be their problem and a by-product of their own baggage since your intentions are only to communicate and not play games or offend.

I would urge each reader to find a good book about communication and really study it with a partner. This is a major stumbling block for most people. Intention behind all communication is important and should be conscious and well thought out. Always make certain you honestly know what your intentions are before you attempt to say anything important. Then choose the right approach; wait for, rather than try to create "the right moment", and then trust yourself and breathe as you speak. Stay relaxed and non-aggressive even if your partner reacts negatively. The inability of your partner to deal with reasonable, open, honest, non-threatening communications is a huge sign of incompatibility if it happens with any even slight hint of regularity.

It isn't possible to be satisfied or grow within the context of any kind of relationship where communication is not possible and constructive. This is true of couples and for couples who are or may become parents. Open, constructive communication about parenting issues is the only way to ever hope to be effective in raising kids. Appropriate and effective communication is equally important in all of the contexts outside of the home/family context. Listen to how offensive many approaches are toward communication, oftentimes setting up cycles of competition, and of defense and offense even between parents and kids, or just between adults and kids in other contexts. Competition should be limited to sports and real games. Just listen to world leaders, politicians, and corporate executives who get nowhere in their efforts to communicate especially when each participant is pissing in the other's ears and calling it rain water – a Southern colloquialism. Everyone could really benefit from studying and practicing the "art" of communication.

One last important factor is to express intimate and/or sensitive subject matter without the expectation of what a response, rather than a reaction, will be. It is okay to have the hope of what a response will be. However, in all situations and contexts expectations limit the range of possible responses the other party or parties are free to make. If the hoped for response isn't received then it is possible your feelings, observations, and statements were unreasonable, unrealistic, or simply incorrect. The only other possible explanation is the indication of serious incompatibility issues. If your efforts to communicate are positive, reasonable, and correct then you could consider factors such as insensitivity, rigidity, and uncompromising as possible personality characteristics of your partner. If whatever you expressed was critically important to you and unchangeable then the relationship is doomed. Remember relationships end simply because partners are incompatible, not because one or the other is good or bad; right or wrong. It just means both of you made the wrong choices in trying to establish a relationship. If ending it is necessary try to do so amicably. Also, make sure your study of communication includes a segment of effective and appropriate patterns of communication between adults and kids. Basically, don't do anything different with kids than you should do in communicating with other adults. The only difference is that with kids, sometimes "no" just means "no".

For a sense of familiarity and comfort to develop and evolve, the two people must be willing to risk being emotionally intimate and vulnerable in addition to the vulnerability associated with sex. This requires both people be fully dressed, unaroused sexually, and even around friends or family members as a test of sincerity. At that time if they can still look each other in the eye and say not only do I love you, I also like who you are, there is an indication of something real and more than just lust. If the idea ever comes to mind that the other person "would be really nice if…," then it is time to run like hell, as this is an indication you don't really like who the person is currently. At that moment you are literally thinking they would be really nice if they were someone other than who you sense them to be. This process is frequently unconscious, but should not be overlooked, as it is clearly a red flag that you and this individual are probably not compatible. Many times people who have FLAGS from abusive backgrounds are motivated to join in a relationship to either change or otherwise rescue an individual. This is not a reason to become involved romantically with anyone.

For many of the years prior to my study and work in the field of psychology and the "helping professions", I had a clear unconscious tendency to look for people who needed to be rescued, believing that if I just loved them enough they would change just for me. How foolish! However, with my role during childhood and within my family as caretaker and rescuer of my mom, I was simply following the only means I had ever learned relative to trying and having my emotional needs met. At times my actions would unfortunately result in favorable outcomes, not enough to make it worth the effort, but enough to make it seem so and, thereby, reinforce the approach.

As I took my first job at the psychiatric hospital I mentioned earlier, I realized I could get paid to take care of others. Please don't misunderstand me. There is nothing wrong with taking of care others *unless* that is your only way of trying to get your own unfulfilled needs met. If this characteristic is as strong a part of your personality as it was for me, then consider finding a job which will allow you to fulfill this important need. You can then look for people in your personal life who can meet you on balanced and equal ground in their ability to provide the same service to you as needed. A failure to recognize this aspect of your personality will result in a lifetime of disappointment and wasted efforts toward establishing and maintaining any healthy and satisfying adult relationships. However, before you join one of the so-called helping professions, make sure all of your personal issues related to limits and boundaries have been completely identified and addressed. A failure to do so will result in a tendency to take responsibility for your clients and even to become inappropriately involved in their lives. Work on yourself first before, or at least while you are training relative to assisting and guiding others professionally.

All too often I see this need to be a caregiver as a motivating factor for people to pair up. This coupled with the mistaken notion that because the sex is good we must be in love, sets up both parties for misery and failure. Remember, seeking out unhealthy and unproductive relationships is one way I have identified through which people tend to act out the emotion-based anxiety created by the FLAGS. This doesn't mean there is something wrong with you. It simply means there is something wrong with where you have come from, not having had the opportunity historically to experience what love and healthy relationships involve. With this in mind it is easy to see that since there is nothing wrong with you, the matter simply becomes that of undoing the past misperceptions. It is then important to seek out and learn new approaches and patterns which can lead to successful outcomes in relationships and in other areas of your life as well. All too often I see people unknowingly wasting precious energy trying to make something work which is doomed before the effort ever begins, given the reality of there being no chance of succeeding at something inevitably impossible. Rather than continue making the same mistakes, seek help in finding ways to channel the energy into something which can hopefully yield a favorable result.

I am always amazed at the rationalizations adolescents use in deciding to pair and/or become parents. Ironically, their reasons are often no more futile or absurd than the reasons and justifications of their adult counterparts. When I talk with kids about sexual activity between males and females, I ask both genders to make sure the person they are having sexual intercourse with is the person they would want to be the parent of their child if something goes wrong and pregnancy results. Most of the time both kids and adults admit they aren't even thinking about that possibility, and would generally answer the questions with a "no". And yet many of these individuals continue to take this risk and are then surprised when the female of the pair gets pregnant.

It is time for everyone to get their heads out of the sand and address obstacles interfering with the opportunities of educators to teach all of these aspects and concepts of sex and sexuality to teenagers. This should be done at least by the eighth grade, and then again during high school as kids gain a higher level of emotional maturity and development. For instance, I am no longer invited to go into high school classrooms and talk only about mental health issues in a required health class because the process required by schools to approve the presentation and then get permission from the parents for their kids to participate is too complicated. The religious issues and other sources of ignorance and stupidity need to be identified and challenged in an effort to be realistic about human nature. Discussions about sexuality do not encourage sexual behavior. In fact health professionals tell me that honest, open discussions and presentations generally make kids hold off longer before they become sexually active. I know this is one of my treatment goals with kids on a one-to-one basis.

With pairing and parenting as such significant issues, it is totally irresponsible on the parts of adults not to allow their kids to make fully informed decisions about issues in their lives, including any form of sexuality, which they have to face anyway. This denial and resistance only leads to kids gaining a lot of misinformation and therefore, making serious mistakes affecting them in many cases for the rest of their lives. Recently I learned that kids believed for a while that a popular soft drink killed sperm either by boys drinking it or by girls douching with it after sex. Another serious yet common misperception is that smoking even a small amount of marijuana reduces a male's sperm count to zero. Kids fail to see the absurdity in these beliefs. Furthermore, by refusing to provide complete educational information regarding sexual issues no one is really thinking about the children born into situations where the parents aren't even able to care for themselves yet, much less for a child. This is no less true for adults than for the kids I work with constantly.

Because parents often fail to address sexuality and other sexual issues at home I do so as part of my professional role as a psychologist when it is appropriate to do so. While I approach sexual topics differently with boys than I do with girls, I still make sure the same information is conveyed. The only time I ever gave a condom to a young female who asked me for one, her mom discovered it. When mom was told that I had given the condom to her daughter, rather than address this issue she reported me to the principal and I almost lost my job at a training sight as a result. When the mother called me I told her my policy was to simply make kids aware that I had condoms available if they were either sexually active or even considering it as an option. Kids had to ask me for a condom to even get one. I suggested the mom go and ask her daughter why she wanted the condom and have a responsible discussion as a parent with her daughter, rather than try to blame me for a decision I had tried to talk her daughter out of making. That was my first and last time to give condoms to girls. Ironically, when parents find their sons with condoms, even if there is some concern, there is generally no big uproar, and the parents readily accept my reasoning and suggestion that it is time to have a responsible parental conversation with their sons. I never ask a kid to lie to a parent, even if it means I may get confronted. I do, however, limit my risk of confrontation by making sure it will be worth whatever issue I will ultimately have to defend. I tell all kids that, like it or not, girls can get pregnant and boys can't.

Take a few moments to go back and reread the vow I presented and proposed at the end of Chapter VI. Really take it to heart as you think about what an awesome and even overwhelming role it is to become a parent. Not enough people put a great deal of thought into what parenting means, given the fact that the role is a lifetime biological commitment, even if the parent role is abandoned on an emotional level. All too often the decision to become parents is made solely for the sake of the individuals about to become pregnant, and not for the sake of the child who will be the result. Such thoughts prior to conception should include a strong emphasis on the preparedness of the individuals to even consider taking on the responsibility, especially when you remember that much of the outcome for that child depends on their qualifications for the job as parents.

This is why it is so critical for people everywhere in other adult roles and with other adult responsibilities for the well being and welfare of kids in addition to parenting, to review the respective lists of unquestionable obligations. I am addressing those responsible for educating and training the very ones who will likely someday make the choice to become parents. A major part of the purpose for writing this book is to offer materials which will be useful in sharing and teaching these concepts to adolescents in middle and high school settings, as well as for adults, even those who are already parents, regardless of age. Something has to be done now to address the responsibility many adults and adults as leaders ignore relative to the world conditions being created in the present for future generations. Adults in all settings need to be held accountable for any failure to honor their obligation to assist children in all arenas and aspects of life. Within contexts outside the home/family a thorough assessment of possible short term and long term outcomes should be conducted before decisions are ever made and implemented. This kind of approach should at least make adults in positions of power and authority stop and think about the impact their actions will have on future generations. Even indirectly we are all paired up with kids regardless of our roles.

Some of this will actually take a great deal of courage and determination if educators and other professionals are to stand up to threats and intimidation blocking their ability to do their jobs of preparing kids to face life as productive adults. People have become too easily scared off by litigation every time someone doesn't like the way things are done given that issues being challenged are being handled appropriately. Obvious publicized mistakes associated with many forms of religious extremism suggest it is time to limit the ability of organized religion to influence and direct the lives of people "paired" professionally with kids and given the responsibility of guiding them into and through life. This is especially true for people who need to be trained in some cases to think for themselves, rather than simply accept and believe everything they are told as long as the word "God" is attached to it.

When any society reaches a point where people are afraid to face realities of everyday living because of domination and misinformation provided by leaders, it is time for some of us to be brave enough to challenge the apathy and passivity facilitating these injustices. Perhaps it is time to get lawmakers at all levels to stop or at least limit the lawsuits clearly blocking progress in the fields of education. Reasonable guidelines are needed, but because education and even the legal systems have become so political, no one knows where to turn or how to act because of a fear of offending even one small group. This is especially true if the term "faith-based" is connected to any group.

When the complaints and opposition of a few block effective and appropriate pairing of adults and kids, I say "SCREW 'EM"! Let those few who cause the greatest amount of opposition retreat to the islands of fantasy created by the groups who dominate their minds and lives for the restricted and biased forms of education they seek. It is obvious that many of these small, yet vocal groups are holding everyone sway in our efforts to move forward. These groups should be forced to be as self-sufficient as they are self-serving, and made to get out of the way for the rest of us who want more than their narrow minded ways. The problem is that many adults are still afraid the "wrath of God" might be real and that we all run the risk of hell if the conservative groups are right. It is time to step up to the plate and establish a means of educating everyone which addresses the real issues of today including a need to understand true adult roles and responsibilities.

With regard to pairing and parenting it is time to address the foolishness with which people in many parts of the world fight for the right to occupy lands, and thereby, people. A piece of land designated in some former time as "sacred" for various groups of people who were each supposedly and reportedly chosen by God to possess the land at all costs does not justify killing each other in order to occupy any territory. Who are we kidding? Where are their gods in all of this? It is so true that many of the atrocities being carried out around the world appear to be based in centuries of hatred and prejudice created, justified, and perpetuated by organized religions. Let it go! Give the lands back to God and share them equally, educating our children about man's inhumanity to man. What good is a concept of divinity that is used to justify murder and other horrific acts of abuse and victimization? We need to identify those issues, such as oil, holding captive different parts of the world and use the technologies already available to free ourselves from such entrapments. People always tend to focus on the more obvious surface behaviors, mistakenly identified as issues, as being the real problems, when in reality the issues fueling the observable behaviors go much deeper and are based in FLAGS and outrageous histories of abuse and victimization. Children are always the most vulnerable in these situations and need to be protected through the healthy pairing with adults acting as parental figures and leaders who care and understand the results of abuse and victimization. This kind of aggression mentioned above is as futile as the gangs fighting over turf in local communities they don't even own.

Pairing and parenting are so much more global than to be seen only as traditional and limiting concepts relative to and restricted to certain contexts and regions. Sometimes leaders as parental figures need to pair properly with others who share the same goals for the common good of everyone, and especially for children who cannot protect and defend themselves. This would result in an effort to unite victims, including the United States and other nations vulnerable to oil-based economies against those trying to abuse and victimize us by keeping us dependent. How foolish is it for us to allow any world leader to try scaring and punishing others by cutting off supplies to anything when we have the means to make ourselves independent. For countries truly dependent on outside support such sanctions can be effective in bringing about compliance. But, how stupid is it for leading nations to allow for such vulnerability when we have the capabilities to avoid it by ending the competition and decreasing exposure to dependency.

These are clearly some of the same tactics used within societal, political, and religious contexts as well. Until all adults are held accountable for our own allowance for entrapment and restrictions on many aspects of our lives, then how can we effectively teach proper adult roles and responsibilities to successive generations? We must at the same time make every effort to protect children around the world and in every context, including home/family, from continuing to be, or becoming victims as a result of vulnerability created by adults. This is where the innocence of children is so obvious. All you need to do is turn on the television to see the suffering of children everywhere who cannot escape vulnerable situations created by adults. This is true even in countries not so blatantly torn apart by war, street violence, and other acts of terrorism. Imagine again how much worse all of this is in the contexts outside of the home/family context if things aren't even stable and psychologically/emotionally healthy in the home and with family members.

Basically we will need three approaches to correcting the wrongs at all levels. The first is that of interventions aimed at recognizing and changing errors currently being made by adults, to include the concepts of leaders within all contexts as having this kind of inclusion as well. Secondly, interventions must be aimed at helping kids and adults from all walks of life heal from the wounds of abuse and victimization caused by the pendulums swinging out of control in numerous contexts and relative to numerous issues around the world. Finally, given the fact that all of these issues are world issues, and the indications that the RFLAGS Model and related concepts are internationally applicable, we must begin to implement and teach as prevention the appropriate and effective utilization and practice of adult/leader roles and responsibilities as a way of protecting future generations from abuse and victimization. In other words it is time to identify, rectify, and learn from enormous errors which keep being repeated throughout history. What is the point in history if not to learn from previous mistakes from every level including personal/individual to more global and philosophical applications on much larger scales?

Pairing and parenting apply to the proper match between leaders and others in positions of power and influence with the people under their domains. As with laws and efforts to protect children in the United States from abuse, effective world leaders have an obligation to work together to stop acts of terrorism which abuse and victimize countless numbers of innocent people. Sometimes, as with consequences for child abuse, abusive leaders in any capacity must be held accountable for the acts of victimization and be punished. This also applies to leaders within the corporate systems. The process of then helping the victims of abuse and horrific acts of violence and injustice becomes a humbling experience of assuming roles as effective leaders who can guide and teach in an effort to heal and rectify. This cannot be done out of arrogance and must be done relative to the realities of the people being assisted, and must be done altruistically. The concept of teaching people to fish rather than giving them a fish clearly applies. Much chaos and conflict is likely to erupt initially, but with the right planning, preparation, methods and efforts eventually pendulums can swing in perfect balance.

Chapter XI
Breaking the Cycles

So far we have looked at a number of issues and different segments of the RFLAGS Model and its components. One of the things we identified is the concept of loss associated with dysfunctional backgrounds relative to abuse and victimization. I have referred to a process of unresolved grief associated with these losses and the resulting FLAGS. Because grief is so often only connected with issues of death and dying, I want to help each reader identify grief as it applies to more non-traditional losses. You might want to refer back to Chapter VI and to the list of losses associated with dysfunctional backgrounds. Also keep in mind the complicating factors making people vulnerable, with the higher number of complicating factors correlating directly to the degree of unresolved grief.

As I indicated earlier some of these unresolved issues can go relatively unnoticed until some traumatic or otherwise significant event triggers an overreaction to a given life situation, or even to some phase of development associated with change. I sat in a seminar a few years ago in which the presenter was talking about some of the same topics I am addressing, specifically applicable to adolescents. He kept using the phrase "for no apparent reason", repeatedly implying that sometimes kids do things without obvious cause or motivation. I was surprised that he never attempted to even suggest what some of these non-apparent reasons might be, so I want to address this issue here.

In both my personal and professional experiences I have come to believe that all behavior is purposeful, even if the purposes are unconscious in nature. The only exception might be relative to those behaviors associated with severe forms of mental or physical illness which are not only unconscious, but also often beyond the control of the individual so impaired. All too frequently people simply observe behavior and accept it as not only the problem, but also as the only issue requiring attention and remedy. This is so far from the truth and so widespread that I find such thinking to be alarming. Sure, in a crisis situation where problematic behaviors are life threatening then the behaviors have to be the sole focus until the person is restored to some reasonable degree of emotional stability. Once this is accomplished then the most difficult part of the process is to identify and resolve the underlying emotions which create emotion-based anxiety/depression resulting in feelings of hopelessness/ helplessness and the need to act out the physical state which feels so bad. This is where the idea originates of knowing how bad it feels to feel bad.

The first step in the process of working through underlying issues is to help people break the automatic cycle of acting out rather than facing the FLAGS. For adults the need to act out will usually be so completely habitual and automatic as to be beyond the conscious awareness of the individual. With older kids it is generally possible to take them back in conscious memory to a time when the acting out behaviors started and to a point where they can begin to relate specific events and emotions to the resulting changes in behavior. Like I said it is much easier to work with kids before they actually develop personality disorders in early adulthood. These disorders are defined and identified as well established, unconscious patterns of maladaptive behavior intended to ease the unresolved grief and stop the bad feelings, if only temporarily and/or in an effort to escape them. The fact there is nothing wrong with us is grounded in the fact that these maladaptive behaviors develop in childhood in an effort to cope with abuse and victimization. In most cases the number of and degree of ineffective coping behaviors observable in adulthood correlate directly to the degree of abuse and victimization experienced in childhood.

One of the best ways to help people identify maladaptive behaviors is to help them identify the ways in which their lives are out of control and the degree to which their lives are complicated. From there it is possible to identify specific actions they are taking which only serve to keep the vicious cycles of complicating factors in motion and even at times increasing. As people begin to see how their lives are out of control and are able to see that nothing they are currently trying to use as remedies or solutions are working, they can then begin to realize that the same effort being wasted in futile attempts to resolve issues can be put to better use. The way to help people realize they are not to blame is to help them recognize the underlying desire to make their lives better and more balanced. It is then possible to help those people begin looking at the FLAGS and to begin seeing how these are connected to the past. The best indication of the existence of a history of abuse and victimization is to have a person try and imagine what would be a reasonable reaction or response by others to the life circumstances they are facing. If the reactions they are having are more extreme than would normally be reasonable then the chances are unresolved issues from the past are fueling their overreactions.

At this point it is time to really begin to help people make real, not imagined connections relative to how the past is living in their present. It isn't necessary to go back and relive the past as I indicated previously; however, it is necessary to identify enough of the details to give the person a clear picture of the enormity of what they may be ignoring. Of utmost importance at this point is to help the individual realize they have been and are doing the best they know how to do; not that it is necessarily the best thing to do, it is simply all they know. The goal is to teach them how to continuously make their "best" better throughout their life process. This emphasizes the fact that it is possible to face all of this and resolve all of the issues to such a point as to begin the process of healing and uncomplicating their lives now and on into the future. This process is intended to help those who recognize their need for professional help is based on two primary reasons: first, because their past is too painful to face alone; and, second, to see that it isn't about them as much as it truly is about where they have come from and what they have been through. This allows the individual to lighten up on themselves and begin to make changes which will lead to a higher standard of living and the resolution of unresolved grief associated with very real looses they have experienced and dismissed as just part of life.

The statement "that's just the way I am" is really a cop out simply because it is sometimes believed to be easier to live miserably than it is to face the past as the source of many of the current ineffective attempts to cope and move forward. The other self-defeating belief is that there is nothing which can be done to change things. While there may be some truth in that statement relative to a few factors such as missed opportunities and other losses which cannot be retrieved, just the awareness that change is possible makes it easier to accept the things which cannot be changed, or at least cannot be changed immediately. Most everyone, and certainly people with extremely intense FLAGS, really should seek out help from a well-trained and highly recommended therapist. Remember, any therapist is being hired by you to help according to your set of actual needs. If you are not simply being resistant to treatment, and the match with a therapist doesn't fit, look for another therapist with whom you feel comfortable and from whom you feel a high level of positive regard. Don't allow fear or denial to stop you from seeking the assistance you need! Also, please don't be afraid to insist they read my book.

As people begin to literally identify all of the things they lost during childhood because of abuse and victimization, even if these only included emotional abuse and emotional neglect, there is a very clear grief response to this reality. The easiest model I have found for understanding grief as a process of recovery is the model presented years ago by Elizabeth Kubler-Ross. The stages of her model are: denial, anger, bargaining, depression, and acceptance. Sometimes people think of the process as being linear. However, anyone who has applied this model to their own process of grief understands that while all of the elements are included, they tend to repeat themselves toward acceptance as the goal. Depending on the significance of the loss and the intensity of the FLAGS, some of these stages can be expected to repeat at different times throughout a lifetime, hopefully less often and less severely with varying degrees of resolution and growth. Acceptance is more along the lines of learning to incorporate the losses in a healthy manner into your history of significant events from which you have learned and grown.

As a side comment, it is a good experience to take the time to sit down and make a chronological list of every significant event that has occurred in your lifetime. Start out by writing down every event, both positive and negative, as quickly as you can remember them. Then go back and put them in order chronologically. This will help you in your therapy and in your life in general. Keep the list and add to it from time to time as you remember or even learn about events and experiences, to include your future experiences and events as well.

It is interesting to me that people often think accepting something means it is also necessary to like whatever it is that is to be accepted. Most things which are grieved are not okay in the sense of being accepted *and* liked. The reality is to simply accept the fact that whatever has happened has happened and needs to be faced and dealt with. Remember as I paraphrased earlier from The Book of Runes, by Ralph Blum: you may not always win in every situation, but you can never lose, because there is always an opportunity to learn something valuable. Many of life's greatest lessons are learned by suffering through, in the sense of going through experiences which are really hard to accept. The successful incorporation of these events and what can be learned from them are immeasurable and build amazing strength and character.

It is critical to help people understand the recovery process from issues associated with a history of abuse and victimization is oftentimes a lifelong process. Realistically, the complicating factors which led to the maladaptive coping styles and influenced the development of the FLAGS and the emotion-based anxiety all occurred during the critical period of childhood. It is unrealistic to think that everything can be resolved overnight. I believe the process of recovery is not the one traditionally used in referring to the process of breaking the cycles of addiction, except as it relates to the physical recovery from damage resulting from such acting out behaviors. Recovery, in my view, is from the underlying factors and FLAGS fueling the desire to drink and use. A failure on the part of many so called recovery programs is the denial that there is an emotional basis to virtually everything we do, even if those things we do are positive and motivated by underlying positive emotions as well. In spite of any possible biological predisposition to drink and use, the choice to start is a conscious one and will likely only lead to addiction if the individual sees substance use as a means of escaping emotional pain. Perhaps the biological basis is not that for addiction, but toward personality traits interfering with someone's ability to effectively cope with and control anxiety and the FLAGS. There may be biological/genetic factors, coupled with environmental factors, inhibiting someone's resilience and the ability to transcend loss and hardship.

As people begin to move into the process of true recovery, it is possible to then give them some skills to reinforce their belief and confidence in their ability to move forward. Most important of all is the need to keep them grounded in the reality that the process of growth and development is truly a lifelong process and should not be seen as a means to an end. Unfortunately organized religions have taught us that "salvation" is simply a single act of acceptance followed by repentance and a promise to never sin again. That approach doesn't work in that context any more effectively than it does in real life. This narrow-minded way of magical thinking sets people up for failure, which is a flaw of many "conversion" experiences. Even true spirituality is a process of growth and development and there is no promise that just because you choose to believe something, life after that choice won't sometimes be difficult. When people are told all you have to do is believe in order to achieve or attain something, they feel they have failed when things don't work out as promised. Imagine how Dorothy would have felt in the land of OZ if she hadn't returned to Kansas when she clicked her ruby slippers together. Such experiences leave people feeling they are inadequate even when it comes to salvation; or they feel they don't deserve even the salvation they sought. This fosters a belief I really believe to be flawed and perpetuates the perception of being unworthy, vulnerable, and weak.

For these reasons I believe people need to be steered away from organized religions, especially those which are punitive and judgmental, preaching hellfire and brimstone kinds of philosophies. I am shocked at the conservative groups which are allowed to go into juvenile halls and tell the kids they are worthless pieces of crap without God. They already feel bad enough without being further victimized and abused. The messages should be along the lines of hope and the reality that everything you need can be found within the soul of any individual. It is just a matter of finding the right guidance to bring into awareness the insights which can then be put into practice. As I indicated earlier, my job as a psychologist allows me to "minister" to people without the need to recruit them or convince them of any particular way of thinking. I can encourage them to discover their own sense of God and Truth.

In the past I have given some of the juvenile offenders I work with copies of The Celestine Prophecy, by James Redfield. The intention is to introduce them to a healthy concept indicating there is a force bigger than we are which has a purpose for each of us which we and only we can fulfill. I can then tell them that things they have done so far in their lives aren't part of that plan, but can be used as a way to learn and grow even from the negative experiences they have had and the negative things they have done. Even if their level of reading skills isn't high enough for the book, many of them will benefit from the concepts taught to us as professionals from within the pages of The Celestine Prophecy and of many other books sometimes incorrectly dubbed as "New Age Spirituality". This is such a misnomer in the sense it perpetuates the views of organized religion that all ancient concepts of spirituality not sanctioned and ordained as acceptable are somehow evil and dangerous. People, it is time to wake up and smell the coffee so to speak, and begin to openly fight the dependency, ignorance, and arrogance fostered and espoused by many religions! Even though The Celestine Prophecy is fictional the main point of spiritual insights being a threat to organized religion is well taken.

The very first insight in The Celestine Prophecy is the idea many things happening in our lives are the result of Coincidence with a capitol "C". The kids I work with are always intrigued by this concept, especially when I point out all of the events which had to transpire for us to be sitting in the same room together. I focus on all of the negative experiences they have had with other adults in the home/family environment, and at least to some extent in all of the other contexts as well. My kids treasure the opportunity to work with someone like me who really is interested in getting to know them as who they really are, rather than judge them by their behaviors and lack of skills in a number of areas, including education. Perhaps no connections with kids are accidents. However, connections frequently become missed opportunities for both kids and adults to learn from each other and grow, especially when adults fail to fulfill their roles effectively and appropriately as outlined within these pages.

So many of the kids I work with either have significant learning disorders and difficulties which have gone undetected, or they are really behind in their skills in reading, writing and math. Any combination of these factors leaves them feeling dumb and stupid. When you add special education to the list of other complicating factors then the mixture of issues only gets worse. Even though special education doesn't have the same connotations as it did in the past, it still carries the stigma in the minds of kids, especially since other kids and even relatives can be quite abusive about it. For these reasons when I interview a new client I always ask for their perception of how intelligent they are. Generally they will tell me something negative, until I ask them what they could do if they really pushed themselves and could get caught up on their skills. Then their answers are much more positive and I can always mark them on the intake form as average to above average, using a letter grade of "C" as average. Most of them can identify at least one area in which they feel they could excel, and all of them agree they could make C's with a few A's and B's thrown in if they really pushed and supported. Therefore, there is nothing phony about marking them as average to above average since this is their own perception. I really believe in the notion kids and adults will perform better if the expectations of educators and trainers are high enough to challenge them without setting them up for failure.

As strange as it may sound, be careful not to overlook the skills kids acquire even from their criminal activity, street life, and gang involvement. By helping them identify skills learned from these very real kinds of experiences, it is possible to capitalize on things they already know and simply need to redirect. Such skills include: marketing, planning, goal setting, follow through, sales, recruiting, procuring, purchasing, importing/exporting, investment, returns, profits, bargaining, bartering, supply and demand, team building, team spirit, artistic ability/creativity, critical thinking, setting ideals and standards, etc. As you can see, and probably have never previously considered, kids often have many acquired skills which would prove very useful in life if used in positive ventures and directions. Never underestimate the opportunities you have to creatively find ways to connect with kids within the context of professional roles. No one taught me what I know while I was sitting in a classroom. I have learned it through some degree of trial and error from the kids with whom I love to work. I will use whatever ethical and legal means I can discover to help me relate to them and to protect them as their advocate whenever necessary.

Let's look at issues relative to breaking the cycles of acting out emotion-based anxiety relative to abuse and victimization in the loftier contexts outside of the home/family. First of all abuse and victimization outside of the home/

family context tends to target groups of people and prey upon their perceived vulnerabilities. Furthermore, some of the complicating factors alone result in abuse and victimization just by virtue of their very existence. While many situations are created by choices, even if they are unconscious, simply making and working toward different choices can change many situations. Frequently the perception of being trapped is a misperception based in the limited ability to even believe there could be other options. Also, the excuse of being trapped can be an act of denying the availability of other alternatives. This is where courage and determination are needed in order to make different choices and move forward.

The point is when complicating factors are either unchangeable, or are perceived as being unchangeable, these factors are experienced as abusive and victimizing. Look again at the list of complicating factors to see those which may be either realistically outside of someone's conscious control, or are perceived as being. Remember one of the ways to act out is to buy into the victim role, which means that sometimes things can be fought and changed with a simple change in perspective and perception. This is what happened during the times of social unrest and change in the United States during the 1950's, 60's, and 70's. People in many different categories and groups who had previously bought into the hopelessness/helplessness position realized they were living in houses without real walls. During these decades of unrest some people had to reach in and pull some of the people out, while others just went with the flow and waited until the imaginary walls were torn down. These are probably some of the people in these different groups who still want to see themselves as victims rather than seize the opportunities to make changes, even if those changes may be difficult to create and maintain.

One of the main things I focus on with clients is the concept of a standard of living. As I said before, even people living below the poverty level can have a relatively high standard of living as exhibited by the pride they feel within themselves and for the material things they have. As one's standard of living improves generally people become more motivated to make additional changes which will continue to improve their situations. I see this in many families who use what they have available to create a good standard of living and at the same time encourage their children to make even better choices than they made or were able to make. Kids accepting this encouragement and way of thinking are the ones who break the cycles of vulnerability and continue to make positive changes in their lives. This again is an example of the importance of the right kinds of conditions within the home/family context if the other contexts are to be navigated and conquered successfully.

One of the biggest mistakes I still see people making is the failure to learn from previous mistakes and from the mistakes of others. I have very little respect for people who irresponsibly create children they are not ready to provide for, or even capable of providing for on all levels. One mistake may be excusable, but repeated mistakes and bad choices without any regard for the impact on kids is unforgivable without some sincere efforts on the parts of both parents to correct things and at least work toward fulfilling their obligations and responsibilities. Laws cannot regulate irresponsible sexual activity between consenting sexual partners. Therefore, I say again it is important to really begin teaching accountability, responsibility, and appropriate values to adults and to kids. Adults in all arenas need to recognize and accept our need to model the right kinds of standards to the kids observing us in all settings. We are responsible and it is time to stop ignoring this reality.

The time has come for adults to address and change all of the faulty perceptions we have established and perpetuate. The time has also come to stand up to any adults who are supposed to be leaders and hold them accountable for their lack of honesty, their deception, and the lack of general concern for all people. This level of accountability goes beyond that represented by such leaders utilizing divisive sets of unethical standards and group membership accepted as "just the way things are". It is time for all of us to stop accepting the hypocrisy and misinformation we are being fed on a daily basis especially in all of the contexts outside of the home/family. People in positions of power and influence are not promoting fairness and sound ethical standards. It seems that so many of the choices and decisions made in the contexts outside of the home/family are motivated by greed and self serving interests, and not for the common good of this country and of the world.

In the 1950's through the 1980's people stood up to things accepted as norms and truth and began to set limits on opportunities for abuse and victimization. This kind of momentum needs to continue by searching out and identifying all areas where deception and secrecy reign. Even in this country people in leadership positions within all of the contexts outside of the home/family get greedy and begin to think they are above ethics and decency if their power isn't open to full review and monitoring. I believe this is true at all of the top levels especially within the corporate, religious and political domains.

Accountability is a must when it comes to answering to the public in general who have reached a point of trusting foolishly that everything is under control, that what we are being told is accurate, and that the best interests of everyone are safe. During the early phases of the "War on Terrorism" I watched helplessly as I our president and others in positions of power and influence made threatening statements only provoking more hatred toward us from the rest of the world. I think if more of us were bold enough to say so we would find few people really trust all of what we are being told is the truth, or that what we are being told is all we need to know. I feel much of what I hear and read from the media is suspect, even if the media personnel believe in what they are saying. In reality, who knows what the truth is anymore? In our desperate struggles to reach the top I am afraid the vast majority of people in this country are at the mercy of external factors we aren't even challenging, and in many cases are actually ignoring. We have grown lazy and complacent in the monitoring of the systems upon which we depend for our very survival.

All of these considerations are logical given the severity of situations around the world and the need to break cycles of ineffective and inappropriate beliefs and actions. I think the Republicans in the U.S. got into the White House and Congress for a period of time so we can finally get to see their true colors and see how ineffective and dangerous their thinking really is. Who in their right mind would stand in the way of reasonably controlled scientific research using dormant human embryos to affect cures for untold numbers of diseases and conditions around the world? While I am pro choice I am not a proponent of abortion as birth control. However I do not see the harm in using nothing more than cells created in a laboratory to make such incredible progress, probably even sanctioned by God, just because of protests made by a few relatively small, yet powerful and vocal groups of conservative extremists. The politicians who need votes are afraid to stand up to these groups even if this stance jeopardizes the welfare of countless others. The midterm election of 2006 sent a clear message that the American majority no longer want this climate of deception and division to continue. The 2008 elections screamed out even louder against lies and abuses of power and authority. Hopefully we will see even more progress in the years ahead.

When anyone gets to the point of crossing ethical boundaries whereby actual human beings are being either destroyed or duplicated within laboratory settings, then there will be cause for concern. Until then get out of the way and let the common good of the vast majority of people who do not buy into narrow-minded conservative views benefit from God-given medical and other technological advances. We need leaders who are more focused on reality than on re-election. I am tired of seeing everything get thrown into chaos and conflict simply because there are political elections coming up soon. The lines were already being drawn for the 2012 presidential election and each of us will pay a price for this, even around the world, until politicians figure out that the political arena doesn't have to be a shooting gallery. They also need to see that religion should not be allowed to influence elections and national/ international interests and concerns. This is clearly spelled out in the U.S. Constitution relative to separation of church and state. Thank God for the victory in Alabama when the monument of the Ten Commandments had to be removed from a government building. If clergy focused on spiritual maters rather than on legislating morality the world would be a better place for all and everywhere. Have you ever tried to imagine how elections would look if lines weren't drawn according to divisive party politics? What would we actually debate if people could begin to identify and agree upon a common good by which everyone could win? Wouldn't this help break the cycles of dysfunction within this country and represent a true moderate stance politicians are supposedly seeking? Again, I think it is time to stand up and demand accountability and ethics in all areas of life. There is no right time to become indifferent and unconcerned.

By recognizing life as the process it is rather than trying to see it as a means to an end, we can begin to see that efforts made toward breaking cycles, and reducing and eliminating abuse and victimization are only stages in a process of evolution – spiritual evolution. Interventions at all levels should be viewed as nothing more than the first steps toward taking our spiritual evolution seriously and beginning to see that each of us must accept our respective roles and responsibilities as part of this process. If we begin to recognize not only our abilities to destroy ourselves individually and collectively, but also the underdeveloped abilities to construct and grow, then our interconnectedness will become more apparent.

We are not separate groups of people segregated and defined by arbitrary barriers, borders, and boundaries as we believe. We are the human race, a rather large group of spiritual beings having, to date, a somewhat negative and disappointing human experience. The extreme advances in recent decades continuing to explode almost exponentially are not accidents. They are Coincidence and Opportunity over which we fight for ownership and recognition. All advancements with the potential to improve the well being and raise standards of living for everyone are to be shared, not owned. Ours is not a process of uniting as one; it is a process of recognizing that we *are* one. With this change in thinking we can seriously begin to break the destructive cycles and promote the process of healthy cycles of living – universal cycles of living - where every ending always mark the beginning of something new.

Chapter XII
Myth and the Need for Critical Thinking

After giving much thought to the content of this the last chapter in my book I have decided to focus on myth and the need for critical thinking. The acceptance of myths as Truth is one of the problems we face, along with the lack of critical thinking in the world representing two major obstacles in our process of spiritual evolution. In my opinion I believe that myths fall into two categories. First, there is the concept of myth as an attempt to explain things which cannot be proven, or are at least not readily understood. Secondly, myth represents the collective group of unchallenged and oftentimes unspoken rules accepted as Truth which determine the flow of life and the zeitgeist of any particular moment in time. In the first application myths are those early attempts within ancient cultures and civilizations to explain natural phenomena, and early perceptions of spirituality and the existence of factors and forces greater than ourselves. The second consideration addresses how early myths get revised to some extent throughout time and get passed along as Truth and traditions which somehow have to be honored and adhered to blindly.

On the other hand we have the concept of critical and creative thinking which to me represents the means by which we can challenge myths accepted as Truth and tradition. By challenging myth we are able to make determinations as to what is no longer applicable and useful, as opposed to other elements which can continue to serve as foundations for growth and exploration. As we look back in time it is possible to identify myths which have existed and only partially evolved within all of the 6 contexts I have identified.

First let's look at the home/family and myths associated historically with this context. Very early myths included barbaric notions of survival needs which were real at the time. These included the concepts of males as hunters and gatherers, and females as caretakers of the cave and children. The grunts of males were taken to be law and the females, while playing important roles relative to survival of the group, were given specific jobs within very confined areas where the groups dwelled. These were clearly male dominated societies, with male behaviors viewed equivalent to the basic instincts of animals, so that the men generally had all of the privileges and freedoms, even sexually, and the females were very subservient. Children and virginal females also made very good sacrifices to the gods whom were believed to control natural phenomena, especially natural disasters such as severe weather conditions, seasonal changes, volcanoes and earthquakes.

Without trying to make this a detailed historical account I will assume everyone reading this book has at least some awareness of mythical roles and responsibilities within the home/family context which had not changed much since the Stone Age until the last half of the Twentieth Century. Clearly there were vast improvements in living conditions and in all areas of agriculture, industry and technology throughout this time frame. However, the notion of traditional male and female roles remained rather unchallenged until the 1950's. During the early years of the Twentieth Century the lives of children improved in this country to some extent with the advent of child labor laws which represented the first identification of a period of adolescence and the need for secondary education beyond the basic "3 R's" of reading, 'riting, and 'rithmetic. These initial changes were partly because of a move away from primarily agricultural-based societies and economies to a more industrialized/mechanized existence. As these changes occurred people were finally able to move around the country and ultimately the world through the advent of automobiles and communication devices, and eventually through extreme advances in transportation and technology. Many professionals of today focus research on how all of these changes have impacted the lives of adults. All too often we fail to recognize the even more tremendous impact of change on kids who have to put up with adults whose lives are in states of almost constant turmoil and transition.

It is possible to see the progress we have made as our needs for survival changed more into opportunities for growth and development. However, it is equally easy to see how the myths of the past are still being clung to and fought for in many arenas all around the world. In the more advanced cultures of the world it is possible to see some critical thinking taking place, challenges being made, and some changes occurring. While these more advanced cultures and societies are beginning to move forward, the "War on Terrorism" since 9/11 and the wars in Iraq and Afghanistan have made all of us aware of the barbaric conditions continuing to exist in geographical regions still dominated and controlled by males and religious extremism even in the United States. The 2008 election of the first African America president caused a whole new uprising based in fear and discrimination, primarily within the ranks of older white Americans.

It is important to recognize many of the myths of the past are still accepted as Truth even in the more advanced societies. Even within the United States and in the home/family context there are still struggles being made to discover and stabilize new male/female roles, and to redefine the adult roles and responsibilities toward children. As I stated previously, any initial periods of radical change seem to be fraught with chaos and confusion. This is clearly represented by the on going lack of stability in any sense relative to appropriate family structure and definition. When people immigrate into this country from primarily male dominated societies, one of the biggest acculturation issues is that of men trying to retain their positions of unquestionable power and authority over women and children. Also, I see a lot of opposition to myths associated with religious extremism from within the country of origin as well. Hopefully as we continue to search for balance we will be able to find a set of standards which work for home/family issues in this and other societies. Because the United States is such a blending of cultures this is likely a good testing ground. So far when my RFLAGS Model is presented in public seminars, workshops and classrooms it is well received and appears to be effective in challenging myths associated with family issues regardless of cultural or ethnic differences.

A few years ago I had an older man from a Spanish-speaking country refer to me as being from "Gringo Landia" or the white man's culture. This occurred during a workshop for Spanish-speaking people and this gentleman was challenging my views on abuse and victimization as they apply to the concept of discipline. He clearly recognized he was alone in his views after I confronted him in front of a group composed entirely of Spanish-speaking people, telling him literally "it takes a lot more time and energy to learn how to be a good parent than it does to hit and yell." The entire audience agreed with and supported me, indicating a clear acceptance of my model and related concepts in spite of the fact I am indeed a gringo, at least on the outside. As the evening progressed my opponent became an ally and was able to see the Truth in my beliefs regardless of our cultural differences.

Now let's consider myths existing within the school context. One of the most obvious is the elitist attitude of educators being part of a closed system and clearly seeing non-members of the educational field as "outsiders". I have experienced this first hand as a representative of kids who are referred to various mental health settings to address psychological needs often accompanying learning difficulties. Many agencies, within all of the contexts frequently have their little song and dance routines they use when no outsiders are around to hold them accountable for misdeeds committed against those who are the most vulnerable.

This is especially true when the parents and kids present are thought to be ignorant (in the sense of being uninformed) and vulnerable relative to a full understanding of rights, policies and procedures, and due process. Because of my reputation of being seen as an advocate for kids and families, as well as supportive of school-based efforts to offer the best options available, I am respected and am not seen as being oppositional. However, there is a fine line I am not allowed to cross. Doing so results in efforts to exclude me from future meetings. My tactics are to empower kids and families by making them fully aware of their rights and by encouraging them not to accept the myth that those in charge always have their best interests in mind. Believe me, many times people in all arenas will only seek to serve and protect their own best interests, especially when the best interests of other parties are likely to cost money over and beyond usual financial considerations. My best efforts are focused on informing people of their rights out in their communities and in my office, rather than during meetings where I might be viewed as adversarial.

The next biggest myth within the school context is that many teachers are victims and therefore, are not able to do their jobs, much less be effective. As with other professions including psychology, most people enter these fields with hopes, ideals and dreams of the changes they want to make in the lives of kids and adults. Unfortunately, the realities of actually trying to make a difference are quite often a stark contrast to the fantasies which motivated us to make the efforts in the first place. Rather than take this as defeat, see it as challenge and opportunity.

There are people within the educational systems who are very effective in spite of some very real odds. Because of the breakdown in the home/family environments kids seem to be more difficult to reach at times, partly because of legitimate trust issues they have with adults in general. Unfortunately with the role of teacher or educator oftentimes comes the myth "I am an authority figure who deserves unquestionable and unchallenged respect. Furthermore, my only job as a teacher is to teach you textbook information and not have to deal with you on a behavioral or relational level."

The reality is that kids today are too sophisticated to fall for this kind of thinking from any adult. This is why I think we have so much defiance and so much poor taste in kids relative to what they consider as funny and appropriate. Kids seem to feel a desire for revenge against adults who continue in many cases to take them for granted and try to push them around. These are not even conscious awarenesses on the part of most kids. Because public school staff members are no longer allowed to use corporal punishment to force compliance, it is almost necessary for all educators to have a back up degree in psychology and human relations in order to be successful. As times change, every system impacted either directly or indirectly by the changes is obligated to shift and adjust to changes as they occur. This is extremely necessary within educational settings which must adapt and grow to adequately keep up with and even try to anticipate and predict changes in the real world outside of the classrooms. It is only through such efforts to adapt and adjust within all contexts that the chaos and confusion can begin to subside and true progress can begin. The myth of a classroom easily and readily conducive to learning no longer applies, so face it and deal with the reality of changes which are occurring. Quite often any successful approaches in dealing with the most troubled kids and problematic behaviors require very different and creative efforts involving communication and shared problem solving processes.

The community context contains numerous myths as well. First of all the myth of communities being equal now that civil rights laws are in effect really needs to be addressed. In the South it is almost comical to watch as white people in different locales and neighborhoods run from blacks who are seemingly believed by whites to be chasing them around simply to destroy their European American existence. Unfortunately and regardless of ethnicity and cultural backgrounds, a few people in any neighborhood who have a lower standard of living than the others can bring down every aspect of that neighborhood. Because of concerns over property values and general pride in any area where people live, the reasonable standards relative to an agreed upon standard of living set by residents in a particular area should be acknowledged, enforced, and accepted by new residents. As I mentioned previously, a standard of living is not determined by socioeconomic status as much as it is established by a sense of pride in oneself and in one's possessions and environment.

I have very little respect for people who have a low standard of living and seemingly have little or no pride in themselves unless conditions exist which are somehow completely beyond their control. I attribute this in part to systems and circumstances helping to remove the concept of a work ethic whereby people work and have an opportunity to feel good about themselves and about what they have gained materially. With community-based programs to facilitate opportunities for education, jobs, and appropriate housing, more people have opportunities to raise their standards of living. Failure to do so or even see the need to change is generally based on faulty value systems and myths people have bought into from the stance of continuing to be victims of various historical factors which no longer exist as the insurmountable obstacles they once were.

Communities are in reality divided into classes whether we want to see that or not. Hurricane Katrina in the summer of 2005 hit all of us in the face with this reality in this country. However, there are many people in neighborhoods who have raised their standards of living and have improved the environments in which they live, allowing them to now take pride in what they have. While it may be difficult for some adults to get additional job training and education, by raising standards of living and teaching kids the importance of dreaming and pursuing their dreams through education and determination, more and more people will be able to give kids a chance to raise their standards of living even higher than those of their parents.

It is only fair that people with higher standards of living than others have a right to protect themselves from being subjected to those with lower, yet changeable standards. Many people even within "inner city ghettos" take pride in their neighborhoods and protect them from decline once the areas are transformed, improved and become free from domination by criminal factions. The acceptance of different groups by others, including groups referred to as "low lifes" or "trailer trash", depends on the acceptance of their responsibility to clean up their acts if they want to stop being looked down upon. While I do not agree with labeling and judging, I do feel an obligation to protect myself and what I have accomplished from anyone or anything that threatens the standard of living I have worked hard to achieve. Believe me, there is a big difference between thinking I am better than others, compared to realizing I am better off than some because of the ways I have pushed myself to gain education, experience and respect. Believe me none of these personal gains were handed to me by virtue of simply being white.

I went to college and graduate school with people recognized as being from different minority groups who had their education paid for at least partially if not fully in some cases. In order to have reached my goals relative to education and profession I found myself heavily in debt, owing almost as much as I paid for the house I was finally able to buy at age 45. If I continue to push myself I hope to pay off my student loans before I turn 77 as the repayment schedule now stands over a 30-year period. Remember, I do not associate myself much with stereotypical European American groups, so I am not obsessing about how to get rich. I am basically hoping to be able to pay myself out of debt before I die. I believe if I could do it without any support from anyone including my family, anyone can do it. None of my efforts were any easier for me than they would be for any others given the opportunities and standards existing in today's society. This is especially true in states like California where there is more financial assistance in advanced educational programs for non-European Americans than for European Americans. These factors help in at least challenging the myth of privilege.

One of the best community-based and federally funded programs available to low-income kids today is Job Corps. The closest one to the desert where I lived and worked in California was located about seventy-five miles away from my base office. Everything, including room and board, education (high school diploma or GED, and college), job training, transportation, basic medical/dental/vision, and clothing is provided without any financial obligation to anyone who at 18 is unemployed, low income, and sleeping in their parents' home. The age ranges for admission are 16 to 24. At the end of their training the trainees, as they are called, are guaranteed a good paying job, and are given a check for a significant amount as starter money.

The job training opportunities offered are very usable skills in today's job markets, with starting salaries higher than for those without the Job Corps training. If you have Job Corps facilities in your area that are not up to the highest standards then start a campaign to make them accountable for a failure to provide the services they are expected to provide. If there isn't a Job Corps facility relatively close to you then check into establishing one. The reality is that in more than nine years of taking a total of probably two hundred kids to see this program only three actually went into the program. This was in spite of my efforts to take them to orientations, for interviews, and for eventual residence once there was a spot for them at the facility, thereby eliminating virtually all external obstacles I could address.

The biggest obstacles for most of the low income kids I work with are the lack of courage to take a favorable risk, and the fact there are rules and structure which are enforced during the time kids are in training at Job Corps. The zero tolerance rules kids hate the most are about the need to stay clean and sober. It is appalling to see how blind kids and adults are to the destructive effects of drugs and alcohol, including marijuana. I can get kids to stop gang banging easier than I can get them to stop using and drinking. Substance abuse and dependence quite often represent the kinds of obstacles people with lower values and standards of living, regardless of socioeconomic status, are not only ignoring, but are able to convince themselves aren't really a problem. These are some of the present day community myths kids and adults need to face and resolve.

How foolish it is to let reasonable rules stand in the way of an absolutely free opportunity to get a good start in life. Job Corps eliminates all of the obstacles and excuses if kids will just make the commitment to attend and accept the rules and structure. The length of stay depends on the individual's abilities and level of dedication which determine the time needed to complete educational and job training needs. This program alone eliminates any excuses on the part of low-income kids who complain about a lack of opportunities. What they are really complaining about is the lack of easy opportunities which never will exist anyway. Even get-rich-quick criminal schemes and ventures come with a price. There is nothing to be lost by making a legitimate investment of time and effort into your future. Any legitimate future created by an individual can never be taken away. In addition to training at Job Corps all trainees are given access to support staff who are there all along the way to help them be successful and to even help them stay clean and sober.

Keep in mind myths are only as strong as the degree to which we accept them as unchangeable and unquestionable truth. Societal myths include such things as: strength in numbers; might makes right; entitlement; some groups being better than others; us versus them kind of thinking; money and materialism will lead to happiness; my well being and profit at the expense of others; lack of responsibility and accountability; it's only wrong if I get caught; interconnectedness and universality don't exist; the environment will protect itself; natural resources are limitless; something for nothing; etc. As you can see there are numerous myths lived out as truth by many adults and kids in all arenas at the societal level. It will take others like myself to begin speaking out about the injustices and erroneous assumptions and acceptance of myths as Truth if we are to finally see progress being made as these myths evolve into more current day realities and applicability.

Many of these societal myths also apply to the contexts of politics and religion as well. I have already addressed these contexts rather extensively. Again, one of the most significant myths to be challenged in the political context is the assumption those in power really have the best interests of society at large in mind. I believe because of the perceived importance of some conservative groups relative to a politician's reelection, these groups are often treated as if they are majorities. If the facts were known, I also believe we would realize that more and more people are actually against the self-serving interests of most conservative groups and issues within this country and in countries around the world.

Unfortunately many of the hippies in the 1960's and 70's became the yuppies in the 80's and 90's by buying into some of the same myths they were fighting against at an earlier time. These are the ones of us labeled as "the baby boomers", and are the ones moving into the retirement age range. Hopefully not all of the baby boomers have forgotten their spirit of radicalism and desire for changes and improvements in the world at large. Having been born in 1954, I am kind of on the tail end of the boomer generation. It may have helped that I got to watch and learn from their efforts before I finally made the choices of how to start my own progresive campaigns against arrogance and ignorance. I take pride in the fact I have learned to recognize and challenge ways of thinking which were never really appropriate anyway. I am fortunate enough to have found the courage to step outside of the boxes I was exposed to as a kid and as a young adult. Hopefully my efforts to write and publish this book and others will inspire people to do the same relative to their own sense of calling and uniqueness.

The last context I want to spend a little more time with is that of religion. In one of the psychology classes I taught at the local community college in California, we talked about myth and how myth applies to issues of sexuality. I always, of course, took an antagonistic approach to challenge what the students accepted as Truth, which included the reality of how extensively the myths associated with organized religion impact and influence virtually every level of our existence.

One of the most obvious and yet infrequently thought about indicators was the influence religion has had on the establishment of Latin-based languages initially within countries and cultures ultimately if not initially dominated by Catholicism. While I am not an expert in linguistics, I have noticed while learning and speaking Spanish how very sexist the nouns are in this and in other Latin-based languages. It cannot be an accident that things associated with the idea of women as being subservient to men are associated with conventional religious thinking. The languages reflect concepts of God being male and the church being female in the sense of being the bride of Christ. Feminine and masculine roles and responsibilities are given either feminine or masculine forms. One of the women in my class who was fluent in Spanish had never thought about this was rather astounded, commenting that I "must have too much time on my hands" to have been able to make that observation. I laughed and pointed out the fact that I don't take anything at face value anymore, and have found the study of Spanish to be an enlightening revelation of cultural nuances and myths within the "Latin" cultures. Remember until recently religious services in the Catholic Church were conducted strictly in Latin. Latin-based languages in Mexico, Central, and South America were introduced by Europeans who spoke languages based to some degree in Latin. Clearly the Catholic Church superimposed its sexism on the cultures they invaded and destroyed throughout the centuries and around the world.

She and a few other class members were intrigued by this reality, and could not refute it as fact. I pointed out the English language has some forms of words that identify gender, but that because of the challenges of myths in the last half of the Twentieth Century, many efforts have been made to correct these. For instance, many words ending with "man" have been modified to "person" or to "woman", such as chairperson or congresswoman. Some words such as salesman have been modified to such an extent as to now be genderless as in referring to someone as a sales associate. In the Latin languages everything related to God is masculine, and to the church is feminine. This is one of the most blatant examples I have found of an ever-present reminder of the myths of gender roles and religion. Words associated with emotions attributed to stereotyped feminine characteristics are also feminine, with harsh emotions being considered as masculine. It is amazing how the Latin languages reflect so many of the cultural dynamics within these countries. Talk about constant "subliminal" reminders for women of position in life relative to men and to religion. Men are constantly reminded of their need to be intense and nasty, with such words for anger, dirty, and bathroom being masculine in form.

I say all of this to point out that it is time to challenge all components of organized religions which try to keep people down, dependent and trapped in their abilities to think and to live. The biggest myth associated with any religion is that of infallibility, along with the myth that religion is to be found in a building or through someone ordained or otherwise blessed, or through some act indicating faith, confession, commitment, and dedication. I am very free as a spiritual being because of breaking away from the teachings of organized religion. It took a lot of courage initially to simply look over the edges of the boxes, much less to actually step outside of and away from what I had been taught as my only salvation and hope of heaven.

Think of how horrible it is for people to believe in any god that would want them to kill themselves and others in that god's name and then be rewarded for doing so in the afterlife. How tragic are the circumstances of vulnerability and abuse/victimization giving people the need to buy into such foolishness, myth and fallacy. The very religious texts believed to be the infallible and literal words of many gods are in many cases the very same books which, when written, allowed for the killing of people (especially women) for what are now considered to be basic human rights. These are the same writings whose authors justified slavery and attended public executions as entertainment and sport when people, usually women were caught in the act of something considered by religion to be sinful. These are the very same writings that promote the abuse and victimization of women and children by insisting on subservience and the concept of "spare the rod and spoil the child". They also promote the concepts of God as being vengeful and judging – something to be feared. One of the abusive statements my Dad used against me as he beat me with a belt was to threaten "to put the fear of God" in me, likening himself at that moment to the image of God.

I am amazed at how ignorantly and arrogantly many religious people, regardless of religious affiliation, claim to believe in religious writings as literal truth and yet pick and choose as it suits their needs what to believe and actually implement in their daily lives. For instance, it is my understanding of Christianity that Jesus came to replace the Law with Love. However, there are only four books dealing with the life and teachings of Jesus. All other books in the New Testament appear to be the creation of new laws for the establishment of "the Church". It is ironic how these new laws lost sight of the spiritual nature of what Jesus was trying to teach, thereby losing sight of the Love. My spiritual beliefs are something I strive to live out in every aspect of who I am and what I do. In recent years I have come to believe so strongly in the concept of Karma and that what goes around comes around, I really seek to limit my exposure to negativity as much as I have learned to do so to date. I have also come to believe very strongly in the concept that I have some purpose in life I and only I can fulfill, and that the only thing making any sense in this existence is to want what God wants at every level of my being.

True spirituality is genderless and yet virtually all of the larger traditional religions are still male dominated. It is about time people are beginning to challenge the myths of celibacy and heterosexual male dominated clergy. These myths are nothing more than laws expressed in ancient Jewish texts and established by early Christian leaders to set standards of the day for the religious institutions they were trying to form. This is likely also true in the Muslim traditions as well. People who are truly spiritual are equal in all regards. Those focused on universal spiritual concepts of One Source, unconditional love and acceptance, being non-judgmental, and truly altruistic, are not self-absorbed, self-serving, or materialistic. Spiritual people are both self and other focused; truly altruistic; see ourselves as connected to everyone and to everything; and are constantly seeking guidance and wisdom through numerous sources including both spiritually strong people and spiritually sane written materials. Unconditional love and acceptance have little to do with literally embracing everyone, and everything to do with recognizing and respecting individual processes.

Think about how the extremists within the three prominent feuding religions – Muslims, Jews, and Christians – all seek to dominate, conquer and control geographic locations basically because of land considered to be sacred to each group. Again, where is God in that? Also consider the reckless use of ancient religious texts in these pursuits to command place and privilege, with the possible end result being that of total annihilation. Who would be on top then? What a horrible way to end struggles needing to end in peace through compromise and recognition that we are all created equally by God. No religious text taken literally in today's times should be used as a basis for anything less than the sense of Spirituality and Soul within each of us. No one knows what the Truth is anyway, so why not take a leap of faith forward and toward a common ground of acceptance of and appreciation for the diversity among all people in all regions of the world.

Each individual based in pure spirituality approaches people only when it is appropriate to do so, and at the same time models the spiritual concepts listed above. People are not recruited into spirituality. Rather, people become spiritually aware as their focus shifts from self to Self in relation to others. Spirituality must be lived and modeled rather than institutionalized, and can only be perpetuated by people who speak out loudly against the injustices everywhere by identifying and challenging all forms of abuse and victimization within all of the six contexts as they exist around the world. None of this can be accomplished through self-serving societies, partisan political factions, or divisive religions. Effective challenging of injustices must be done through the power of the Originator of the Universe — the Creator and Voice of "one-song" (uni-verse) as taught by Dr. Wayne Dyer, a man deeply grounded in non-religious Spirituality.

Even publishers and distributors of printed materials have a responsibility to market materials promoting healthy spiritual and psychological growth. Writers and other professionals who are truly spiritually based must take the lead in teaching spiritual concepts which can be grasped by individuals at all levels according to their own needs and abilities relative to each respective process. Basic spiritual concepts can be easily understood and are universally acceptable. Every human being, including children and adolescents, responds favorably to unprejudiced love, acceptance, and altruistic assistance intended to strengthen and nurture, rather than dominate and control. Predators are those individuals, groups, organizations, institutions, and governments who prey upon the innocence and vulnerabilities of others. Those of us who are focused on spiritual growth and development must become the promoters of universally applicable spiritual concepts.

Retrospectively I have learned that once I broke free from misleading and dangerous myths accepted by many as truth I have been able to move forward and grow at a phenomenal rate. Not that life has been easy or always fun, but that my life now has a feeling of purpose and direction I never had in the past. I want to optimize this existence as much as I can on a spiritual level so I can follow the process to become the best I can become, whatever that involves.

When I was a child growing up in an abusive and chaotic home/family environment in the Deep South, also being victimized by religion, I couldn't have ever imagined I would be where I am now in terms of my life experiences and philosophies. As a child I always said I wanted to be a doctor when I grew up so I could help people who "felt bad". I thought the only kinds of doctors were MD's, so I gave up on that notion until in 1993 when I walked across the stage during my graduation ceremony and was announced and hooded as Dr. David L. Roberts. I started crying from sheer joy, wishing that my family had cared enough to attend my graduation, but realizing that in spite of all of the hardships and disappointments in my life I had beaten the odds. I had actually achieved the professional status my soul whispered to me even as a young child and all because I jumped out of the boxes and sought my own TRUTH which then became my freedom.

I live, work, write, and teach from somewhere very deep within my Soul. This is also the place where I process information in an effort to turn the good stuff into wisdom and insight which I can then share with others. At the beginning of each semester as a professor I began my college classes by telling the students that "if I do nothing more than teach you to think critically, then I will have done you a great service." I believe that I have gained a tremendous amount of wisdom through the experiences life has offered me, and even more importantly from the experiences which I have searched for as I changed my belief systems, values, and perception of Spirituality. For the first time in my late 20's I gained sight of the person I really could become, realizing that all of the lies I was told as a kid through the abusive statements and actions of my parents were simply just lies. I am so glad I found the courage to act in spite of fear, and the determination not to allow my feelings to interfere with my goals.

One final litany about the kids I serve. My job and work with kids at risk are my passion. I consider myself to be a very fortunate man and am always awed and humbled by the opportunities to connect professionally with kids often thought of by others as unreachable. At times I wish I was a man "of color". But, the amazing thing is that I get to reach out to all cultures and ethnicities as a European American male who doesn't fit any of the stereotypes currently associated with those within my own culture/ethnicity. I know many people in various settings look at me as just "another f-----g white guy", oftentimes assuming, because of my shaved head appearance and without knowing me, I represent some branch of law enforcement. There is no greater satisfaction in the world for me than to be able to connect with and reach out to kids who have no real reason to trust me in the first place. It is heartbreaking to me when I learn I am the first person in a long lineup of adults with whom a kid has been able to talk and not feel judged or labeled. There is no excuse for this reality, and as for adults who have any regular contact with kids, we need to feel shame for any ineffectiveness. This sense of shame should serve as a motivator to make the necessary changes which would facilitate our opportunities to make positive differences in the lives of kids who are so much in need of support and understanding.

Within twelve months spanning 2002 to 2003 three of my kids have been murdered as the result of gang related violence. These were the first out of hundreds I have met and served since starting my training in 1990. I was deeply saddened by their deaths and at the same time harshly reminded of the fallacies residing in the myths associated with the streets and so-called street justice. I watched as the brother and friends of the first kid polished the black casket with their blue "rags", ignoring the reality that the kid in the casket died for no other reason than that of foolish and desperate choices he had made along the way. With the second kid I looked into his dead face and recalled the promise and potential which was buried with him and all for nothing. The third death occurred in August 2003 and I was given the awesome and extremely difficult responsibility of giving this news to a group of twenty minors court ordered to a lock-in placement where I had the privilege of being their psychologist. All but two of these kids knew the kid who died and were frightened and horrified by the gruesome manner in which he died and manner in which his killers disposed of his body. The kids and staff all referred to me as "the Doc" and each of us shed tears together over the loss of one who tried so hard and yet faced unimaginable odds. As a unit of staff and kids we celebrated the life of this kid through a moving and memorable flag ceremony whereby the flag was lowered to half-staff, a ceremony repeated for several days. Until just six weeks prior to his death, and for a period of eight months we gave this kid something he had never had in his entire life – an environment of unconditional love, support and safety in which he clearly knew people cared for and about him. What a sad tribute to say that this kid had been in virtually every system available since birth and yet never encountered anything positive until he reached our unit.

In all three of these cases I was able to remind myself I had given these kids everything I had to offer professionally and to some extent on a personal level. One of my closest colleagues told me she respects me most for my willingness to give my heart to my kids. These kids – my kids - would have told you the same thing. While I cannot mention these guys by name I dedicate this book partly in memory of their lives and the connections we shared. I was also reminded by their deaths that I can only do so much, and that the effort is worth every moment of frustration and even sorrow I may experience along the way. I thank God often for the chance I have been given to make a difference in the lives of kids basically thrown away by most of society and in some cases even by their own families. Because of the extreme nature of the populations I generally serve the indications of progress are sometimes hard to find. But every time I see a kid in the streets who is glad to see me, or have a kid return to me in later years for additional guidance and support, I am reminded it is all worthwhile. I was favorably known within all of the gangs in the areas where I worked and I am proud of that fact. The respect I receive from these kids is immeasurable as is the satisfaction I receive simply from doing a job I truly love. There is no doubt in my mind I am fulfilling the purpose for which I was called to serve.

The completion of this book is another of many significant milestones in my life. The only thing I take credit for is my discovery of and willingness to live out my Spiritual beliefs. It is amazing me to realize this venture is the culmination of a process which began in 1986 as the idea for an undergraduate research project I mentioned earlier in this book. I am awed by everything this manuscript represents. I am also humbled by the many experiences included within and stand behind the insights I have gained throughout my entire professional training and work experience as a psychologist. I thank the Source clearly at work in my life and through me as I believe this and all I have to offer is truly a gift to the world from God and through me. I cannot begin to imagine how or why I was given this assignment, but I am very grateful for the opportunity and the privilege, and I am proud of my willingness to commit myself to this calling.

Believe me the feelings I often experienced of **F**ear, **L**oneliness, **A**nger, **G**uilt, **S**hame, frustration, doubt, uncertainty, and insecurity could easily have destroyed my determination. As I said earlier I never ask anyone to do anything I haven't done in one form or another relative to taking risks which ultimately will result in growth and accomplishment. I challenge each of you to find the same place deep within your Soul where you can begin to search for and process new and productive ways of living. Remember, one of the biggest factors is the ability to think critically. I truly wish you the best as you discover and facilitate your own process toward a clear awareness of purpose and direction. Hopefully you have discovered that one of the main themes of this entire project is to never forget how bad it feels to feel bad, and to never make another living creature, human or otherwise, feel that way. Furthermore, when you see people hurting in a way with which you can identify, if it is appropriate to do so, and after you have successfully addressed your own issues, help them. Memorize both this concept and the vow from adults to kids found toward the end of Chapter VI. These factors alone will give you a solid basis from which to right the wrongs in your life and in the lives of kids who are directly and indirectly in your care.

Appendices

Appendix A

ROBERTS FLAGS MODEL

Negative Emotions	**Anxiety/ Depression**	**Hopelessness/ Helplessness**	**Acting Out Behaviors**

FEAR

LONELINESS

ANGER

GUILT

SHAME

Appendix B

DESCRIPTIVE TERMS AND PHRASES USED TO DESCRIBE ANXIETY AND ANXIOUS DEPRESSION

Bored

Angry/mad

Annoyed

Burned out

Overwhelmed

Stressed out

Anxious

Tired/exhausted

Down

Confused

Can't cope

Uptight

About to lose control

Need to get away

Falling apart

Anguish

Depressed

Frustrated

Pissed off

I've had enough

Ready to explode

Nervous

Apprehensive

I'm in a bad mood

Trapped

Can't take it anymore

Losing my mind

Tense

I'm backed into a corner

Desperate

Disappointed

Irritated

Appendix C

ACTING OUT BEHAVIORS AND IMPULSIVE REACTIONS

Drinking/using
Using tobacco products
Sex
Eating too much/little
Sleeping too much/little
Self-mutilation
Suicide
Taking risky chances
Head-banging
Biting fingernails
Self rapproach/loathing
Withdrawing
Isolating
Somaticizing
Playing the victim
Shopping/spending money
Gambling
Exercising
Reading
Watching TV
Working
Running away
Pretending
Manipulating
Blaming
Scapegoating
Subverting
Gossiping
Fantasizing
Thrill-seeking
Always going out
Being unfaithful
Divorce

Avoiding
Being overly materialistic
Hoarding
Excessive cleaning
Organizing
Obsessing
Exhibitionism
Being arrogant
Feeling superior
Shunning/rejecting
Violence (all forms)
Criminal acts
Discrimination
Judging
Victimizing others
Yelling
Hitting
Destroying things
Rape
Molesting
Being self righteous/pious
Denying reality
Arguing
Becoming divisive
Hating
Making drastic changes
Undermining
Searching
Day dreaming
Partying
Dating recklessly
Controlling
Greed

Intimidation
Living irresponsibly
Being unjust/unfair
Being cruel
Playing games
Joining negative groups
Being needy
Being rude/crude
Procrastinating
Mislead/deceive
Unyielding
Living as a slob
Disorganization

Bullying
Living an unethical life
Demanding/ordering
Being hurtful
Thinking irrationally
Getting pregnant
Disregarding rights of others
Being inconsiderate
Acting without thinking
Adopting extreme beliefs
Uncooperative
Vicious and mean spirited
Rigid and uncompromising

Appendix D

PROBLEMS/ISSUES WE SEEK TO ESCAPE OR ACT OUT

Emotional pain
Abuse/victimization
Hatred
Anxiety/Depression
Perceived Reality/Truth
Sexual orientation
Abandonment
Neglect
Self loathing
Underachievement
Financial problems
Lack of moral values
Poor coping skills
Mistakes
Lack of a support system
Dysfunctional childhood
Poor family relations
Societal taboos
Being judged by others
Environmental factors
Lack of perspective
Lack of opportunities
Lack of understanding
No sense of belonging
Ignorance
Lack of forgiveness
Limited view of the world
No sense of purpose
Personality problems
Fear of losing control
Unfulfilled needs
Fear of success
Boredom

FLAGS
Trauma/Loss
Hopelessness/helplessness
Sadness
Poor self image
Identity issues
Failure
Denial/Repression
Rejection
Overachievement
Being or feeling trapped
Low self esteem
Bad decisions
Negative consequences
Conflict
Loss and grief
Prejudice, racism, bigotry
Poor judgment
No future dreams or plans
Biological factors
Lack of alternatives
Employment problems
Lack of acceptance
Appearance
Persecution
Lack of self-control
No sense of spirituality
No sense of direction
Mental/Emotional problems
Sexual issues
Lack of patience
Illness
Lack of challenge

Lack of motivation
Lack of creativity
Doing nothing
Lack of involvement
Isolation
Deprivation
Lack of pride
Lack of courage
Fear of taking risks
No desire to learn/explore
Disappointment
Negative beliefs
Divorce/breakup

Lack of inspiration
Lack of critical thinking
Lack of interests/hobbies
Fear of the unknown
Unpredictability
Lack of trust
Lack of accomplishments
Lack of strength
Comfort in stagnation
The need to be desired/loved
Frustration
Negative perceptions
Infidelity

Appendix E

ADULT ROLES AND RESPONSIBILITIES

Love

Care for/about

Encourage

Support

Teach self control

Teach morals/ethics

Teach values/work ethic

Model appropriate behaviors

Assist

Increase self esteem

Support individuality

Instill hopes/dreams

Listen

Avoid judging/labeling

Avoid being abusive

Give attention/time

Answer questions honestly

Encourage openness

Encourage trust

Challenge appropriately

Control

Punish/give consequences

Watch/observe

Accept responsibility

Apologize

Compromise

Comfort/soothe

Respect privacy

Encourage responsibility

Teach conflict resolution

Teach planning skills

Nurture

Provide for

Empower

Teach limits

Teach respect for self/other

Teach appropriate behaviors

Teach priorities

Guide

Believe in kids

Increase self confidence

Maximize potential

Teach courage

Accept

Discourage abuse

Protect

Create a safe environment

Communicate with kids

Encourage honesty

Defend kids

Respect

Discipline

Reward

Supervise

Allow appropriate expression
of emotions

Reward extra effort, not what is
expected

Forgive

Teach effective coping skills

Teach spirituality, not religion

Teach decision-making skills

Teach problem solving

Learn from mistakes

Always consider kids
Correct/improve conditions
Teach humility
Provide traditions
Share activities
Validate feelings
Be fair
Encourage education
Be realistic
Encourage respect for natural
environment
See kids as human beings
Avoid labels
Promote acceptance
of self and others
Encourage healthy exploration
Encourage social responsibility
Don't be arrogant
Avoid the need to dominate
Praise kids
Appreciate kids
Don't push extreme conformity

Model appropriate choices
Alter maladaptive patterns
Avoid creating FLAGS
Encourage fun/play
Develop talents and abilities
Be reasonable
Encourage independence
Encourage achievement
Seek guidance and education
Discourage negativity

Be psychologically healthy
Promote inclusion
Teach appropriate use of time

Be real/genuine
Support uniqueness
Avoid the need to be right
Don't always need to be liked
Respect/love yourself
Don't spoil kids
Teach balancing and centering

Appendix F

FACTORS CONSTITUTING THE 'IDEAL FAMILY'

Loving parents
Consistency
Mutual respect
Consideration
Connection
Unconditional love
Self control
Work ethic
Higher standard of living
Ability to learn
Ability to teach
Reciprocity
Appropriate role modeling
Encouragement
Acceptance
Reward
Healthy degree of privacy
Assistance
Fun
Traditions
Goal setting
Foresight
Responsibility
Safety
Non-judgmental
Belongingness
Continuity
Honesty
Togetherness
Cooperation
Aesthetics
Appreciation
Well being

Stability
Predictability
Nurturing
Communication
Peaceful environment
Trust
Spirituality
Quality of life
Moral values
Sharing
Mutual concern/regard
Balance
Individuality
Empowerment
Recognition
Reasonable limits/boundaries
Age-appropriate expectations
Mutual caring
Excitement
Planning
Forethought
Appropriate structure
Protection
Non-threatening environment
Humility
Assurance
Reality
Freedom of expression
Compatibility
Support
Education
Willingness
Adaptability

Flexibility	Dependability
Resilience	Compromise
Healthy involvement	Sense of roots/ancestry

Appendix G

MISTAKES OFTEN MADE BY ADULTS

Lack of unconditional love
Bad choice of partners
Dependence on welfare
Domestic violence and chaos
Promiscuity
Family secrets
Non-acceptance of individuality
No future goals or plans
Self-loathing
No sense of a work ethic
Little or no self pride
No pride in possessions
Questionable moral values
Abandonment
Poor eating habits
No limits or self control
View children as nuisances
Resent and blame your kids
Poor parenting style
Not encouraging kids
Poor judgment
Place too much responsibility on kids
No desire to improve things
Unresolved issues from the past
Adults who act like kids
No sense of responsibility
Treating kids like adults
Unpredictability
Obsessed with what others think
Poor impulse control
Playing the odds
Denial of reality/truth
No respect for kids

Becoming a teenage parent
Families with multiple parents
Drugs and alcohol abuse
Frequent relocations
Lying/deceit
Abuse/neglect
Broken promises
No self respect
No self confidence
Low standard of living
No pride in living situation
Lack of cleanliness
Poor communication skills
Poor hygiene
Substandard living conditions
Inconsiderate of children
View kids as income potential
Focus mainly on self
No nurturing or bonding
Negative outlook/worldview
Mood swings
Instability
Self-defeating attitude
Displacing emotions onto kids
Lack of emotional maturity
Blaming others for problems
Inconsistent parenting
Deprivation/neglect
Pettiness/jealousy/envy
Poor coping skills
Self destructive lifestyle
Unresolved grief
Poor problem-solving skills

Judgmental
Kids not viewed as priorities
Not teaching kids to dream
Teaching shame
Using kids as pawns
Failure to protect kids
Making kids feel obligated

Competition of wills
Stubbornness
Won't admit mistakes
Not emphasizing education
Whining
Refusing help
Do as I say, not as I do
Disregard a kid's need to know
Not caring
Strong need to control
Threatening to remove love
Not separating actions from identity
Teaching prejudice/hatred
Living life through your kids
Giving up
Keeping kids dependent
Ignoring spiritual needs

Holding grudges
Poor role models
Failure to instill hope
Jealousy toward kids
Using kids as weapons
Viewing kids as property
Double standards between sexes
Cultural clashes
Unable to forgive
Unable to apologize
Playing the victim role
Not seeking help
No honest self-assessment
Unfair to kids
Poor listening skills
Strong need to be right
Strong need to be liked
Labeling
Extreme religious beliefs
False sense of pride
Setting unrealistic goals
Breaking kids down
Creating FLAGS
Not being true to self

Appendix H

KIDS ROLES AND RESPONSIBILITIES

Grow
Mature
Play
Bond
Avoid stress
Have fun
Love
Listen
Observe

Learn
Achieve
Explore
Do not worry
Feel safe/secure
Do chores
Respect human rights
Trust
Copy/mimic appropriate behaviors

Be honest
Be loved
Feel confident
Follow reasonable rules
Develop positive self-concept
Be considerate
Learn good social skills
Appreciate nature
Avoid being selfish
Avoid becoming materialistic
Learn morals and values
Value personal property
Stay out of trouble
Think before acting
Accept responsibility
Avoid drugs and alcohol
Report problems created by adults
Be themselves
Recognize appropriate behavior
Express emotions appropriately
Become independent
Seek answers

Be open
Feel proud
Understand limits
Respect themselves
Care for and about others
Learn to cope
Appreciate things and people
Tolerate frustration
Avoid being self-centered
Learn to be spiritual
Value life – self and other
Avoid violence
Learn from mistakes
Accept reality
Learn limits and self-control
Choose friends wisely
Report abuse/victimization

Understand sex and sexuality
Understand love
Express their individuality
Question
Plan ahead

Avoid expecting too much/little
Dream
Develop talents and skills
Make friends
Use good judgment
Respect reasonable authority
Avoid/resolve conflict
Ask for help/guidance
Develop their bodies and minds
Learn to be independent
Take responsibility for actions

Accept consequences

Find hope
Allow room for mistakes
Study
Make good decisions
Appreciate diversity
Recognize unfairness
Talk about problems
Help others
Learn to be self-sufficient
Learn about adult issues
Separate sense of self from actions
Gain insight

Appendix I

NEGATIVE/HURTFUL STATEMENTS
OR THE ANSWERS TO THE QUESTION:
"WHAT"S WRONG WITH YOU?"

You are lazy, fat, ugly, dark, stupid, etc
You will never amount to anything
I am ashamed of you
Why can't you be more like...?
God is watching you
God will punish you
You act just like a girl
You act just like a baby
I'll beat the hell out of you

Because I said so that's why
You should be ashamed of yourself
You are so hateful
You are not worth my time or energy

No one else will ever want or love you
I am going to tell everyone what you did
You cause all of my problems

No one will ever believe you
Don't you talk to me that way

Don't give me that look

You will do what I say or else
If you don't like my rules there's the door
You think everything is so easy
My mom/dad would have killed me
You better make me proud

I'll box your ears

You are good for nothing
I wish you were never born
Everyone is looking at you
You are just like....
God knows everything
I wanted a boy/girl instead of you
You act just like a boy
I'll slap the crap out of you
This hurts me more than it hurts you
Don't argue with me
Your face will freeze like that
You are nothing but trouble
Get out of here, I am tired of looking at you
You'd feel bad if I died
You are killing me
You are more trouble than you are worth
You little liar
Don't use that tone of voice with me
You will respect me or I'll show you
You don't appreciate anything
You don't appreciate me
When I was your age....
Don't ever think I'm stupid
I'll give you something to be afraid of/cry about
I'll knock you into tomorrow

What, are you dumb/retarded?

Wait until I get you home
You thought I forgot didn't you
If you…, I will….
Dry it up or I'll let you have it again

Do you want a diaper and a bottle?
You were adopted

You are not welcome in this
house/family
I am going to teach you a lesson

I'll show you who's boss
You have no right to be angry with me
My life is none of your business
That's not normal
That's nasty
Sissy
You're no son/daughter of mine
I don't care what you think

You are my child, not theirs

You are never satisfied
I am glad your…isn't here to see this
You better ask God to forgive you
All you do is whine
Don't tell me how to run my life

Shut up

I am going to leave you

I have no life because of you

I'm going to give you away
If you tell anyone, I'll…
I taught him/her better than that

Boy, don't think I can't take you
down
Wait until your ….gets home
The boogeyman will get you
Don't get smart with me
I'll beat you until you can't sit
down
You are no longer my child
If you do that I won't love you
anymore
Get a good education because
you will never…
You have to break down a boy's
will
I'll take you down a notch or two
Don't ask any questions
You wouldn't understand anyway
You're too young
Cry baby
Fag/Queer
Have you lost your mind?
I don't care what other people
think
No one will tell me how to raise
my child
Want. Want. Want.
Nobody likes you
You bother everyone
Do as I say, not as I do
You better learn to keep your
mouth shut
Shut your mouth or I'll shut it
for you
Get out of my sight and don't
ever come back
If I didn't have kids I could meet
somebody
You can't leave; I need the money
He/she gets that from his/her.…
If I want your opinion I'll ask for it

You owe me

You are not really my child

You are going to be just like your…
Your mom/dad was….

Look at you
I'll show you
Children are to be seen and not heard
Just pray about it
When I get through with you…
You have to earn my love
I know you are doing something bad
Don't come crying to me
You are mine and I can do what I want
I don't know why you were ever born
It's going to get worse before it gets better
You better listen to me

If you go out that door don't ever
come back
Your mom/dad never loved you,
as much as I do
Shut up or I'll do it again
You are a disgrace to the family
and me
How could I love you?
Don't speak until spoken to
Don't embarrass me
You are going to pay for that
You don't deserve anything
You are always sick
You have no common sense
You are nothing unless I say so
You are from the devil
I wish you were never born
Your daddy/mama is a….
I told you so didn't I?

If we were back in…, things would be different
You think you have problems now? You just wait
You don't know your ass from a hole in the ground
You are nothing but a troublemaker and a loser

Appendix J

PURPOSES SERVED BY ABUSE/VICTIMIZATION

Control

Sexual gratification

Create fear

Displaced anger/aggression

Break someone's will

Act out anxiety/tension

Punish/hurt someone close to the victim

Express non-acceptance

Enforce rule compliance

Instill guilt

Enforce silence/secrecy

Force conformity

Enforce religious beliefs

Force dependency

Force obedience

Rule over

Force submission

Continue the abuse

Direct attention away from self

Blame

Fulfill selfish needs/desires

Feel better than another

Squelch emotional expression

Squelch self-expression

Enforce any belief system

For pleasure

Keep someone from leaving

Prevent abandonment

Reminds the abuser of someone else

Destroy self concept

Reduce fear of exclusion

Act out regret

Act out the FLAGS

Punish oneself (self abuse)

Control other compulsions

Dominate

Intimidate

Exploitation

Demand respect

Force change

Revenge/getting even

Express hatred

Express dislike/disapproval

Shame/humiliate

Secure a bond

Squelch individuality

Squelch intelligence

Keep someone down

Brain wash

Force loyalty

Enslave

Meet a need for power

Protect one's position

Scapegoat

Reduce boredom

Feel important

Establish separation

Eliminate/annihilate

Squelch creativity

Cruel and sadistic

Prove a point

Prevent rejection

Reduce personal fear

Self-loathing

Deny a right to privacy

Act out resentment

Act out jealousy

Guard against loneliness

Control other impulses

Dictate

Appendix K

ABUSIVE BELIEFS AND STATEMENTS FROM PEOPLE IN POSITIONS OF POWER AND INFLUENCE

They are dumb/stupid
We know your weaknesses
They need to believe us
You can trust us
Don't think or ask questions
We are better than you are
We are above accountability
We are wiser than you are
We are above scrutiny
No that's not what you really see
We wouldn't do you wrong
We did "it" for them
You didn't ask the right questions

What we really meant was ___.
Money and numbers are all that matter
You don't need to know everything
We are sorry. No, *really*, we are sorry
They will never know
This is good enough
This will teach them a lesson
It is always the luck of the draw
No one tells us what to do

What they don't know won't hurt them
We don't need to be team players
It's not any of your business
Who are they to tell us what to do?
We will handle this our way
We serve the best interests of everyone

They will believe anything
We know your vulnerabilities
We wouldn't mislead you
We know what is best for you
Accept what we say as truth
You are all fools anyway
You can't touch us
We are above the law
You can't outsmart us
That's not what we really meant
What do they know anyway?
It was in the small print
We didn't really do anything wrong

We are too smart to get caught
It was only a few little white lies
It is only wrong if we get caught
Might makes right
It is better to cover up than own up
This is all they deserve
We didn't mean to
We have legitimate power
We must get them before they get us

Why should we answer to them?
Our way is the only way
Strength in numbers
Let's just change the rules/laws
Oh well!
Follow us

If it is in the Holy Writings it must be truth
Let's see how many ways we can interpret that
What do you think they would believe?
Rules/laws don't necessarily apply to everyone
Deny guilt and hope for reasonable doubt!
You should be ashamed for suspecting and doubting
You put us in power; how could you have been wrong?
How can I say this so it at least sounds legal or ethical?
You have only the rights we are willing to give you
It is their fault because they gave us the power

Appendix L

FAULTY THINKING BY VICTIMS OF
LARGE SCALE ABUSE/VICTIMIZATION
(In all of these statements "I" and "we" are interchangeable)

There is nothing we can do
This is just the way things are
They are important people who
wouldn't lie to us
They are supposed to respect the law
People in positions of power
are honorable
They are stronger/bigger than we are
No one will listen to us
Our voices/votes don't count
It has been this way for a long time
This is what was prophesied
Pray and everything will be fine
This is good enough
They said they were sorry
Things will only get worse
if we oppose them
It is better to be nice/polite
It doesn't really matter anyway
I don't have the time or
the energy to fight
Time will tell, so let's just
wait and see
If it is in the Holy Writings
it must be true

We have always been persecuted
We are at their mercy
It is okay as long as they apologize

They are smarter than us
We are powerless

No one will believe us
No one will help us
Nothing ever changes
Might does make right
This is God's will
They are scholars
This is all we deserve
This is just our luck
It is best to suffer in silence

They are too powerful
Let someone else handle it
That doesn't really affect me
anyway
They wouldn't really do that

Some things are better left alone

It is not worth the hassle
Let's see how many other ways we can interpret that
They are religious leaders and would never do anything wrong
We can only hope they have our best interests at heart
Things have to get worse before they can get better

Profit and personal gain can't possibly be more important than the common good
Powerful organizations are okay as long as they provide financial support to our cause

Appendix M

COMPLICATING FACTORS/RISK FACTORS

Low socioeconomic status
Religious affiliation
Gender
Low or high intelligence
Poor impulse control
Appearance
Being unwanted
Dysfunctional family
Unpopular beliefs
Mental/emotional problems
Negative personality traits
Being spoiled
Lack of education
Lack of planning skills
Lack of personal choices
Speech problems
Acculturation issues
Unrealistic expectations
Limited support/encouragement
Limited coping skills
Low tolerance of frustration
Need for instant gratification
Poor decision-making skills
Unemployment
Unpredictability
Abandonment
Isolation
FLAGS
Inability to care
No sense of life purpose

Ethnicity
Sexual orientation
Cultural differences
Non-conformity
Unattractive/very attractive
Medical conditions
Being unloved
Extreme beliefs
Perceived as being different
Being abused/victimized
Negative outlook
Where someone lives
Lack of hopes and dreams
Lack of internal control
Physical impairment
Language differences
Unmet needs
Limited opportunities
Sexual acting out
Poor management of anger
Lack of patience
Low self-concept
Peer pressure
Deprivation
Loss/death
Rejection
Self-doubt
Lack of motivation
Hopelessness/helplessness
No future goals

Appendix N

RESULTS OF ABUSE/VICTIMIZATION

Negative self-concept
Confusion
Need to protect oneself
Criminality
Adjustment disorders
Depression/anxiety
Victimization of others
Sense of impending doom
Poor sense of internal control
No awareness of choices
Poor communication skills
Suspicious/paranoid
Violent/aggressive fantasies
Rebellion
Boredom
Lowered expectations
Inappropriate morals/values
Lack of joy/passion
Lack of dreams/goals
Not learning from mistakes
No universal perspective
Feeling at the mercy of...
Inability to forgive
Inability to trust or love
Distorted sense of reality
Fear of emotions
Denial
Continued deprivation
No sense of purpose/direction
Constant search for meaning
Ongoing vulnerability
Inability to question/discern
Limited creativity

Helplessness/hopelessness
Becoming deceitful/deceptive
Need to separate/isolate
Personality disorders
Psychotic disorders
FLAGS
Maintaining victim role
Self-defeating attitude
Inability to make changes
Problematic relationships
Blame self and others
Lack of assertiveness
Numerous ways of acting out
Frustration
Desperation
Needing instant gratification
Poor coping skills
Lack of contentment
Searching for "the answer"
Repeating mistakes
Absence of spirituality
Poor physical health
Inability to move forward
Inability to attach/bond
No self assessment
Fear of the past/future
Lack of courage
Fear of unpredictability
Limited life satisfaction
Easily mislead/deceived
Easily controlled
Difficulty saying "NO"
Inability to plan

Difficulty prioritizing

Uncommitted and unmotivated

Obsessive

Easily traumatized

Inability to take criticism

Judgmental

Jealous/envious

Procrastination

Become a poor role model

Seductive

Provocative

Limited sense of right/wrong

Fear of losing

Emptiness

Limited initiative

Driven

Compulsive/impulsive

Extreme self criticism

Taking everything personally

Petty

Poor use of time

Inability to relax and enjoy

Easily riled

Overly emotional

Cold/insensitive/uncaring

Unresolved grief

Fear of losing control

Negative relationships

Appendix O

LOSSES ASSOCIATED WITH ABUSE/VICTIMIZATION

Childhood
Security/Safety
Peace
Hopes/dreams
Assurance
Healthy development on all levels
Healthy self concept
Identity/individuality
Positive regard
Consideration
Trust of self/others
Pride
Excitement
Positive role models
Broken will/character/spirit
Positive outlook/attitude
Spirituality
Happiness/joy
Knowledge/learning
Friends
Understanding (Why me?)
Privacy/boundaries
Nurturing
Healthy desire
Commitment
Ability to cope/soothe
Ability to concentrate
Ability to leave/escape
Support system
Good judgment
Ability to help
Ability to reach out for help
Positive self concept

Innocence
Love
Self
Ideal family
Assistance
Self confidence
Sense of future
Respect for self/others
Control
Communication
Opportunity
Fun/play
Imagination/creativity
Personal growth
Acceptance/fitting in
Morals/values
Belief in others
Healthy perspective
Curiosity/wonder
Sanity/emotional stability
Home
Possessions
Caring about self/others
Motivation
Predictability
Ability to control/influence
Achievement/success
Social interaction
Openness (many secrets)
Decision-making skills
Ability to stop the abuse
Ability to question/discern
Positive recognition

Praise/reward routines

Ability/desire to look forward

Sense of importance/significance

Encouragement

Value for life

Friendliness/kindness

Honesty/trustworthiness perception

Belief in goodness

Accurate sense of responsibility

Satisfaction

Positive fantasies

Quality of life

Healthy daily habits/

Confirmation/validation

Reason to live

Courage

Remorse

Getting needs met

Clarity of thought/

Positive worldview

Feeling wanted

Healthy reality

Healthy sexual development

Higher standard of living

Appendix P

FAMILY FACTORS

Violence
Neglect
Public assistance/disability
Few limits/boundaries
FLAGS
Divorce/separation
Alcohol/drugs
Role reversal
Feeling trapped
No work ethic
No sense of ethics
Lack of mutual respect
Money/affluence
No regard for children
Safety issues
Kids taking care of kids
Multiple fathers/mothers of siblings
Personality disorders
Emotional distress
Bad neighborhood conditions
Outcasts
Uneducated
Foster home placement
Teenage/immature parents
Family secrets
dysfunction
Multigenerational problems
Dishonesty/deception
Stunted emotional development
Lack of adequate supervision
Materialism
Lack of regard for others
Exposure to weapons

Abuse/victimization
Conflict
Fraud
Total control/rigidity
Absent parent(s)
Poverty/low SES
Criminal activity/history
Hopelessness/helplessness
Lack of future plans/goals
Low morals/values
Discipline
Low standard of living
Sexism
Acculturation issues
Single parent
Pregnancy
Negative role models
Mental illness
Chaos
Targeted by society
Low class/classist society
Poor self concept
Lack of security
Unsanitary conditions
Family history of

Prejudice
Trust issues
Deceased parent(s)
Privilege
No sense of balance
Lack of value for life
No interaction/togetherness

Appendix Q

GANG/GROUP FACTORS

Criminality as a badge of honor
No limits
Death as honorable
Parties/socialization
Physical injury
Girls/sex
Money
Sense of family
Loyalty/solidarity
Respect
Goals/plans
Acceptance/belonging
Cars, clothes, etc.
Identity
Prejudice/hatred
Lack of remorse
Structure
Addiction to risk and the rush
Heroism
Praise/recognition/reward
No respect for outsiders
Chance to prove oneself
No work ethic
Occasional in-fighting
Accountability
Comradery
Hierarchy
Heroes
Awed/feared by others
No sense of future
Personality disorders
disorders
Chance to become an "adult"

Freedom
Drugs/alcohol
No responsibility
Violence
Popularity
Back up
No school
Trust
Courage
Hope/help
Love
Excitement
Status/importance
Self-focused
Disregard for enemies
Strength in numbers
Attitude/defiance
Antisocial behavior
Elitist existence
Instant gratification
Secrecy
Fearlessness/courage
Victimization of self/other
Discipline/consequences
Code of ethics
Mission statement
Leadership
Success/accomplishment
Copied by others
Peer pressure
Mental/emotional

Safety and security

Mediation
Pro-criminal thinking
Planning
Defending
Defiance

Abandonment of family
Competition
Organizing
Offending
Regrets